GEORGE MÜLLER (1805-1898)

George Müller is noted for his care of orphans in England, his long evangelistic career, and above all, for his commitment to prayer. Converted at the age of twenty, he founded orphanages in England, depending strictly on faith and prayer for the support of his work.

This inspiring story of how one man's faith so completely changed thousands of lives encourages the reader to trust in God and obey. Whatever the circumstances, even through the darkest valleys, George Müller's message is best captured in Psalms 37 — as true today as it was in the mid 1800's — commit your way to the Lord, trust in Him and He will act . . . .

HEROES OF THE FAITH has been designed and produced for the discerning book lover. These classics of the Christian faith have been printed and bound with beauty, readability and longevity in mind.

Greatest care has gone into the selection of these volumes, with the hope that you will not only find books that are a joy to read, but books that will stir your faith and enlighten your daily walk with the Lord.

Titles available include:

John Bunyan

Fanny Crosby

Charles G. Finney

David Livingstone

Martin Luther

Dwight L. Moody

George Müller

Mary Slessor

John Wesley

George Whitefield

The Life of George Müller

William Henry Harding

*"Ask, and it shall be given you; seek,
and ye shall find; knock, and it shall be
opened unto you: For every one that
asketh receiveth; and he that seeketh
findeth; and to him that knocketh it
shall be opened."*

Matthew 7:7,8

Barbour Books
Westwood, New Jersey

ISBN 0-916441-13-X
(Canadian ISBN 0-920413-89-7)

Published by: **Barbour and Company, Inc.**
164 Mill Street
Westwood, New Jersey 07675

(In Canada, HEROES OF THE FAITH,
960 The Gateway, Burlington, Ontario L7L 5K7)

EVANGELICAL CHRISTIAN PUBLISHERS ASSOCIATION [ECPA] MEMBER

Printed in the United States of America

CONTENTS

CHAPTER I

The Converted Student

THERE arrives in London, early in the year 1829, a young Prussian, level-headed, earnest, and thoughtful. Although he has been a student for long years, and has distinguished himself at the University of Halle, he has come to England for a further course of study prior to devoting himself to missionary work among Jews. His name is George Müller. He is destined, under the direction of the Spirit, to inaugurate a spiritual movement which shall bring men back into an atmosphere of trust, and, standing by the eternal verities declared of old, to witness against the deadness of formalism, and the fanaticism of revived mediævalism, and the iciness of unbelief, that God is, that His Word is truth, and that He is the Hearer and Answerer of prayer.

George Müller was born at Kroppenstadt, in Prussia, September 27, 1805. A few years later the family removed to Heimersleben, four miles away, Müller, senior, having been appointed a collector of excise there. In 1821 there came another removal, for a similar reason, to Schoenebeck, near Magdeburg. Young George Müller, as his own confessions show, in their Augustinian frankness, mingled folly with study. The mad ways of an ungodly world fascinated him—indeed, he seemed a little madder than the rest, in his pursuit of pleasure. No Monica poured out her soul in prayer for him. His life, in its eccentricity of headlong adventure, might have suggested new wine-stained fancies and intricacies of intrigue to Wycherley or Congreve; and perhaps there is no more striking instance in modern history of the transformation that is wrought by grace, the power of the Spirit, through faith, than that which is furnished by the contrast between George Müller, the reckless libertine, the devotee of Horace and Molière, and George Müller, the saint of God, the student of the Word, the tender shepherd of the lambs of Christ's flock.

The night his mother died, George, all unaware of her prostrate condition, was playing cards until two o'clock in the morning; and when day came he and his dissolute companions went roistering in a tavern and were seen rolling, in a drunken condition, about the streets. At this time he was but fourteen years old. As the years came and went, he still squandered time and money in the riotings of vice. He made, indeed, some formal recognition of Christianity, and in the midst of Bohemianism studied much, preparing for the University, it being his father's ambition for him that he should ultimately become a clergyman, "not indeed," as George himself naively remarked, "that I might serve God, but that I might have a comfortable living."

Acquiring a considerable education, he began to take pupils, whom he instructed in languages; and, to recover the lost confidence of his father, he strove to maintain a semblance of respectability. At length he entered Halle University as a Divinity student, resolved to quit for ever the primrose path of dalliance—not, however, from a godly fear, but lest he might otherwise experience difficulty in obtaining a pastorate; moreover, the highly paid places in the ministry, upon obtaining one of which his heart was set, could only be hoped for by those possessing important degrees; wherefore he was determined to give himself to studious days and nights.

In such a spirit he arrived in Halle, but his resolutions failed him. The sense of freedom to follow the dictates of a rebellious heart, and the fascinations of a life of indulgence, arrested and quenched his new devotion to, at any rate outward, decency. The tavern and the gaming-table renewed their hold, and the Divinity student quickly became a bondslave of iniquity. Directly he obtained money, it was squandered in wickedness. Telling the truth was a rare thing with the George Müller of those days. There was little in University life to help him struggle out of the slough, for, of nine hundred Divinity students, all of whom were allowed to preach, scarcely any had tasted the heavenly manna. He read Voltaire and Cicero with delight, but the words of eternal life held no attraction for him ; indeed, he did not even possess a Bible.   George Müller, of all men, without a Bible !

This night of sin was dark, but the dayspring was at hand.   One day, Müller, with some of the rabble rout of the ungodly, was drinking in a tavern, when he recognised a former schoolfellow whom he calls "Beta."   The two were at once attracted to seek one another's company, drawn by oddly antagonistic ideas that might in other days have supplied a subject for Molière himself, were it not that an element of spiritual tragedy also entered thereinto.   Müller, still anxious to preserve an appearance of society polish and moral respectability, with an ultimate view to the loaves and fishes of ecclesiastical appointment, desired the company of "Beta" as a steadying influence ; "Beta," on the other hand, was a wretched backslider, intent upon pursuing the frivolities of the world, and seeing in Müller one who would guide him gaily into the circles of wine-bibbers and gamesters.

The two, accompanied by a couple of other students, went upon some wild pleasuring journeys through the country, their sight-seeing being attended by a good deal of drinking.   Of the widely diverse anticipations cherished by Müller and "Beta," it was inevitably the latter's that was realised.   They had pawned their books to obtain money for these jaunts, and had obtained the necessary passports by means of forged

THE CONVERTED STUDENT

letters—ostensibly written by their parents. In such a spirit, these four made a tour of Switzerland; and Müller, in carrying the purse, not only undertook a task similar to that of Judas, but executed it in a like spirit, for he so manipulated the accounts that, to put the matter delicately, the journey cost him only two-thirds of the amount which each of his friends contributed. He oscillated between repentance and indulgence. Now a sense of grief for his ways of life would afflict him; now he would plunge deep into dissipation. Going home to see his father, he resolved to live differently; returning to Halle, he was at once back in the taverns.

While struggling vainly with the sins of his heart and the misery of his mind, he was seized with a sudden wish for yet another "pleasure journey." This time he was set upon going to Paris, and in order to raise the necessary money he undertook to translate a French novel into German, for a newspaper. It must be remembered that at this time he had never really heard the Gospel presented as a living message, nor had he met with one person who lived, or expressed any desire to live, according to the rule of Holy Scripture. Despite his studies in Divinity, the idea of the New Birth was a startling novelty to him, his conception of Christianity being merely a mental acceptance of certain dogmas and statements. As to the personal experience of the joyful knowledge of sins forgiven, and of regeneration by the power of the

Holy Spirit, he was in utter darkness. Religion was a matter of " doing one's best." The difference between himself and the rest of his circle, in morality of life, was simply one of degree, and, actually, this was so, for, with darkened hearts and lives, they were, with the exception of "Beta," entire strangers to God.

All this time, "Beta" was writhing under conviction of sin. The memory of the Swiss expedition was like a blight upon his life. With a broken heart he confessed his guilt to his father, and on returning to the University carried with him a letter of introduction from a Christian friend to a Halle tradesman, named Wagner—at whose house meetings were held for prayer and praise. In a happy moment, Müller one day accompanied " Beta " on a stroll. Possibly " Beta " perceived in his friend some glimmering of desire after the truth ; possibly Müller remained silent on the subject of worldly pleasuring, owing to the evident change in his companion's demeanour ; in any case, "Beta" told Müller of the meetings in the tradesman's house, and explained the procedure : " they read the Bible, sing, pray, and read a printed sermon "—meetings for expounding the Scriptures being illegal in Prussia, if no ordained minister were present. A few weeks before, such a programme might not have exercised any fascination upon Müller, but now, directly he heard of such a meeting, the thought of it fired his soul. The poor weeds of earthly folly began to appear in their true aspect. The cap and bells lay among the dust ; the river of pleasure was silvery no more, but a nauseous stream. He felt instinctively that he had "found something after which he had been seeking all his life." It was Saturday afternoon; a meeting was to be held at Wagner's that evening; would "Beta" kindly take him?

"Beta" was at first a little deprecatory, thinking that "Bible-reading and prayer and a printed sermon" would scarcely harmonise with the flippancies of the French novel and the vapourings of beer-halls. Müller, however, was eager, and "Beta" promised to call for him in the evening.

Instinctively feeling that there was something to be found at the tradesman's that all the University dignitaries and professors had failed to impart, Müller went accordingly to this humble gathering of believers, and, being utterly in the dark as to the delight of Christians in seeing the ungodly manifest an interest in spiritual things, he began to stumble out an apology for attending. "Come as often as you please," responded warm-hearted Wagner, "house and heart are open to you." Müller was profoundly touched. He surveyed the little assembly with new and heavenly thoughts illuminating his mind. A Christian brother named Kayser[1] fell upon his knees to pray—greatly to

[1] Frederick Gottlieb Kayser, afterwards a missionary. He was appointed, in 1827, by the London Missionary Society, to Kaffirland. After arriving at Cape Town he pushed forward to found a new station on the Keiskamma River, but in 1836 he removed to a more suitable locality up the river, founding the station called Knapp's Hope. In 1846 the

Müller's amazement, for he had neither seen any one kneel to pray nor done so himself.

Next, Kayser read a chapter and a sermon ; a hymn was sung, and then Wagner led the little company in prayer. A plain man, this Wagner: his portrait may yet be seen—a shrewd, far-seeing man of affairs; kindly withal; taking life seriously; he had learned also to walk with God, and was taught of the Spirit; hence Müller, coming into the gentle dawnlight of the Gospel, realised that there was much more in real prayer than literary phraseology or graces of diction. "I could not pray so well, though I be much more learned," he concluded.

The humble little meeting wrought a revolution in Müller's experience. He was happy—he knew not why. The peace of those who love the law of God was on his soul. To wait a whole week, for a second meeting, was impossible. The next day, and the next, and again and again, he went to Wagner's, to read the Bible with him. The idea of the Paris trip was given up, and though he did not immediately disentangle himself from the novel-translating affair, but concluded the work, he realised the impossibility of touching pitch without being defiled and accordingly burned the manuscript, instead of selling it.

Now came the terrible struggle, with inbred sin,

Kaffir War broke out, and Kayser found it necessary to retire to the Kat River; but in February, 1848, he was back at work at Knapp's Hope, where he remained until his death, which occurred in 1868, about nine years after his retirement from active service for the Society.

of a man who sees the highest towering in the front of his life, loves it, is determined to follow on, and yet finds his own heart is in league with things evil. Müller broke loose from the tipsy wits of the tavern; he almost, but not quite, conquered the habit, which had unhappily laid so powerful a grip upon his life, of telling falsehoods. Now, when he fell into open sin, he found no satisfaction therein. His lament might have been fitly expressed in the Pauline cry that so many, down the centuries, have echoed, striving to conquer without the aid of the conquering Christ: "O wretched man that I am! who shall deliver me?" He prayed, read the Scriptures, meditated, went to church.

Meantime, the students laughed uproariously. "George Müller a saint! Müller of the gayest company; Müller of deep drinks and madcap adventures!" Nevertheless, Müller heeded neither their sarcasms nor their invitations back into folly—

> Reply not to me with a fool-born jest:
> Presume not that I am the thing I was;
> For God doth know, so shall the world perceive,
> That 1 have turn'd away my former self;
> So will I those that kept me company.

At length, too, he saw that for the renunciation of sin and folly he required the aid of a Greater than he. That aid he sought; that aid he found graciously given. There could be but one Way of Life for him, and as he entered in he declared: "The individual who desires to have his sins forgiven, must seek for it through the blood of Jesus. The individual who desires to get power over sin, must likewise seek it through the blood of Jesus." It was in November, 1825, that he found peace with God, though not until July, 1829, did he make what he called his "full surrender."

In the period between these two dates he fell occasionally into coldness, and into sinful ways, yet his heart was set upon doing the will of God. He hoped to be a missionary, stimulated by the example of a godly youth who, leaving circumstances of wealth and ease, went out to preach the Gospel among Jews in Poland. In order, however, to obtain admission into any Missionary Society in Germany it was necessary for Müller to obtain his father's permission, and this he sought, but only to be met with indignant refusal. "Was all the money that had been spent upon his education to be wasted? Was he not, after all, going to secure some well-paid post in the Christian ministry?" Reproaches, however, proved unavailing to move this singular son to alter his views; the father wept and entreated—although his urgency, it must be confessed, was caused by the passing of the hope that in some "comfortable parsonage" of his son's he might himself pass life's evening in quiet ease. Müller returned to Halle, resolved upon doing the will of God; deciding at the same time, although he greatly needed money—having yet two more years at the University—not to ask his father for any, it being no longer an ambition of life to secure a "comfortable parsonage."

George was now without means, but the Spirit taught him to walk in the path of faith; and all needs were supplied. Three American ministers, visiting Halle but not understanding German, desired to be taught the language, and Dr. Tholuck, the famous and godly Professor of Divinity who had now come to Halle, advised them to employ Müller. They did so, and paid him so well for this and for translation work, that his embarrassment was removed: "Thus did the Lord richly make up to me the little I had relinquished for His sake."

In view of Müller's experiences and position at this time, it is desirable to bear in mind two men—Tholuck and Francke. Tholuck was, of course, an Evangelical champion of world-wide reputation, both in class-room and pulpit, as Francke had been before him. Halle was the headquarters of German Rationalism; yet it seems not too much to say that Tholuck, by the power and sympathetic nature of his teaching of Christian truth, entirely changed the condition of affairs. He was intimately known and highly esteemed in England and America, and was an ardent member of the Evangelical Alliance. By reason of his gifts and godliness he was an admirable instructor and guide for an eager seeker such as George Müller; moreover, he was keenly concerned in the welfare of orphan children, having formed a home for such in Berlin, where, also, he had evinced a particular interest in advising and helping young men who desired to give themselves to the work of the Christian ministry. Tholuck restored Halle University to the position which it had attained, immediately upon its organisation—in 1691, by the Elector Frederick III. of Brandenburg—as a lively centre of Evangelical zeal and fervour; which original position was created chiefly by the Christian devotion of August Hermann Francke.

To turn for a moment to Francke himself. His spirit and life were early manifested in his preaching. Philip Jacob Spener and he may be described as the two chief figures in the so-called Pietistic Movement in Germany, which, when the Lutheran Church had backslidden into cold intellectualism, reaffirmed the great truths of saving faith and the New Birth and the priesthood of believers. The designation "Pietists" arose as a term of reproach; actually, it signified a new protest against spiritless orthodoxy and a return to apostolic principles and methods. So large were the crowds, including many Roman Catholics, who thronged to hear Francke at Erfurt, that a fierce opposition arose, as an outcome of which he was expelled from the town. Prior to this, his lectures at Leipzig had created such offence that he left the city, but a few weeks after quitting Erfurt he was appointed to the chair of Greek and Oriental languages at Halle, where "Pietistic" principles triumphed, the theological professorships being filled by men who held the "new" views—which, however, were just as old as Christianity itself. Francke afterwards became Professor of Theology; but also laboured, all the time, as pastor of a church in the neighbourhood. Scarcely, however, had he settled to his duties at Halle, when, stirred by witnessing the lamentable condition of outcast children, he began to gather them into a meeting-room, feeding, clothing and teaching them. Next, it became necessary to take a house, and gradually this remarkable philanthropy, commenced as a sort of Ragged-school, greatly developed, so that Francke established an Orphanage, with Day-schools as an auxiliary, where hundreds of poor children received Scriptural instruction and physical benefit.

To return to Müller. On the advice of friends, he decided to take no immediate steps towards becoming a missionary, but the call to give himself fully to the work of God sounded in his soul: he distributed missionary papers and, above all, sought to win souls for Christ amid the darkened people around him. The field was large and difficult; in Halle "all the ministers were unenlightened men"; but he sought out the saints, had sweet fellowship with "Beta" and the rest, and at the invitation of a schoolmaster preached his first sermon, in a village near Halle. That is to say, he first secured a printed sermon, fashioned it afresh in manuscript, and committed it to memory. At eight o'clock in the morning he gave this address, in a chapel of ease; at eleven o'clock he gave it again, in the parish church. He afterwards confessed : "I had not light enough to see that I was a deceiver in the pulpit, since everybody supposes that the sermon a man preaches is his own." There was yet another service to be held, in the afternoon. George need not have taken part, for his friend the schoolmaster might have read a printed sermon, but there was bubbling up in the heart of poor, repentant, earnest George Müller a love for the Lord that inspired him to preach again. "I had it in my heart to preach !" Here is the secret : what matter how stumblingly he goes to work? True, he has no other printed sermon, no other manuscript, no other address learned by heart ; but he breaks out in a suitable word upon Matt. 5 : 3—"Blessed are the poor in spirit : for theirs is the kingdom of heaven." The people listen with new interest, and the joy in his own soul is deep.

It is a delightful study to trace, in his personal experiences at this time, how wonderfully he was being taught by the Spirit the supreme lessons that were necessary in the shaping of his life according to the Divine plan. For example, in his poverty he was glad to take advantage, for a time, of certain free lodgings for poor students of the University. The lodgings, a foundation of Francke's, were specially for Divinity students, Francke, as we have seen, having been Divinity professor. What was of peculiar importance, however, in Müller's case, was the position of the lodging-place; it was in the great Orphan Houses which Francke had not only, by the grace of God, erected, but had maintained in simple faith in Him. Thus, Müller's hour of need took him to the very place where he would come into immediate and intimate relationship with the work of sheltering and educating orphans, a work essentially Christian in its aims, and depending for its support solely on the daily provision of Him who sent the ravens to Elijah.

Another profound lesson regarding the finance of faith was received in connection with the asking of a small loan which he wanted for helping a poor relative and for defraying a debt remaining from his days of extravagance. Müller had not yet learned that, to use one of his own expressive phrases, " There is no ground to go from the door of the Lord to that of a believer." Hearing an excellent account of a certain wealthy and aristocratic lady he decided to ask her to lend him the required sum. In the course of his letter he told the story of his conversion, and, in case she should be a stranger to the Lord, he endeavoured to lay before her the way of salvation.

His good opinions of the lady were erroneous ; she was neither godly nor charitable ; nevertheless, the exact sum for which he asked was sent him as a gift, in silver coin, by an anonymous correspondent, who wrote : " A peculiar providence has made me acquainted with the letter you have written. You are under a mistake concerning her, but, that I may lessen in some measure the difficulties in which you seem to be, I send you the enclosed small sum, for which you must thank, not the unknown giver, but the Lord, who turneth hearts like rivers of water."

Overwhelmed with gratitude to God, and recognising also the force of the letter in adding homely admonitions to "beware of vanity and self-complacency," he walked out of Halle, seeking some solitary place where he might commune with the Lord. It was winter, but, behind a hedge, although the snow lay a foot deep, he fell upon his knees and, with a blessed realisation of his Heavenly Father's goodness and mercy, poured out his soul in prayer and praise, dedicating himself afresh to the service of God.

During these days of preparation, one other foundation principle came into being, of exalting and studying the Bible. His long neglect of Holy Scripture meant that he understood it comparatively little and found it easier to read biographies and sermons. Thus, for the four years following his conversion, he "preferred the works of uninspired men to the Oracles of the Living God." While winning knowledge of the victories of the warriors and pilgrims of faith he yet neglected the study of the great essential facts, of man's ruin and God's redemptive purpose and work in Christ, which are basal for the acquirement of an intelligent understanding of Divine truth. The meetings at Wagner's helped him much by their simplicity and directness; and a gathering of Christian students, equally instructive, was providential, for it guided him into the apostolic way of assembling together to praise God, in humble, brotherly fashion, which must have lived in his memory and had important results in after days. These meetings for students were for some months held in Müller's own room—up till the time he left Halle; and they were meetings around the open Bible.

Müller, nearly twenty-two years of age, was now considering the great question of his life-work. He had acquired a sound education, and was endowed with a remarkable faculty for teaching. The Word of God was in his heart; the service of Christ was his chief joy; he was determined to follow the light. First, there seemed to be an opening to proceed to Bucharest as assistant to an Evangelical preacher; indeed, he was actually accepted for the post, by an English Society, but the breaking-out of war between Russia and Turkey [1] led to the cancellation of the arrangement. Just previous to this, the Sunday evening meeting in Müller's room was attended by his friend, the young missionary to Polish Jews, who expressed a fear that, owing to ill-health, he would be obliged to give up that particular branch of service. This led Müller to study Hebrew, in which language he delighted, and Dr. Tholuck one day pointedly asked

---

[1] That is, the war following the " untoward incident" of the battle of Navarino, centring in the question of freeing Greece from Turkish domination and resulting in the erection of the Danubian Principalities into practically independent States and in the creation of the modern Kingdom of Greece.

him : Had he ever thought of labouring among Jews? An opening might possibly occur in connection with the London Society for Promoting Christianity amongst the Jews, of which Society Tholuck was himself a representative. To this Müller naturally replied that it would scarcely be proper to think of that, all arrangements being made for going to Bucharest. Tholuck assented, but, on the war breaking out, he recurred to the subject, whereupon Müller, after consulting with more experienced brethren, resolved to offer himself. Upon this, Tholuck communicated with the Society's headquarters and eventually a conditional acceptance was received : Müller would be regarded as a missionary student, for six months, on probation, providing he would make his way to London. There was somewhat of gall in the cup. Müller had passed through the University and was not without fine opportunities of utilising his scholarship in the educational world ; yet he was asked to become a student once again. But, since this seemed clearly to be the will of God, he agreed. Yet there was one apparently insuperable barrier to his departure for England : it was the Prussian law demanding universal military service.

Some prominent officers who were also men of God became interested in him on learning his object, and sought to help him. Nevertheless, exemption was refused even by the King of Prussia himself ; Müller, it seemed, must yield the demanded three years' service ; yet at the last moment he was declared, on being medically examined, to be physically unfit. A second military physician gave a confirmatory verdict, and the commanding officer issued him a "dismissal" for life from military service; adding, as a Christian intensely interested in the conversion of the Jews, a few hints as to the most suitable Scriptures, particularly Rom. 11, for impressing upon rebellious Israel.

On March 19, 1829, Müller arrived in London His mind was set on the evangelisation of Jewry, although, all unconsciously to himself, God had equipped him for a different field; however, he was determined to be obedient to the heavenly vision—and in his heart he carried the sweet memory of the Halle Orphan House.

CHAPTER II

Müller and the Brethren

IN an ecclesiastical sense, it was a disturbed and distressed England to which Müller came. Spiritually and socially it was, taking a wide view, a "dead" time. The example of the Court made for profligacy. The Napoleonic wars had left the nation a heritage of military and naval glory; but social conditions were developing which, unless speedily remedied, were bound to generate intense misery and degradation and a spirit of revolution, the end of which no man might foresee.

The Evangelical party of the Church of England, however, was making a splendid struggle, cherishing glorious hopes of the evangelisation not alone of Britain itself but of the world's untouched heathen in other lands.[1] Only two years later, Exeter Hall was built, becoming at once a rallying-place for godly Anglicans, and, with expanding usefulness, for good

[1] It is well to remind ourselves that the " Evangelicals " and the " Low Church" were distinct groups. As Balleine says (see *A History of the Evangelical Party*) : " The clergy, whose churches were falling to pieces through dirt and dampness, the fashionable, card-playing clergy of the towns, the port-loving fox-hunting squarsons of the villages, were all Low Churchmen. But they hated Popery even more than prayer-meetings."

causes innumerable, particularly of missionary enter-
prise; its name also becoming an offence and byword
to the ungodly all the world over. How much the
upraising of a flag of righteousness was needed in those
days is sufficiently demonstrated by the bitter hostility
which was displayed, equally among Churchmen and
Nonconformists, against the attempt of zealous men
and women to carry the message of Redeeming love to
the "regions beyond."

The Oxford Movement was beginning to sound its
melancholy call back to the bogs of superstition, under
Newman and Keble and Richard Hurrell Froude, and the
rest of the Anglican mediævalists who, with Faber,
were vowing that life should be "one crusade against
the detestable and diabolical heresy of Protestantism";
or, like Ward and Dalgairns, were panting for the
day when "the ears of Englishmen should become
accustomed to hear the name of Rome pronounced
with reverence." Yet, at the same time, there was
being raised up of God a body of witnesses whose
testimony—all drawbacks of fleshly confidence, human
disputation, and doctrinaire hair-splitting to the
contrary—has been of enormous and world-wide importance in the revival of apostolic ideals, and in the
honouring, not of the traditions of men but of the

Here, of course, was an opening for Ritualism with its numerous services,
activity in the restoration of fabrics, archæological tastes, and its gorgeous
vestments and embroidered altar-cloths. Here was the opportunity, not
merely for the Pugins, but chiefly for the industrious "Puseyite" priest,
whose activity thus presented a contrast with the habits of dashing vicars
whose chief ambition was to shout "Tally ho!" and "be in at the death."

Holy Spirit Himself, as Guide and Instructor. These witnesses were the early Brethren.[1]

We are not so much concerned to trace the precise beginnings of what became the mighty Movement of Brethrenism : the Movement itself, as it was used of God in the accomplishment of His gracious purposes and plans, is what matters. Not that Brethrenism was a swiftly formed force. At first it grew slowly, but the rivulets of earnest thought and holy aspiration to return to the simplicity of the early days of Christianity, trickled together and formed a river deep and powerful. The Tractarians, in their journey back through the ages in the quest of truth, stumbled in the morasses of mediævalism, and chased will-o'-the-wisps instead of following the true light ; the Brethren went back all the way to the little company that gathered in the Upper Room, or that stood upon Olivet, watching the disappearance of Christ in the clouds, and hearing the sacred assurance of the heavenly visitant, that in like manner He should return.

The Assemblies at Dublin and elsewhere were a

---

[1] The title, "Brethren," might be accepted (the qualifying term, "so-called," must inevitably drop out of use—in fact, is well-nigh dead), yet there remains the present-day necessity of differentiating between the "Open" and the "Exclusive" Brethren. The latter term, in particular, sounds a little offensive, yet both designations are tersely descriptive, and have long been used in ordinary conversation ; they become recognised titles whether we will or no. After all, "Quaker" and "Methodist" came as popular nicknames. The names in common use at least get rid of the localising term "*Plymouth* Brethren"—which, however, arose naturally enough, through the early origin and the strength of the Plymouth Meeting.

protest equally against priestism and worldliness; they were necessarily a protest against the Mass-offering priest of Ritualism, the hunting parson of the Low Church, and the latitudinarian, theatre-going Nonconformist who preached polished moral sermons and made glowing social appeals, but seldom touched upon soul-winning. The Brethren, however, were not people of negations. They stood for simplicity of life and for missionary zeal at home and abroad, for devotion to Christ, for loyalty to the Scriptures of Truth : and this, not for the furtherance of a theory, but because, following the Lord, they realised that the promise made in the Temple was theirs, that out of their innermost being should flow rivers of living water.

The brethren who became prominent in the Assemblies were not only zealous and self-sacrificing; they were gifted and able members of Christian churches. Anthony Norris Groves, the Exeter dentist, and John Gifford Bellett, the Irish lawyer, were, like John Nelson Darby — the curate from Wicklow — of the Anglican Communion ; Edward Cronin was a Congregationalist. Groves had purposed to go to the foreign field, in connection with the Church Missionary Society. However loosely they held together at first, the Brethren, particularly when Darby's influence became prominent, at Plymouth, speedily made a deep mark upon Christian life and thought throughout the world. "This, I doubt not," said Groves to Bellett, while they walked together along a Dublin street, "is the mind of God concerning us : we should come together in all simplicity as disciples, not waiting on any pulpit or ministry, but trusting that He would edify us together by ministering, as He pleased and saw good, from the midst of us."

Groves' practice as a dentist was worth fully £1500 a year. Money, however, was dross to him. He lived to do the will of God, and forsaking all, went to Bagdad as what the world elects, not without a touch of satirical amusement if not of superior scorn, to style a "free-lance" missionary—which is to say, he looked only to God for his support. The circle of Brethren also came to include : Dr. Samuel Prideaux Tregelles, the distinguished Biblical scholar ; J. L. Harris, an Anglican clergyman, and son-in-law of Legh Richmond ; Benjamin Wills Newton, Fellow of Exeter College, Oxford ; Francis William Newman, the brilliant but erratic brother of the brilliant but erratic Tractarian ; and the Hon. John Vesey Parnell, afterwards (succeeding his father) Lord Congleton.

The influence of Brethrenism upon the religious life of the United Kingdom and indeed of the world, proved powerful at a specially momentous period. The Oxford Movement was essentially one from the Bible to ecclesiasticism : the Brethren Movement was essentially one from ecclesiasticism to the Bible. Tractarianism found its emblems in the Mass and the Priest : Brethrenism stood for the common gathering around the Lord's Table, and the priesthood of believers. If the Ritualists' badge was, fitly enough, a wooden cross with an image of the dead Christ thereon, the Brethren's was an open Bible, telling of Atonement for sin, of Resurrection and Return.

A common criticism of the Brethren among the Churches of the Nineteenth Century was that they were "disturbers of the peace"; but the Brethren, eager for holy endeavour and for fresh proofs of loyalty to the Saviour's commands, might well retort upon many that the "peace" which was "disturbed" was simply that of selfish apathy. It must inevitably happen when a new spiritual movement—not a mere fantastic craze—arises, that zealous men and women in the churches, whose righteous souls are vexed by the melancholy spectacle of nominal Christians being absorbed in worldly pleasure and indulgence, break away, and throw in their lot with the new movement; whereupon the fashionable religionists, instead of repenting in sackcloth and ashes, retort upon holy zeal with cries of "sheep-stealers" and "fanatics." So it was, to a considerable extent, with the Brethren, who, we must ever remember, stood for a return to first principles, and were therefore desirous of being, simply, Christians, and could not admit the impeachment of being a sect: indeed the idea was of necessity obnoxious; "sect" they were not: not to be a sect, not to form a new "system," but to follow, by God's grace, the apostolic order, as Christians, only: this was the aim.

Apart even from the contributions of Brethren to

Theology and Bible exposition—evidenced chiefly, perhaps, in the teaching and writings of Tregelles and William Kelly and Darby and C. H. Mackintosh —the Movement rendered enormous service to the Christian cause. It created a body of men and women against whose faith and zeal the devastating winds of destructive criticism and the sapping waves of sacramentarianism beat vainly as against a house built upon the Rock. It moreover raised up, among the Open Brethren, a new and living force of Evangelism, founded upon the plain truths of the written Word, which recognised no boundary of nationality, but was occupied, albeit often under circumstances of difficulty and danger, with the proclamation of the Gospel. So unostentatiously do Brethren work that the world takes little account of them, except when one of them flashes back into Europe after long years of incessant toil in the heart of Africa, or the interior of China, or the swamps of Guiana.

In order to an intelligent understanding of George Müller's life-work, it is necessary first of all to grasp the main facts and characteristics of the Brethren Movement, remembering always that in the early days it consisted of believers who were members of this or that denomination, and who had no settled idea of separation, and were far from contemplating any new organisation, but yet, here and there, realised the desirability of gathering together in the Name of the Lord. Then, a little meeting, held in the house of Francis Hutchinson, in Fitzwilliam Square, Dublin, developed in size and influence when John Vesey Parnell hired a room in Aungier Street.

Müller, on coming to London, was, by his connection with the London Jews' Society, linked with the Evangelical section of the Church of England. He pursued the study of Hebrew, committing to memory portions of the Old Testament in that tongue; and he also made a commencement with Chaldee. While following his studies, he learned how Anthony Norris Groves, giving up all for Christ, had gone forth to Bagdad, looking only to God for his support. Another providential incident in Müller's life was his going to Teignmouth for a change of air, following an illness. At the little Devonshire resort he attended Ebenezer Chapel and there came into contact with Henry Craik, thus beginning one of the most remarkable of spiritual alliances in religious annals.

A profound scholar and an able teacher, Craik had been private tutor in the family of Anthony Norris Groves.[1] Later he was tutoring two sons of Mr. John

---

[1] In 1849, St. Andrew's University intimated to Craik that it was proposed to confer on him the degree either of Doctor of Divinity or Doctor of Civil Law. Craik courteously declined on his own account, but suggested the name of a friend " to whom, being an author, a degree would be welcome, appropriate, and serviceable." The University accepted the suggestion, but some years after repeated the offer to Craik, upon which the humble-minded scholar declined a second time, being, says Müller, " stedfastly purposed, in his own heart, not to seek the honour that comes from man." The incident illustrates the spirit of the early Brethren. Craik must not be set down as suffering from the " pride, that apes humility," but as a heavenly-minded apostle of—as he hoped

Synge, an Irish gentleman, who was himself zealous in the study of the Scriptures. The party lived in a house near Teignmouth, and, the Greek Testament occupying a considerable part of the studies, Craik's mind was largely occupied with the primitive truths of Christianity and the teaching of the apostles. He was also engaged, in addition to occasional preaching, in the preparation of a Hebrew Lexicon. A little later, on taking the oversight of the church at Shaldon, he drew up a few rules for the "better conduct of the future," which afford insight into his character, and show how natural it was that George Müller and he should be drawn together.

After so strenuous a time of study, Craik regarded the quiet mornings of study as opportunities to "prayer and meditation and the reading of the precious Word"; and in the rules of life he wrote: "Let me be more and more impressed with the necessity of 'redeeming the time'; and, for this purpose, avoid all food, etc., which may clog the exercise of my spiritual powers, or produce tedium of body or mind. Let me be kept daily waiting for my Lord's Return, and steadily examine my readiness to meet Him. Let me keep my heart with all diligence. Let me remember that I am nothing, have nothing, can bear nothing, and that my

—a new era, to whom even the distinctions of St. Andrew's were of small account. Müller's testimony regarding him was: "Whilst endowed by God with such great mental powers, he did not use them to get a name among men, nor to be admired, but to throw light on the Holy Scriptures, and to set forth the truth" (see Müller's Introduction to *Passages from the Diary and Letters of Henry Craik, of Bristol*).

depending upon self is madness, and my depending on the Lord is heavenly wisdom." Such were the thoughts, such the out-breathings of soul, of the man whose spirit was so akin to Müller's.

Müller, already prepared for the Brethren view, by his own independent thinking, and by the simple and direct methods of action which, in his zeal for the work of God, he had adopted in his native land, was also impressed by Craik's powers of mind, but more particularly by his guilelessness and humility, as, trusting in Christ for all, he sought to return to apostolic methods and rule. After returning to London, Müller realised that the ideas and plans which had governed him on leaving Germany could no longer exercise a dominating influence upon his life. For example, he could not accept from any Society whatsoever an appointment to preach the Gospel, his call being of God, and not of men.

Accordingly, he began to distribute tracts, which bore his name and address, and invited recipients to call upon him, for conversation. He preached in places of public resort, and also read the Scriptures with Jewish boys. Yet he was in a dilemma : while conscientiously unable to accept the rule or the money of the Society, he could not fail to recognise that, the Society having brought him to England, he was under considerable obligation to the Committee—earnest and godly men, anxious for the evangelisation of Israel. Hoping to fulfil his duty to them, he offered to labour under their name, but without receiving salary, if they would allow him to go from place to place as God might lead him, preaching both to Jews and to professing Christians. There could, of course, be but one answer. The Society, with its plain rules to be observed by all, could not possibly retain in the ranks of its evangelists one who in essential principle could recognise no rule. In kindly terms, the Committee intimated that, while Müller held the opinions which his letter expressed or implied, they could not consider him as one of their students.

The matter was bound to end thus. Probably the leaders of the Society felt somewhat relieved when the Gordian knot was cut; certainly Müller felt delighted at gaining freedom while yet retaining the respect of the Committee.

Meantime, he had gone west again—on December 30, 1829, first to Exmouth, and then to Teignmouth, and was once more in close association with Craik. "We were now drawn more fully together," Müller wrote, "for between July, 1829, and January, 1830, I had seen the leading truths connected with the Second Coming of our Lord Jesus Christ; I had apprehended the All-sufficiency of the Holy Scriptures as our rule and the Holy Spirit as our Teacher; I had seen clearly the precious doctrines of the grace of God, about which I had been uninstructed for nearly four years after my conversion; and I had learned the heavenly calling of the Church of Christ, and the consequent position of the believer in this world." As for questions of denominational position and government, he evidently held with Groves, who said: "As for order, if it be God's order, let it stand; but if it be man's order, I must examine whether or not it excludes the *essence* of Christ's Kingdom; for, if it does, I remember that word: 'Call no man your master upon earth; for One is your Master, even Christ, and all ye are brethren.'"[1]

Briefly, the new convictions which had come to him bore upon the doctrines of election, particular redemption, and persevering grace. He concluded, too, that the Scripture gives no warrant for expecting the conversion of the world before the Return of Christ; and he saw that in that glorious Return there lay the "Blessed Hope" of the Christian, since His appearing alone would end the chaos of human existence and bring in the glory of the true Church— the Body of Christ. Let it be clear, however, that Müller rested in no theory, however splendid, however sound. To rejoice in the grandeur of salvation's plan, to look for his Lord's Coming in clouds of glory, to anticipate in faith the triumph of the adorable Redeemer—these things were indeed enough to thrill his rapt soul in blessed seasons of holy contemplation; but this was not all. Coming down from his

---

[1] Letter to "his friend, Mr. Caldecott," Dec. 16, 1828. Groves added, moreover: "For the mystical Body of Christ my prayer is that I may gladly spend and be spent, even though the more abundantly I love, the less I am loved."

"Mount of Transfiguration," Müller spoke of his experiences as being "like a second conversion"; he came down in the joy of a dedicated life, to toil, to suffer, to sacrifice, to give.

After preaching at Ebenezer Chapel, he was invited by some of the brethren to stay on, as pastor; but, while his preaching delighted some, it was an offence to others, who became bitterly opposed. With engaging candour—which is really to say, however, with the disregard of men's opinions, which follows on clearly apprehending the will of God—he says of his first service: "My preaching was disliked by many of the hearers"; but he can also add: "The Lord opened the hearts of not a few to receive the truth."

When he preached again, on the ensuing night, his doctrine and his faithfulness had the same dividing effect: "The word was disliked still—perhaps *more*—though the few who received the truth in the love of it increased in number." The third service had had the same effect: "dislike on the one side, and joy and delight on the other." Reasoning with himself as to the cause of this, he notes one peculiar fact — those who were his special friends, on the occasion of his former visit, are now his opponents, which simply means, as he calmly recognises: "They were friendly to me when I was less spiritually-minded and understood much less of the truth; hence, I can only explain their opposition on the ground that the Lord intends to work through my instrumentality, and that Satan, fearing this, seeks to raise opposition against me."

The outlook might have appeared depressing to a man of lesser faith. Unbelief would have said that, so far as mundane matters were concerned, the prospect was not so much of "living by the Gospel," as of starving by it. But Müller was no church-splitting crank. The notion of "Aut Cæsar, aut nullus," was not merely repulsive to him but utterly alien to his principles. He wished for no Cæsars—nor to be one himself. He stood for apostolic truth—for the Book of God; and was entirely fearless; wherefore he held on his way and preached faithfully; a spirit of inquiry arose, and souls turned to Christ.

For close upon three months he preached, prayed, and hoped, two of the brethren deeming it a privilege to supply his temporal needs; finally, the tiny church—of only eighteen members—gave him a hearty invitation to the pastorate. He was to have £55 a year, which sum was afterwards increased somewhat as the church grew. "I now had Teignmouth for my residence," he says, "but I did not confine my labours to this place; for I preached regularly once a week in Exeter, once a fortnight at Topsham, sometimes at Shaldon, often at Exmouth, sometimes in villages near Exmouth, regularly once a week at Bishop's Teignton, where a part of the church lived, and afterwards repeatedly at Chudleigh, Collumpton, Newton Bushel, and elsewhere."

On October 7, 1830, Müller was married to Mary

Groves, sister of Anthony Norris Groves. In the circumstances which led up to the engagement, the two recognised the ordering of the Lord, and regarded the marriage as being truly "made in heaven."

When going on his second journey to Devonshire, Müller had carried with him a card, given him by a friend, on which was written, as a reminder, the name and address of Miss Paget, a zealous lady to whom references frequently occur in the early history of Brethren in the West. Attaching no great importance to the matter, Müller did not call on the lady for some weeks; then, making her acquaintance, he received an invitation from her to preach in a small Assembly-room at Poltimore, near Exeter. Rejoicing in any fresh opportunity to set forth the precious truth of the Lord's Return, and the other great doctrines which at this time were newly thrilling his soul, Müller at once accepted the invitation, and received from Miss Paget an intimation that during the visit arrangements had been made for him to stay with William Hake,[1] a

[1] Hake and Robert C. Chapman were yoke-fellows in the work of the Lord at Barnstaple, where they had charge of two houses (one of them the property of Miss Paget, who lived there, and who, dying there, bequeathed it to the work), as places of rest for Christian workers and of resort for young Christians desiring spiritual help and instruction. The "two patriarchs," as Chapman and Hake came to be called, continued in this joint ministry until 1890. On November 4 of that year, wrote Chapman: "At our tea-table we had a goodly company of young disciples of Christ, to whom Brother Hake spoke joyfully on the words: 'Peace I leave with you, My peace I give unto you.' At a meeting afterwards, Brother Hake drew contrasts with the walking, sitting, and standing of Ps. 1: 1—Enoch walked with God; Elijah stood before the Lord; David sat before the Lord. After he had been for about an hour

particular friend of Groves, who was carrying on a boarding-school in the house which Groves had himself formerly occupied. Mrs. Hake was an invalid, and Miss Groves was giving assistance in household affairs. Müller, realising that it was well for him, as a young pastor, to be married, and being strongly drawn to Miss Groves, wrote her a proposal. A few days after, he made a call, to receive her answer. She accepted, and, says Müller: "The first thing we did was to fall on our knees and to ask the blessing of God on our intended union."

The marriage, which took place on October 7, 1830, was entirely devoid of the characteristics of fashionable weddings. There was no orange-blossom wreath, no carriage and pair, no "drinking the health of the young couple," no showers of old boots. The young people walked quietly to church. Wedding breakfast there was none. "In the afternoon," to give the bridegroom's own account, "we had a meeting of Christian friends in Mr. Hake's house, and commemorated the Lord's death; and then I drove off in the stage-coach, with my beloved bride, to Teignmouth, and the next day we went to work for the Lord."

This was the day of simplicities, of return to the spirit of the Upper Room. "All ye are brethren": it was "beloved brother Craik," and so forth. The

the brightness of the assembly, his speech failed. . . . A young brother, in faithful love, sat up with him. I joined them about four in the morning. Brother Hake grasped my hand and held it till he could hold it no longer, and breathed out his spirit to the Lord."

atmosphere was one of love. And this happy company lived in that atmosphere to the end; of whom was George Müller. We may think of them as a delightful group of godly souls, entirely free from a desire to impose any human yoke, but quietly and humbly seeking to glorify God. Sweet is it to note the earnestness, the devotion, the plainness of life of the early Brethren, as they sought to dwell in harmony with the idea of the Second Advent: of men like Lord Congleton, who lived, at Teignmouth, in a house of which the annual rental was £12, the equipment including a deal table and pewter teaspoons, and the floors being carpetless. Müller's life was entirely in keeping with the idea of primitive simplicity and self-denial. It was no Spartan infliction, but a joy in the Lord. Surveying the Movement as a whole, we are bound to recognise, despite all weaknesses, that it marked a renaissance of holy energy and godly living, of zeal and fervour and brotherliness. Upon that deal table of Lord Congleton's (afterwards stained, in order to lessen the scouring labours of the housemaid) lay the open Bible, the fit emblem of the rule of life which prevailed beneath that roof. The homes of the Brethren, indeed, were in many instances Bethanys; peer and tradesman, scholars and the unlettered, would meet in humility in some quiet parlour, around the Bible, to hear what God had to teach them, by His Spirit, regarding the Work and the Kingdom of His Son.

Müller was now embarked upon a career of pastoral

usefulness, and yet the important feature of his life at this time was not so much what he did, as the formation of his own strong, Christian character. He was a young pastor—only twenty-five years old. He gave himself ardently to prayer and the study of the Bible— hard, close study, winning treasure from the mine; treasure that was all the dearer because, through the Spirit, it was gotten by himself—and studying to know the will of God, that he might do it and declare it.

During these days of pastoral activity there came to Müller much concern regarding certain points of belief and doctrine. For instance, he had repeatedly spoken against Believers' Baptism, but, urged by a Christian lady who took exception to his views, he determined to study the Scriptures and prayerfully weigh the respective doctrines of Infant Baptism and Believers' Baptism. His conclusion was that believers are the only subjects for baptism, and immersion the only true Scriptural mode: accordingly, he was baptized —by Craik. A second conclusion was (from Acts 20 : 7) "that it is Scriptural to 'break bread' every Lord's Day, although no absolute command is given."

A third opinion was that, at any rate at certain of the meetings, opportunity should be given, according to the general Pauline teaching—of, for example, Rom. 12—and indeed according to the spirit of the Christian faith—for any brother, convinced of possessing a message, to deliver it, whether by teaching or by exhortation, "that there should be room given for the Holy Ghost to work through any whom **He** pleased to use." Fourthly, he resolved to discontinue accepting a stated salary, being convinced that (1) the pew-rent system by which the salary was mainly raised was, according to Jas. 2 : 1–6, directly against the mind of the Lord, since, obviously, the poor Christian could not afford so good a place as the well-to-do one ; (2) that money given to " make up " the salary was grudgingly given ; and (3) that the pew-rent plan was a temptation to the preacher to be lacking in faithfulness to the people and to his own principles. Conviction was immediately followed by action. Only about three weeks after his marriage he cut himself off from a regular income. He notified the brethren of his views, and a box was accordingly placed in the chapel, with a notice stating that it was placed there for the reception of voluntary gifts for the pastor's support.

The decision to ask no man for help, but to look to God alone, applied even to the matter of expenses incurred when travelling on the Lord's service. Müller was highly regarded, as indeed he might well be, for his expository preaching, nor did his foreign accent prove any drawback ; he received numerous invitations, and was delighted to be of service to the saints. " Let us know, dear brother," friends would say, " what your travelling expenses are ; do not fail to acquaint us." Such expenses were more than his meagre resources could supply, yet he resolved to make no more applications for money, for, "unconsciously I had been led, in some measure, to trust in an arm of flesh ; going to man instead of going to God at once." To take this step, he plainly stated, required more grace than to give up his salary. Silence might easily be construed as meaning that he required nothing ; for, if he did not ask, even when kindly invited to do so, he would scarcely appear to be in need. Others might urge that such a proceeding was contrary to common-sense, since there could be nothing objectionable in making known the expense incurred in accepting an invitation to preach.

Müller evidently felt all this keenly. The money itself was a small matter as compared with being misunderstood by his brethren. Nevertheless, he was resolved, and he acted upon his resolution, finding, in a sense of entire and direct trust in the provision of God, the joy of spiritual freedom. But the question of income was by no means all ; that of expenditure was equally important in his view ; if he was to do the will of God in what he received, so was he to do with what came to him. Thus, there came to his soul a new, tender, and lovely realisation of the fact that he *possessed* nothing : he was a *steward*, and he resolved by the grace of God so to give as to demonstrate, in the light of God, the force of the apostolic reminder that "it is required in stewards, that a man be found faithful."

To say that Müller resolved on such-and-such action,

and gave up this or that, is perhaps a little suggestive that he possessed indomitable will that was not to be judged by the ordinary canons of everyday life that apply to average mortals. Müller, however, was by no means free from the temptations common to man. The whisper comes to him, as to others: "*Hath* God said?" The enemy comes in like a flood; and the melancholy thought afflicts him: "God richly helped me in 1830; but—what about 1831?" These wonderful deliverances, these marvellous and soul-subduing instances of God's kind provision: how can such miracles continue daily? Only for a brief space, however, is the cloud upon him: "For *about five minutes*, I was so sinful as to think it would be no use to trust." Later comes another assault of the tempter, and a great wrestling. An hour afterwards, "the Lord gave me another proof of His faithful love. There came, from some sisters in the Lord, £5, with these words written on the paper: 'I was an hungered, and ye gave Me meat: I was thirsty, and ye gave Me drink. Lord, when saw we Thee an hungered and fed Thee? or thirsty, and gave Thee drink? The King shall answer and say unto them, Verily, verily, I say unto thee, inasmuch as ye have done it unto one of the least of these My brethren, ye have done it unto Me.'"

That mortal man, gathering gold into his fist and glorying in gain, should hold or spend his money for his own ends was entirely natural, the fleshly mind being enmity against God: but the heaping together of riches, as an end in itself, by a converted soul, was a contradiction in terms. Hence, Müller took as a literal command for the governing of his life, our Lord's command : "Sell that ye have, and give alms." In recording this, in the "Narrative," he quoted only the clause in which the word occurs (in Luke 12 : 33), but it is illuminative to note that the remaining portion expresses the thought which became part of the very fibre of Müller's being : "Provide yourselves bags which wax not old, a treasure in the heavens that faileth not, where no thief approacheth, neither moth corrupteth."

"Treasure in heaven"! Who shall say how many poor souls, how many struggling ones of the household of faith, George Müller cheered by gifts from his little store? Little "store," do we say? Nay, no "store" in the sense of hoarding or keeping, for he immediately distributed of that of which God made him steward ; not "little," either, when we total what this man of God gave away during his long life. Not only did he give to the great institutions which he founded, not only gave he quietly to the work and personal needs of missionaries in all parts of the world, but he ministered to the poor and needy around, in ways of which we only occasionally gain a glimpse, but of which the aggregate amount was undoubtedly very large. Wherefore the name of George Müller is still potent to inspire the children of faith to deeds of mercy and sweetest charity. "Treasure in heaven"!

CHAPTER III

Müller and Craik at Bristol

IN these days at Teignmouth we see Müller in constant fellowship with Craik—who had the oversight of the Lord's work carried on near by in a Baptist Chapel, at Shaldon. The two were in terms of warm friendship with Robert C. Chapman, and it was through this association that Müller took his next important step in life, by leaving Teignmouth for Bristol.

Chapman, a member of the Established Church,— a convert of Romaine, whose faithful preaching was a feature of the Eighteenth-Century Revival,—visited Teignmouth in quest of health. Disappointed with the preaching in the Anglican churches, he made a round of Nonconformist places of worship, and thereby came upon Craik, at Shaldon, and urged him to remove to Bristol. In due course Craik did so, and pressed Müller to join him.

Desirous in all things to be obedient to the will of God, Müller waited and prayed, thinking rather to commence a preaching tour in the South-west; but the guiding cloud stood over the city on the Avon; it was time to move forward. On preaching, on April 22, 1832, in Gideon and Pithay chapels, Bristol, he was convinced that a new opportunity opened before him, in the will of God, and accordingly he went back to his old sphere of labour only to bid the flock farewell. He preached at Bishop's Teignton and Exmouth, visited all the brethren at Teignmouth, and concluded by taking leave of the friends at Shaldon. The deep and mutual affection between the saints and Müller was demonstrated by the tearful character of the farewell. They would not hold him back, feeling that God was calling him; but he could scarcely tear himself away. Journeying by way of Exeter, Müller and his wife reached Bristol on May 25.

Here, then, we mark another "parting of the ways." George Müller, young as he is, has passed through some notable experiences. The profligate of other days is now a humble follower of the Nazarene; his conscientiousness in detail is as thoroughgoing as his loyalty to the faith once for all delivered to the saints. It is with equal simplicity that he confesses his failures or records to the glory of God how sinners, under his preaching, turn to the Lord.

A famous preacher of the Victorian era once confessed grimly, in private, that he "found the life of faith very fatiguing." So does not George Müller, in these days of his early experience, whether at Teignmouth or at Bristol. On the contrary, he finds it delightful to wait, as it were, at the door of the All-sufficient One, and take the generous and unfailing bounty. Literally, he has "cast all his care" upon the Lord, and therefore is just as content with an empty cupboard as a full one. God will provide—what more assurance can man need than this?

Sometimes he and his wife are without a penny; yet they lack nothing. On one occasion two friends are staying with them, at Teignmouth. The store of provisions in the house is so reduced, on a Saturday, that there is only just enough butter to last their visitors for the Sunday: consequently, butter will be required for Monday morning's breakfast. What shall be done? Drop a gentle hint in a meeting? Ask of man while yet deprecating all asking of men? No. Müller quietly prays that God will cause the brother, whose business it is to "open the box" at "Ebenezer," to do so. That night, the brother in question and his wife are so deeply impressed that the Müllers need money, that they can scarcely sleep. Next day, the Müllers go to the meeting, and are handed £1. 8s. 10½d.—the contents of the duly-opened box. The visitors do not go butterless.

Again, there is not enough bread in the house to provide for the necessities of the day, and the stock of money in hand amounts to 2½d. After the midday meal the resources are scanty indeed, and Müller prays, with literal meaning: "Give us this day our daily bread." While he is yet praying, a certain poor woman brings part of her own dinner and a gift, from another poor sister, of five shillings: later, as if to answer absolutely the prayer of the Lord's servant, she returns, this time bringing a large loaf, Müller mildly remarks to his wife: "The Lord has not only given us the bread, but money beside."

In such experiences, there is no touch of unreality or of super-sanctity. Müller does not speak or write in the style of one who claims patent rights in the power of prayer, superior to those of other mortals, or to be the particular favourite of Heaven. There is nothing of loftiness about this godly, earnest preacher of the Everlasting Gospel. He simply takes the position into which the holy oracles of the Word invite him—the position of belief that God delights to have His children come to Him for the supply of their needs, and that He blesses them in their attitude of obedience and their prayers of faith. This trustfulness is combined, in Müller, with a rigid sense of duty.

For example, he has £40 in cash, but it is set apart for the payment of certain accounts, hence he will not consider it as his own; rather than touch the money, he will be content with dry bread with his tea—and in fact is so, for when he was a little concerned about butter, it was not for himself but for his visitors. In humble ways, in regard to such matters as bread and butter and tea, the Lord is trying His servant, leading him out into the highway of faith, wherein pilgrims journey pleasantly, or encounter grim foes only to conquer them. Once, the assets of the household are reduced to three pence and a small piece of bread, but the Müllers are quite content; they are not thinking merely of "the bread that perisheth," theirs it is to work for God, and, in doing so, food and raiment will be provided; presently a few shillings are sent in— plenty to go on with; so, all is well.

Once he is reduced to a single halfpenny, which is spent in milk. True, there is a matter of £7 in the house, but this, being put by for paying an account that is due, may not be counted an asset. A ha'p'orth of milk will scarcely make a meal for two; is there aught in the cupboard? Yes, a little cold meat, left over from the previous day. If any miserable critic, of unbelieving heart, would fling a dart of sarcasm, let him first see George Müller's serene devotion to the work, though there be only a few slices of cold meat in the cupboard. He is busy—visiting the sick, comforting the struggling believer, preaching Christ to the ungodly. God will provide dinner. About noon comes a knock at the door: two Christian women have called; they leave a parcel, which, being opened, proves to contain two pounds of sugar, one pound of coffee, and two cakes of chocolate. So, these gentle Christian women, giving of their scanty means, are, even with cakes of chocolate, building up George Müller in a mighty faith, whereof the fruits shall one day surprise the world.

Some blind souls might deem Müller's chronicling

of gifts of a loaf or two, of quarter-pounds of tea, of bags of potatoes and so forth, as trivialities, too petty for a man of serious outlook. To Müller, however, the bread, the eighteen-pence, the cakes of chocolate, are more precious than golden ingots, being sent directly by God, albeit through some humble child of His, whom men slightingly call, peradventure, Jimmy the road-sweeper or Mrs. Higgins the washerwoman. Shall George Müller hold the gift and the Giver in less honour because the messenger who carries it is clad in corduroy or wears a rusty bonnet?

The writing down of these grocer-and-oilman, butcher-and-baker facts of everyday domesticity illustrates the development in Müller of that principle and power of faith which, in the plan and purpose of God, was to be the great feature and lesson of his life ; but it is not to be regarded as occupying an undue part of his busy hours. The young man is full of godly energy ; he arranges preaching services, visits the people from house to house, prays much, finds more and more treasure of truth revealed by the Spirit as he studies Holy Writ. The recording, moreover, of gifts received, is no introspective mania, created by nervous doubt as to whether after all God will prove faithful. Far from such hysterical notions, which can only be the outcome of unbelief or an unhealthy condition of soul, the serene saint has no thought of himself in the matter : his aim is to encourage his fellow-pilgrims and to demonstrate the faithfulness of

God. Hence is it that he takes pen and makes the simple entries regarding sugar and butter and beans—sent by the Lord. In all this, the Spirit is educating him and moving him forward to mighty accomplishments in the realm of faith, as we shall presently see.

The actual beginning of the Craik and Müller ministry at Bristol is on July 6, 1832, in Bethesda Chapel. Deep interest was at once aroused, and Bethesda was crammed with people, Sunday after Sunday. There was indeed an element of peculiarity in this ministerial partnership, in that Craik had something of a Scottish accent, and Müller was pronouncedly German, but, looking beyond personal traits, the spiritually-minded could perceive that these two ministering brethren were men of apostolic zeal and insight into Scripture.

Bethesda is taken for a year—a brother paying the rent in advance—so that the prospect of a useful ministry is enlarged. Neither at Bethesda nor at Gideon are there to be pew rents, but free-will offerings are to be received. Craik and Müller are beautifully united in spirit and aim. Many people prefer Craik's preaching; but there is no trace of jealousy in Müller. "See how these Christians love one another" is a godly phrase so caught up by the world, in acid criticism, as to become almost a cliché of the journalism—small and sour—of Secularism. Well, let those who think brotherly love died with apostolic days, take to heart this record of Gospel partnership between Henry Craik and George Müller.

Speedily does the blessing of God rest on the labours of His two zealous servants. Ten days after they have commenced their ministry of the Word, they devote an evening to conversing with the anxious, when there are so many seeking guidance that four hours are gone before the last inquirer is satisfied. A church fellowship is formed, in the simplest fashion, of a little group of believers who, without any set rules, "desire to act as the Lord shall be pleased to give us light through His Word." The group consists of Craik and Müller, one other brother, and four sisters, one of whom is Mrs. Müller—"the first member of the church assembling at Bethesda." Here is the beginning of that Assembly of Brethren whose zeal for the Bible, for the proclamation of the Evangel at home and abroad, and for the upholding of apostolic ideas in faith and administration has made the name of Bethesda to shine in the religious annals of England.

These are solemn days. Cholera, in the first of its great Nineteenth-Century invasions of England—whither it has swept, from Persia and the Caspian, through Russia—ravages most of the cities and large towns. Bristol is so smitten that great numbers die. The maintenance of good sanitary conditions and an alert sanitary administration shall in future times check the disease, but in these dark "Thirties," the word "cholera" recalls something of the story of the Great

Plague, when the legend, "Christ have mercy on us," was scrawled in red chalk on the doors of the afflicted, and the sole sound of wheels heard in the street was that of the cart which rumbled to the accompaniment of the cry: "Bring out your dead." The ungodly, at such a time, prove peculiarly susceptible to the Gospel appeals of Müller and Craik, nor is the interest all evanescent, for sterling converts are won.[1]

The sick and dying are visited; many are thinking of the eternal verities, and listen to the story of Redeeming Love, even amid scenes of suffering and woe; there is a peculiar significance in the preacher's coming from a church meeting at a place called "Bethesda." The number of deaths increases daily. The funeral bell is heard almost continually. Craik and Müller are visiting the sick by day and by night; and, as he faces the terrors of the plague-smitten city, Müller's words are: "Into Thine hands, O Lord, I commend myself. Here is Thy poor, worthless child. If this night I should be taken in the cholera, my only hope and trust is in the blood of Jesus Christ, shed for the remission of all my many sins." And these are days of domestic anxiety also. On September 17,

---

[1] The position was paralleled in the United States, where, also, the disease made its appearance about this time. Charles G. Finney, who was then preaching in New York, counted, from his own residence, five hearses drawn up at the same time at doors within sight. Finney was himself smitten, but recovered, and upon his resuming his campaign, in the following spring, a revival broke out, the remembrance of the epidemic and of the many deaths adding point to the preaching.

1832, a daughter is born to the Müllers. She is named " Lydia."

A spirit of inquiry is upon many hearers at Bethesda and Gideon. When a meeting is held for those who seek to enter the Way of Life, Müller is impressed by the fact that " many more are convinced of sin under brother Craik's preaching than my own " ; and, studying to find the reason, he concludes : " Brother Craik is more spiritually minded, prays more for conversions, and more frequently addresses sinners as such, when speaking in public." This example is followed, and the simple plan proves potent, for soon Müller is rejoicing that the blessing of God, in this respect, rests upon his own preaching also.

Early in 1833 comes a request from the missionary brethren at Bagdad, that Craik and Müller should join them ; bank drafts to the amount of £200 being enclosed, for travelling expenses. The two prayerfully consider the matter, but the way does not seem clear. True, the circumstances of the little company at Bagdad are pathetic indeed. Parnell, who married Miss Cronin, at Aleppo, on the way out, lost her by death within a few weeks. Mrs. Groves, seized by plague, died within a few days. Three months after, Groves endured the further trial of losing their baby girl. The state of Bagdad itself was terrible. Thousands died from plague or through the inundations. On the house-top which was Groves' sleeping-place, rained cannon balls and bullets from the besieging forces: to crown all, he was laid low by typhoid.[1]

That this is a sphere in which Müller and Craik would feel quite at home is shown by their labours during the cholera outbreak at Bristol. Nevertheless, neither of the two feels that God would have him quit the field at Bristol. On the contrary, they have a sense of some larger work opening out before them. The fiery pillar moves not. Indeed, we note, a few days after, that Müller writes in his diary: " I read a part of Francke's ' Life.' The Lord graciously help me to follow him, so far as he followed Christ." Müller, we remember, was himself a debtor to Francke, having enjoyed the hospitality of the free lodgings for Divinity students at the Halle Orphan Houses.

But Francke was not only Divinity Professor, not

---

[1] Groves eventually "moved on" to India; he also travelled home to England to kindle missionary enthusiasm; indeed, scoured Europe with that object. Men's judgment might define the Bagdad Mission as a failure, but—who shall say what is failure or success in the eyes of the All-seeing? Groves' biography has bright gleams amid the darkness; some were won for Christ, despite the seemingly impenetrable hedge of pride and scorn presented by Mohammedanism. One other word: it seems impossible to leave the subject of the Bagdad Mission without recalling that, here, Francis William Newman drops out of the story of the Brethren. He went home, in order, as Henry Groves believed, to obtain fresh workers; but his biographer, I. Giberne Sieveking, suggests that a love interest was involved. In view of the common acceptation of the story that this brilliant but disappointing man died an unbeliever, it may be well to quote Dr. Martineau's admission, three or four years before Newman's death: "I had a letter from Frank Newman saying that, when he died, he wished it to be known that he died in the Christian Faith." One of Newman's final words of testimony was: "Christ is more and more."

only friend of orphans and of poor students; he was warmly concerned in Missions to the heathen, and it was largely through his efforts that, in 1705, the two first Protestant missionaries to India, Bartholomew Ziegenbalg and Henry Plutschau (both of them students under him at Halle), went forth, at the proposal of Dr. Lutkens, chaplain to the King of Denmark, to commence, under Danish auspices, the pioneer Mission at Tranquebar. Doubtless the two aspects of Francke's life are considered and weighed by Müller at this time; and here, doubtless, he drew inspiration for missionary endeavours—opening the way for others while himself engaged in numerous activities at home.

Face to face with the wretchedness of the poor of England, Müller adds, as he ponders the great facts of Francke's life: "The greater part of the Lord's people whom we know in Bristol are poor, and if the Lord were to give us grace to live as this dear man did,[1] we

---

[1] Francke died, June 17, 1727, aged sixty-four, leaving a rare and stimulating memory. It is impossible to estimate the influence of his teaching. Not a few of his students rallied to his side, in the schools, the Bible-printing works, and the Orphan Houses; others, like the two young missionaries referred to, carried the Good News to other lands. One of the most notable of those who studied in one of the schools was Count Zinzendorf, upon whose estate, at Herrnhüt, the Protestant refugees from Bohemia found shelter; and so, under his leadership, the Moravian Church, or "Unitas Fratrum," was renewed. Zinzendorf is also familiar to us as author of the glorious hymn, "Jesus, Thy blood and righteousness." It was at Halle that he founded among his schoolfellows the famous "Order of the Mustard Seed," for soul-winning. Without overmuch "embroidery" of the subject, it is well to note the doctrines, and the men, and the spirit of Halle, as Müller studied them, and to trace the influence upon his life of the Halle teaching and traditions.

might draw much more than we have as yet done, out of our Heavenly Father's bank, for our poor brothers and sisters." Whereby we may judge that some large vision of practical good, perhaps of an Orphan House, is looming before his eyes, in England, rather than in the East, as he seeks God's guidance.

The condition of the poor, more particularly of the rural districts of England, was lamentable indeed. In some parts, a penny loaf of ordinary white bread was a startling luxury to a labourer's child. Children were commonly fed on bran dumplings. A rustic, uniting a taste for variety with a chirrupy humour, would declare : " We had ' roast,' ' baked,' and ' boiled '— roast turnip, baked turnip, and boiled turnip"; but, " another way," as the cookery books say, was simply to have the turnip uncooked. A four-pound loaf cost eleven pence halfpenny or a shilling. In place of tea, said an old labourer who recalled these grim days : " what we did was to toast a bit o' bread at the fire until it were as black as coal, an' put it in the taypot an' pour water on't. . . . 'Taturs 'twas that most folks lived on in them days. What did we do when there were no 'taturs ? Well, we'd to do wi'out 'em." [1] No matter how kindly a squire might be, no matter how filled with loving sympathy the parish clergyman and his wife might be, the melancholy conditions were too widespread to be removed by a system of doles. Yet, what Christian could look upon the misery around

[1] *The Hungry Forties.*

him, upon suffering childhood, upon men and women prematurely aged, without being touched by intense compassion?

Müller betakes himself to prayer. Many a utilitarian, doubtless, scoffs at the idea of reforming earth by way of Heaven. Diogenes Smith, Brown, or Robinson, hunting around for an honest man, will fall into an ecstasy of laughter at this Anglo-German's ideas of reforming England, in all its roaring, tumultuous excitement, with its flaming rick-yards, Chartism, and incipient rebellion, by—prayer. Well, an't please thee, good Master Diogenes, tarry a little to see how the method works.

In the quiet of his own little room, pleading with God for some brethren in poverty, he cries: "Oh that it might please Thee to give me means to help them!" No man of insincere ejaculations is Müller. He means it. It is not: "Oh, that I had Lombard Street for mine own!" He is not thinking of himself, but of yonder poor brethren; but, how long thinkest thee he must pray, honest-man-seeking Diogenes? See, the Divine messenger is even at hand—in postman's uniform. "Before they call I will answer." In less than an hour he receives a remittance for £60, placed at his own disposal by a Christian whom he has never seen and whose home is thousands of miles away!

Be of good cheer, poor Christian brethren, succour is at hand! In a certain little pocket-book, Müller carefully keeps account of all that he receives and expends. His pencil is busy—so are Bristol bakers and grocers in the poorer parts of the city. The spirit of love and sympathy spreads; the Brethren give daily bread to poor boys and girls, and Müller asks himself: "Why should not schools be established for such, that they may hear the Scriptures, and learn the way of righteousness?" Which schools he presently establishes, all, O Diogenes Smith, Brown, or Robinson, being, dear but unbelieving sir, all in answer to prayer.

Teaching, preaching, visiting, Müller sees the work of God prosper mightily. Sinners, hearing the piercing word, are smitten with conviction and brought to taste the sweets of the Redeemer's love. This is to be preferred to controversial victories. A certain lady—a butterfly votary of pleasure—goes to a meeting at Bethesda, having understood that " one of the preachers there speaks with a German accent, and mispronounces some of his words." It will be a humorous experience, subject-matter for gay anecdotes and vivacious burlesque of Müller's mannerisms. To her discomfiture, however, it speedily becomes clear that God, "who hath made of one blood all nations of men," can thrust home the truth, even when preached with a Prussian accent to the British. The lady slips away, but carries a dart in her heart. The follies of this present world have for ever lost their fascination for her. Cleansing away the rouge and the face powder, she hurries back to Bethesda, and—is converted.[1] Her relatives, naturally enough, are astonished at the miracle, and, in response to her entreaties, six of them also go to Bethesda; also find mercy.

Many more, too, find their way to the Fountain of Grace, so that Craik and Müller, full of praise, hold a public thanksgiving "for the great success which it has pleased God to grant to our labours, and for confession of our sinfulness and unworthiness, and to entreat Him to continue His goodness towards us." The happy crowd of four hundred believers continue in praise and prayer for five-and-a-half hours, not finishing till past midnight. There are no engineered newspaper paragraphs, no patronising speeches by wealthy foes of God; only the songs of grateful hearts: "He brought me up also out of an horrible pit."

While the work thus goes on, Müller is as honest in his confessions as David Brainerd or Henry Martyn —who, amid wrestlings with triple forces of evil: Hinduism, the missionary-hating East India Company,

---

[1] Of how many stories of soul-winning does the instance remind us! For example; a gay crowd of young men were met in a London coffee-house. Wesley was to preach in the neighbourhood, so the festive company dispatched their chief wit, Martin Madan, to listen to the preacher and hasten back to entertain them with some delicious bit of mimicry. Madan went; as he entered, Wesley announced the text: "Prepare to meet thy God." Madan was smitten; he listened, and was converted. As a matter of courtesy he returned to the coffee-house. "Have you 'taken off' the old Methodist?" laughed the sparkling crowd. "No, gentlemen," replied Madan; "he has taken me off." Madan's powerful and attractive preaching style made him one of the most prominent of the earlier Methodists.

and the latitudinarianism of Evangel-detesting ministers, would suddenly turn upon himself, crying: "My own heart is at present cold and slothful. Oh that my soul did burn with love and zeal!" It is customary to brush aside the self-reproaching cries of such men. "They do not really mean it," says the literary critic, in effect; or: "These passages of gloom were doubtless written in moments of nervous prostration." They were doubtless written in humility before the Lord, and represent the simple facts. "For several weeks," says Müller, "I have had little real communion with the Lord. I long for it. I am cold. But I am not—yea, I *cannot* be—satisfied with such a state of heart. Oh that once more I might be brought to fervency of spirit, and that thus it might continue with me for ever!" Crushed by a sense of unworthiness before God, he cries: "I long to go Home, that I may be with the Lord, and that I may love Him with all my heart!"

No mere monastic longing is this to escape the dire conflict of the soul with the world, but rather the sigh of the soul to be where he may perfectly love and perfectly serve. "Oh that I had wings like a dove! for then would I fly away, and be at rest"—in God. But will George Müller go Home? Nay; these struggles of soul are but preparatory to the commencement of great things for God, in the witness of faith, which shall rivet man's attention on the building sites of Ashley Down. The Lord hath need of thee, beloved!

MÜLLER AND CRAIK AT BRISTOL

The Divine Potter is completing His work of moulding thy soul for a mighty embassage.

Next day comes such relief as tears can give—"on account of the state of my heart." Activities at Bethesda and among the poor notwithstanding, he condemns himself bitterly, and is less concerned about *doing* than *being*. Then the flame of hope blazes high again: on February 21, 1834, when he is "rather in a better state of heart than for some time past," he broods over the possibility of forming a "Scriptural Knowledge Institution." Thus, although Apollyon wounds him sore, he rises again. Apollyon might indeed seek to discourage him at this wonderful moment, when a great thought of world-evangelisation—which, broadly, the Scriptural Knowledge Institution is designed to be—is by the grace of God taking shape.

Carefully studying the experiences of George Müller in these stirring days, we note, in the thoughts which he expresses, the growth of this great idea, which is to be so fruitful of results. The chief obstacle in his way is the heavy pressure of pastoral duties. Nevertheless, we trace the powerful workings of his mind: to help missionaries in other lands, even if he is not himself free to go; to give instruction, particularly in the Gospel, both to children and adults; and to further the circulation of the Bible.

This same February 21, 1834, Müller is meeting and counselling inquirers for four-and-a-half hours;

even so, the time is too short to converse with them all; hence the next day finds him advising yet more, for a space of three hours. But, in spite of these calls of pastoral duty, his mind is working actively regarding the Scriptural Knowledge Institution, and he prepares a preliminary statement of principles and methods.

Thus, in the inspiration of this penniless Anglo-German preacher, there commences a Gospel work which shall affect human society in all parts of the world. The plans are admirable, the anticipation glorious. This man is a Missionary Society in himself. However; what "financial backing"—to use one of the world's phrases—has he? None whatever. Not a farthing, O gentlemen of finance! Not a farthing, O experts of Capel Court! Then he is "doomed to failure," as newspapers say? H'm. Not necessarily. There were men of old who went forth so, quite moneyless. "When I sent you without purse, lacked ye anything? And they said, Nothing." The force of the question lies in who it is that does the sending. The *sent ones* shall lack no good thing; and Müller argues, in the common sense of the spiritual plane, which is the absurdity of the plane of human shrewdness: "Is not God rich?"

Truly, George, He is rich: the world admits it—with a smile—in theory, but will hugely scorn this notion of thine that God Himself shall provide the means for a great scheme of Gospel-declaration, no man being asked to contribute. George Müller, however, takes no account of the views of the world; it is sufficient for him to do God's will and serve Him, and march forward. "What powerful men have joined the committee? Any millionaires?" None, according to the reckonings of Exchanges and Bourses. "What 'good names' have you, George Müller?" "Good names"? George Müller has Names that transcend all: they are the names of the Blessed Father, the Blessed Son, the Blessed Spirit. "Names"? "Instructions"? "Go ye into all the world, and preach the Gospel to every creature"!

The document wherein the principles of the Institution are set forth is one of the most uncompromising that ever man drew up. In essence it is a direct challenge to the world and to worldly influences in the Kingdom of God. The basis is that every believer is bound to help—is bound to be delighted to make holy sacrifice—in the cause of Christ.

The scheme, Müller admits, is open to the objection that there are Societies already existing "for the spread of the Gospel at home and abroad"; but "acknowledging, by the grace of God, the Word of God as the only rule of action for the disciples of the Lord Jesus," he sets forth some striking contentions in reply to such objection:—

1. The end which religious societies propose is, that the world will gradually become better and better, and that at last the whole world will be converted. To this end, there is constant reference to Hab. 2 : 14 : "The earth shall be filled with the knowledge of the

glory of the Lord, as the waters cover the sea"; and Isa. 11 : 9 : "The earth shall be full of the knowledge of the Lord, as the waters cover the sea." But it is clear, from many passages of the Divine testimony, that these passages can have no reference to the present Dispensation, but to the one which will commence with the Return of the Lord; that in the present Dispensation things will not become spiritually better, but rather worse; and that in the present Dispensation it is not the whole world that will be converted, but only a people gathered out from among the Gentiles for the Lord (see, for instance, Matt. 13 : 24–30 and 36–43 ; 2 Tim. 3 : 1–13 ; and Acts 15 : 14). A hearty desire for the conversion of sinners, and earnest prayer for it, are Scriptural, but it is unscriptural to expect the conversion of the whole world.

2. The connection of religious societies with the world is contrary to the Word of God (2 Cor. 6 : 14–18). When the work to be done requires that those who attend to it should be possessed of spiritual life, the children of God are bound, by their loyalty to their Lord, entirely to refrain from association with the unregenerate. But the connection with the world is so marked that every one who pays a guinea is considered a member; although he may manifest to every one that he does not know the Lord, he has a right to vote.

3. The unconverted are asked for money: how should we do this, who are not only forbidden to have

fellowship with unbelievers, but are also in fellowship with the Father and the Son, and can therefore obtain everything from the Lord which we can possibly need in His service, without being obliged to go to the unconverted world?

4. Even members of committee who manage the work are not rarely unconverted persons, if not open enemies to the truth; and this is suffered because they are rich, or "of influence," as it is called.

5. It is a common thing to endeavour to obtain, as patrons, presidents, and chairmen at public meetings, persons of rank or wealth, to attract the public. Never once has George Müller known the case of a *poor*, but very devoted, wise, and experienced servant of Christ being invited to fill the chair. Surely the Galilean fishermen, who were apostles, or our Lord Himself, who was called the Carpenter, would not have been called to this office, according to these principles. We should not judge a person's fitness for service in the Church of Christ by the position he fills in the world, or by the wealth he possesses.

6. Debt is contracted, contrary both to the spirit and letter of the New Testament (Rom. 13 : 8).

It is not to be thought that Müller is sour and fault-finding. Craik and he heartily recognised that there were many true servants of God among the various Societies. With such they remained united in brotherly love. Nevertheless, to go forward involved doing so on strictly Scriptural lines, and along such lines only they would go, although admitting they would "be considered as singular persons," or that it would seem as if they "despised other persons or would elevate ourselves above them." These principles are of course not merely those of Müller and Craik; they are the principles of Brethren; wherefore in the formation of the Scriptural Knowledge Institution for Home and Abroad, we recognise the further outworking of the missionary spirit already evidenced in the going forth of Groves and his associates to Bagdad.

The work was first entitled a "Society" instead of an "Institution," but, said Müller, explaining the alteration, "as the Institution never was a Society in the common sense of the word, there being nothing like membership, voting, a committee, etc., it appeared better to alter the name, for the sake of avoiding mistakes."

About a fortnight after these fundamental statements have been settled upon, a public meeting is called, and Müller and Craik describe their proposals. Next the Principles are drawn up; a positive statement of which the substance lies in the glorious sentence: "'In the name of our God we will set up our banners' (Ps. 20 : 5); He alone shall be our Patron." The document might well have for its motto the word of the Lord unto Zerubbabel: "Not by might, nor by power, but by My Spirit, saith the Lord of hosts." Of the inaugural meeting, Müller quietly says: "There was nothing outwardly influential, either in the number of people present or in our speeches."

Such being the Principles, what are the definite objects? Briefly, to establish Day-schools, Sunday-schools, and Adult-schools, all upon a Scriptural foundation; to circulate copies of the Bible and Gospel tracts; to further missionary effort. Such simple terms suffice to describe the Institution. Actually it is to become one of the most potent evangelistic and instructional forces of the century. In such days, State-provided education being a far-away goal indeed, the ignorance of the young is truly appalling. The recognition of the conditions does not imply the least belittling of the old-fashioned charity-schools, or the strenuous endeavours, on an extensive scale, of the National Society or the British and Foreign School Society.

Not a moment is lost; yet it is necessary to take time to secure able and godly teachers. Ready-equipped schoolmasters, who grasp the idea of capturing the children for Christ, are not so very plentiful. Müller prays, inquires, interviews, uses his common sense, of which excellent commodity he has a large fund. A suitable brother is secured for the chief post; then a suitable sister to be governess in the girls' school. All this time, events seem to be forcing Müller to take action regarding the welfare of orphans. For example, a little boy attends the school, and is not only instructed in secular knowledge, but, under some pointed word of Müller's, comes to desire to know and serve God. The poor child, however, is taken away to the poorhouse, lamenting his separation from the school and from the teacher he loves so well. Müller, also sore at heart, sees in the occurrence a lesson for himself—that he should do something to supply the temporal needs of poor children, the pressure of which has resulted in his losing an eager and promising young scholar, who might perhaps have been trained in the service of the Lord.

Opportunities multiply around him, but he acts ever upon the fixed principle, neither to lag behind the will of God, nor to run ahead, but ever to be just where that will would have him. In the duties of the day he is assiduous; in matters of "launching out" he waits to be sure of the Lord's dealings, and then moves swiftly and resolutely. His chief enemy, he frankly concedes, is George Müller himself; in a matter of constitutional irritability. George Müller, it seems, does not always "suffer fools gladly." Now and again his temper momentarily slips into the place of authority. However, he does not label it as "righteous indignation," but honestly confesses the imperfection.

There is indeed much to harass, much to tax the heart and brain. The increasing responsibilities in ministry and philanthropy and missionary extension might well exhaust the physical resources and excite nervousness. Biography, as a rule, would pass over matters of a momentary passion as too trivial for notice; but Müller, "nothing extenuates." A lady calls upon him and wastes his time with her chattering—despite his assurance that he has only a few minutes to spare. He is irritated, and humbly registers the fact: "I have sinned thus against the Lord. Help me, Thou Blessed Jesus, in future." And again: "These last three days I have had very little communion with God, and have therefore been very weak spiritually, and have several times felt irritability of temper."

The remedy is not far to seek: the wise and holy counsels he gives to others he applies also to himself —"May God in mercy help me to have more secret prayer!" Next day, he rises betimes, spends two special hours in prayer and meditation before break-fast, crying to the Lord thus early for grace to walk before Him that day, to learn His will, and do His work, being kept from evil, and preserved in peace.

Bethesda and Gideon flourish: hundreds are added to the fellowship—not that Müller or Craik gauge real spiritual results by mere arithmetic: for where men's lists show addition, God's may show subtraction. Selling or distributing Bibles, seeking new scholars, conversing with men and women regarding the Good News, working himself and setting many another to work, Müller is labouring with energy. Amid all, he ponders on the condition of orphan children in these dark and troublous days.

Some question does indeed arise in his mind,

whether, after all, he shall leave all these activities and go out to the East as a missionary, for his brother-in-law is at home seeking recruits for India. Careful, however, to do the will of God, he feels no leading to leave England, and resolves to stay in Bristol. By the end of February, 1835, there are five Day-schools—two for boys and three for girls. Yet much more remains to be done; this is only a beginning, excellent though it be, for troops of wretched, ill-fed, uneducated little ones have still to be gathered in. And if the condition of these, who have parents living, is so lamentable, what shall be said of the forlorn little creatures, parentless, neglected, wandering at large in the streets, and what of the children of the struggling poor who, if suddenly left without father and mother, find themselves homeless and helpless?

Müller's thoughts are often on this subject; often, too, upon the godless state of this same realm of Great Britain and Ireland; and he is praying much. Pray on, O dauntless one, pray on—for, truly, much shall come to the world through thy prayers—Prussian accent as thy tongue undoubtedly has!

CHAPTER IV

The Venture of Faith

A VISIT to Germany, in January, 1835, undertaken in company with Anthony Norris Groves, who is still seeking missionaries, brings Müller back to the scenes of early life. In all his journeyings he is talking of the love of God. A student tells him of certain "peculiarly good and cheap wine, which is to be had at Weinheim, near Heidelberg"; to which inspiring information Müller mildly retorts: "Years ago, when, a student like yourself, I came through the place, I cared about such things; now, however, I know that which is much better than wine." Small wonder that a volatile Frenchman in the coach finds Müller's serious testimony "too dull," and moves to an outside seat. "This," says Müller, "gave me a blessed and most refreshing opportunity to pray for about an hour aloud in the coach, which strengthened and refreshed my soul."

Presently he is at Halle; visits Dr. Tholuck, who treats him with loving tenderness and encourages him with accounts of former fellow-students converted to God and pointing sinners to the Lamb. Inevitably also, a visit is paid to the Francke Orphanage : his business is to visit a friend—the son of a former neighbour in the old days at home. Likewise he goes on pilgrimage to the room at Wagner's where God began the work of grace in his heart. Then he visits his father at Heimersleben, shows him kindness and attention, walks in the fields with him. "May God help me," says father Müller to his son, "to follow your example, and to act according to what you have said to me."

But, Craik being ill, it is necessary to hurry back to Bristol, and to attend to the ministry of the Word. Bristol, clearly, is God's place for Müller. The Scriptural Knowledge Institution is doing so well that the five Day-schools have a total of nearly 450 children. On June 22, Mr. Groves, senior (Mrs. Müller's father), passes quietly away; three days after, the little boy who has been born to the Müllers, dies also : the remains of grandfather and grandson are buried in the same grave.

So goes the round of life : battlings with physical weakness; still more serious wrestlings of soul on account of "inward corruptions, and carnality of heart"—all this, however, being relieved by seasons of nearness to God in prayer, and the shining into his soul of the Sun of Righteousness. It is not difficult to trace the Divine workings which lead him forward. For example, on November 20, 1835, he takes tea at a sister's house, and comes across—of all books—the biography of Francke ; whereupon he records that he has frequently

thought of labouring in a similar way, albeit possibly
on a smaller scale : not, indeed, in slavish imitation of
the Halle philanthropist, but to glorify God. The
little seed sown in his heart by the Spirit is beginning
to germinate ; next day, he is resolved, or rather, to
put it in his own exact way, ascribing all to the
gracious operations of the Spirit, he "has it very
much impressed on his heart," no longer merely to
think about the establishment of an Orphan House,
but actually to commence it. Two days later, the record
is that he is still more stirred up to think and pray ;
and the remarkable gifts that come in for the Scripture
Knowledge Institution encourage him.

Moreover, Müller sees that God has specially
helped him forward to the point of being able to take
Him at His word, and to rely entirely upon that
word. Is this gift to be deemed a small thing? Nay,
in regard to it he judges himself to be verily the
servant of the whole Church of God; the gift is
to be used to demonstrate that God has not changed.
Believers, he sees, are ofttimes brought into bondage
and by unbelief deny their name. Business men
shiveringly fail to be faithful, lest they should lose in
trade ; elderly folk tremble in view of the workhouse ;
all is gloom and depression, as though God has no
existence or has left the universe to chaos, and aban-
doned His people to the winds of adversity and
the laughter of demons. It is, in fact, time for fresh
proof, and such proof must surely be admitted as

tendered if he, George Müller, poor man and humble preacher, can, without asking one person for so much as a farthing, be the means of establishing and carrying on an Orphan House. He loves children tenderly and desires to train them in righteousness : but the main purpose is that all may see the faithfulness of the Living God.

With this dominating thought upon him, Müller arranges for a public meeting, at which he will put the matter before his brethren. Meantime, pondering upon the Scriptures, he is impressed by the Psalmist's word : "Open thy mouth wide, and I will fill it." "Open *wide*"? Then, he will pray for a house "to be loaned, or that some one may be led to pay the rent for one, or that one may be given." Also there must needs be considerable initial outlay, so—"Open thy mouth wide"—he will pray for no less than a thousand pounds sterling. Further, what are money and buildings and even troops of orphans in training unless there be godly teachers, well able to train children in ways of industry and, more especially, to win them for the Lord? Accordingly, he prays whole-heartedly for helpers. Two days afterwards he receives the first donation—one shilling, accompanied by another shilling for the other activities of the Scriptural Knowledge Institution; and the humble donor, in the simplicity of Christian giving, adds: "In the name of the Lord alone lift up your banners, so shall you prosper." A shilling, given him by a German missionary,—and the blessing of the Lord : here is the foundation of the Orphan Houses.

Müller is perfectly quiet before the Lord ; can He not rain down, for that matter, a million shillings, yea, cover Ashley Down with them ? Here is a second shilling : next, three more are placed in the money-box. Two days pass and the post brings nothing, but a friend gives a certain bulky wardrobe by way of beginning the furnishing. In a meeting, Müller tells his story and describes his ideals. No collection is taken ; there are no bursts of enthusiasm, no shouts of fervent saints touched with the fire of Christian philanthropy ; but ten more shillings are given. Next day, a Christian couple write proposing themselves "for the service of the intended Orphan House," devoting their furniture also to the work and being prepared to labour "without receiving any salary, believing that if it be the will of the Lord to employ us, He will supply all our need." Truly the Lord is working in His own way—which is the best way.

Here, too, is a brother who has apparently been making a collection, if not in cash, at any rate in goods ; he delivers up the proceeds of his toil, and Müller placidly inspects them and takes specific note of them, to the glory of God. There are : three dishes, twenty-eight plates, three basins, one jug, four mugs, three salt-stands, one grater, four knives, and five forks—and it is significant of Müller that, all through his career at the Orphan Houses, he never fails to set down each little gift in kind ; for is it not the offering of some humble saint, given in the name of Him who pronounced the lovely " Inasmuch "? It is not in George Müller to enter up a thousand-pound donation but yet forget the "four knives and five forks." No, he will pray a blessing on all—down to the odd fork—and on the cheerful givers thereof.

Next day, again, Müller is early at prayer, seeking that God would give a fresh token of His favour regarding the Orphan House. While he yet prays there comes a visitor—bringing what ? " Three dishes, twelve plates, one basin, and one blanket." Unbelief would say : " A pile of rubbish from a third-rate sale-room ! " To Müller, the bale is one more answer to prayer : he thanks God and still prays for yet another encouragement : it comes, for a person who was one of the unlikeliest to be able to do so, gives £50. This is indeed a day of prayer and answer, but Müller is back again on his knees, crying : "Lord, give still more ! " In the evening comes " twenty-nine yards of print ; and a sister offers her services for the work." All the gifts, all the offers, are precious to Müller.

To other items we add, December 18, 1835, no less important matters than : a counterpane, a flat-iron stand, eight cups and saucers, a sugar basin,—who dares grumble that the list suggests an auctioneer's catalogue, or that the enumeration is petty ?—a milk jug, a tea-cup, sixteen thimbles, five knives and forks, six dessert-spoons, twelve teaspoons, four combs, and two little graters. All are down on Müller's list: mark the pathos of that last item. Here is a man whose demonstration is to be of God's faithfulness, on a grand scale: he is of the true apostolic line, knowing that by faith "all things are yours" for "ye are Christ's; and Christ is God's"; wherefore he realises full well that the circle-sweep of that mighty compass-pencil which brings "all things" into the range of the child of faith includes also the "two little graters."

To the graters and their like add, however, £100, the gift of—a successful merchant, or an alderman at least? No; of a lowly seamstress. The Lord be with thee, gentle, godly seamstress of Bristol city; truly thou art one of the elect, shining out in the annals of philanthropy like that sister-seamstress-in-the-Faith of thine, Sarah Martin, of Yarmouth, who when asked: "Can you spare so much time to visit poor prisoners?" replied: "I can *sacrifice* it!" See, now, this Bristol seamstress. Her average earnings are three shillings and sixpence a week. Her father dies, and she comes into £480, of which the father has had the interest. Her brother and two sisters each inherit an equal amount. The father is heavily in debt at the time of his death; has been, indeed, a drunkard and ne'er-do-well. The seamstress says to herself: "However sinful my father has been, yet he was my father, and his debts ought to be paid." Her brother and sisters are by no means so enthusiastic, but think the case would be met by paying five shillings in the pound.

The delighted creditors, having not the slightest legal claim, immediately agree to the five shillings offer, and are paid on that scale; but the seamstress goes round to each and gives them the full balance of the debt.

Not a little unready to accept so much money from one whom he has always known as poor, Müller questions her as to her motives in giving; he is anxious that she should not give in a moment of enthusiasm, only to be sorry afterwards. But he does not need to converse long; she is, he pronounces, "a quiet, calm, considerate follower of the Lord, who desires to act according to the blessed word : 'Lay not up for yourselves treasures upon earth.'" This "calm, considerate," sickly seamstress has truly apprehended the genius of Christianity; she is Spirit-taught; finally she declares : "The Lord Jesus has given His last drop of blood for me ; and should I not give Him this £100 ? Rather than the Orphan House should not be established, I will give all the money I have." And by way of clinching the matter, she leaves "an extra £5, for the poor."

Such is the spirit in which the Orphan Houses are founded; such is the character of these glorious givers. Every penny, every bank-note, every flat-iron, has been brought in unasked. A plain statement in a meeting, and the simplest of printed letters setting forth the proposals, have been the sole means of publicity; and in neither has money or furniture been asked for; if people would give let them do so, to the glory of God ;

but no request would be made to any living soul.
With such responses being received—signs, assuredly,
of the blessing of God upon the scheme—Müller de-
velops his plan of campaign, resolving that, if no other
place is available, he will rent certain premises, which
can be had for £50 per annum; to commence, he will
take girl orphans, "because they need more particularly to be taken care of."

It is intended to open in April; meantime the
premises which he had thought of having been let, he
resolves to rent the house in which he has himself been
living, as the first Orphan House. But—where are
the orphans? On this point, Müller makes a singular
but characteristically honest confession. He has prayed
for means, for furniture, for teachers of a godly frame
of mind, and for guidance to the right premises; but,
while praying for a Home for children, he has omitted
to pray for children for the Home. It might well have
seemed superfluous; it might easily have escaped his
thought in a populous city and in a day when homeless
and orphan children were so numerous. Nevertheless,
if an Orphan House is to be raised in answer to prayer,
every detail must be "atmosphered," so to speak, in
intercession. "I took it for granted," he admits, "that
there would be plenty of applications." At the same
time he has had a secret consciousness that the Lord
might in some way disappoint his natural expectations,
in order to show him that there could be no prosperity
in any single thing without Him.

Lying low before God for a whole evening and examining his own heart, he comes delightedly to this self-abasing conclusion, that he can rejoice in God being glorified, even though it should be by the whole matter being brought to nought. Yet, he pleads before the Lord, the establishing and prospering of the Orphan House will be to His glory; and he cries to God not only that applications of some sort may come, but that *He* will send them. Next day the first application duly arrives, and very speedily there are enough cases accepted to fill the institution.

The premises, 6 Wilson Street, Bristol, are rented, and in due course furnished for thirty orphan girls, between the ages of seven and twelve. On April 21, 1836, the Home is opened, to the sound of praises offered to the Living God who has so wonderfully supplied the means.

Yet, this is not enough. Among the applications received are several on behalf of tiny girls—and boys also—who are not yet seven years old. What shall be done for these helpless little creatures? Müller is greatly concerned, remembering: "It is not the will of your Father which is in heaven, that one of these little ones should perish." Accordingly, he decides to establish a second Orphan House, for infant children; money comes in; further applications are received; but the difficulty is to find a suitable matron. No hireling will do, no cold official, no person who looks dreamingly to the sky but forgets that the kitchen needs scrubbing and that Tommy's shirt is short of its back collar-button.

For four months, Müller waits upon God : at length the right lady, godly and capable, is found for a matron. Then, within a week, premises are secured, of which Müller himself says : "To-day [October 25, 1836] we obtained, without any trouble, through the kind hand of God, very suitable premises for the Infant Orphan House. If we had laid out many hundreds of pounds in building a house, we could scarcely have built one more suitable for the purpose. How evident is the hand of God in all these matters ! How important to leave our concerns, great and small, with Him ; for He arranges all things well ! If *our* work be *His* work, we shall prosper in it." Had he gone rushing ahead of God's will in the matter of the matron, the suitable premises would also have been missed ; as it is : "All things work together for good." The Infant Orphan House, 1 Wilson Street, Bristol, is opened, November 28.

One concern still lies heavily upon Müller ; of the £1000 for which he started out to pray, it appears, on a reckoning being made, that there is a " balance outstanding," so to speak, which has not yet been received, in answer to the prayer of faith. He is about to publish, for the edification of God's people, a " Narrative of the Lord's Dealings with George Müller "; and it would be sweet indeed could he intimate therein—by no means for the advertising of George Müller, but for God's glory—that all the money has come in. Wherefore, he prays, and God answers. A lady who is a total stranger calls to give £40. Gradually the total mounts up. Then comes a supreme day of wrestling in prayer that the remainder shall be given, and in the evening a gift of £5 is brought, completing the sum. The prayer is answered: the "mouth" that was "opened wide" is "filled." For eighteen months and ten days that prayer ascended, in the full assurance of faith, and all has been given spontaneously, in love and obedience to God.

Far from entertaining any boastful spirit, Müller is prostrate in humility and gratitude, calling upon his friends to give glory to God, with him, for the condescension shown to "such a worthless, faithless servant as I am"—terms which he uses with all plainness and sincerity. Herein, too, he sees encouragement for all. If he, so little conformed to the mind of the Lord, has his prayers answered, what might not others expect? Faith, he confesses, has sometimes faltered. Not always has he been able to fulfil the condition of Mark 11 : 24 : "What things soever ye desire, when ye pray, *believe that ye receive them*, and ye shall have them"; and the distinction he draws is between the two positions: (1) being unable to praise God beforehand, in the triumph of faith, and (2) being as sure that God will enable him to meet, for example, rents that fall due, as he would be were the money already in his pocket. He is not professing by any means that he has attained perfection in faith or walk—far were this from George Müller; but, while declaring his weaknesses and failures, he points to the evidences all around of the faithfulness of God and bids his fellow-believers march on to victory over unbelief.

While looking to God in confident expectation for the £1000, Müller had also to sustain the responsibility for maintenance, and in this matter also he demonstrates the inter-relation of prayer and experience. Duties, administrative and pastoral, press heavily upon him, and, while by no means forgetting prayer for the blessing of God to rest upon the work, he somehow does not pray specifically for funds for upkeep. Not long can a poor man with heavy responsibilities omit finance from his petitions, hence, in urgent need he cries out to the Lord for deliverance. Next day—it is an exquisite task to trace how in Müller's experience "next-day" answers follow hard upon evenings of prayer—a brother who has long intended to contribute but has hitherto lacked the means is—just at this moment—enabled to give £10. The evening of the same day brings a letter, enclosing £5, from a lady who, strongly impressed that God would have her send money, and that there must therefore be a special need, has gathered all the money she has in the house, and has sent it forthwith, promising also to send as much more, if it is required.

The same faith is applied to his own daily needs,

and it is good to note, also, the fine recognition of personal duty that pervades all he does. Upon the principles on which he expects others to act, he first acts himself, faith and sacrifice being indissoluble.

One day he is at the end of his resources; shall he pray for special help? Well, he bethinks himself of sundry silver spoons which are somewhere packed away in the house. They were a marriage gift, at Teignmouth, but have never been used, for the excellent reason that the Müllers, having sold their own plate, years before, as savouring somewhat of the fashions and ways of the world, do not wish to use any silver, even though it be the gift of personal well-wishers. But how, while these spoons lie there untransmuted into bread, is it possible to offer the prayer of faith that the plain needs of everyday life may be supplied? There is only one way: the spoons must go, the consoling thought remaining that the giver, if he knew the circumstances, would by no means be offended. So, the spoons go their way to the dealers', and Müller's soul is free once more to soar in prayer and rapture to the Throne of God.

Again, in that time of sorrow—and also of inevitable expense, when Mrs. Müller's father, and also little baby-boy Müller, have just died, there is a subtle temptation to run into debt for new clothes. To go shabby to the funeral of his loved ones might be misunderstood; however, he resolves that he will on no account run into debt, so the rusty clothes do duty.

A fortnight afterwards he has a new suit given him; there is no record whether they were ready-made or not, but even if so, Müller was doubtless able to say, as did the noted " Billy " Bray upon a similar occasion : "They are sure to be all right; the Lord knows my measure."

This principle of "no debt," indeed, is applied under all circumstances, both personally and in the Orphan Houses. Just after the conclusion of a prayer-meeting, on the last night of the year 1839, Müller is about to go home, happy in soul, but knowing there is not enough money in hand to meet the orphans' requirements, on this New Year's Day, when a packet is given him containing money for the work. Far from acting on the apostolic injunction to "owe no man anything," the donor is a person well known to be in debt, and whom creditors are dunning in vain. Shall the work of the Lord be dishonoured by money being received for it which in honesty does not belong to the donor at all ? No ; the packet is returned forthwith, on the ground that " no one has a right to give whilst in debt." This occurs between one and two o'clock in the morning ; about eight o'clock a gift of £5 arrives for the orphans, sent by a lady, her own son being the messenger. " Observe," says Müller, " the brother is led to bring it *at once.* The Lord knew our need, and therefore this brother could not delay bringing the money."

As the Orphan Houses come to be known and

applications come in, it is evident that further development must follow. It is not possible to rest satisfied with a Home for girls and another for infants, and to neglect the needs of boys. More than this, Müller must ere long be practically forced into commencing a Home for boys, for a number of the little ones among the infants *are* boys, and when these come to be, say, seven years of age, it will be desirable to remove them so as to keep the institution really an Infants' Home. But whither shall they go? And how shall so busy a man as George Müller undertake further responsibilities? He is fully engaged in the ministry of the Word, and in attending to the affairs of Bethesda and Gideon—which means, chiefly, the oversight of a fellowship of three hundred and seventy persons, beyond which regular duties comes the responsibility for the Day-schools and Sunday-schools and other activities of the Scriptural Knowledge Institution. How, then, is it possible for this much-worked brother, despite his willingness, to start yet another Orphan House?

However, the things which are impossible with men being possible with God, Müller decides that if his Father should send the means for such an enlargement then the enlargement shall be made; and in the true "Müller way" he comes to a sort of understanding between his soul and the Lord: "If there could be found a brother who could keep the accounts and attend to applications; if a pious schoolmaster and other helpers could be secured; if there should be forthcoming such a sum as is necessary to furnish a Home for forty boys, and to clothe them, and leave a little in hand for necessary expenses, then I will take it to be God's will that I should go forward."

And, as he hopes and waits, he still holds to his primary idea : " If I, a poor man, simply by prayer and faith, obtained, *without asking any individual,* the means for establishing and carrying on an Orphan House, there would be something which, with the Lord's blessing, might be instrumental in strengthening the faith of the children of God, besides being a testimony to the consciences of the unconverted, of the reality of the things of God.   I certainly did from my heart desire to be used of God to benefit poor children, to seek to do them good in this life ; I also particularly longed to be used by God in getting the dear orphans trained up in the fear of God ; but still, the first and primary object of the work was, and still is, that God might be magnified by the fact, that the orphans under my care are provided with all they need, only by *prayer and faith*, without any one being asked by me or my fellow-labourers, whereby it may be seen that God is faithful still, and hears prayer still."

CHAPTER V

God's Faithfulness

PURSUING the main theme of Faith Triumphant, we see Müller cogitating much upon this Home for boys. Blessed thoughts of the mercies of God encourage him; in effect, he reminds himself: " I have been kept in the ways of God; I desire more than ever to live for Him, and to have a heart filled with love toward Him. While some have fallen into grave errors, I have been saved therefrom, have been more and more established in the fundamental truths of the Gospel, and have seen more minutely the mind of God concerning many truths. I have been kept in uninterrupted love and union with Henry Craik: this union has sprung from God and Him it has glorified. Men of inconsistent life who were seeking to be proposed for fellowship at Bethesda or Gideon have had their sins found out, or, under the constraint of the Spirit, have confessed. Despite the physical weakness of Henry Craik and myself, we have been helped through much work. When trials have come upon us, the Lord has mercifully supported us and speedily delivered us. As to temporal wants, these have been richly supplied; not once have I lacked necessaries, and generally I have abounded—and all without having one shilling ^f regular income."

Turning, in this Psalm of Retrospect, to the story of progress, he finds delight above all that, during these five years, it has gone continuously forward. In the three years and four months since the Scriptural Knowledge Institution was started, over four thousand copies of the Scriptures have been circulated; four Day-schools have been established; and the missionary cause has been furthered at stations in India and Canada, as well as on the continent of Europe. There is a dew from the Lord: the Good Seed yields abundantly.

Inevitably, an increasing measure of publicity attaches to Müller's sayings and doings. In his preaching, Bible teaching, and visitation he becomes widely known in Bristol and the west. The place of Bethesda among the assemblies of the saints, the zeal and simplicity of Müller and Craik, and the publication of the "Narrative," in its captivating ingenuousness and spiritual charm, combine to give the Scriptural Knowledge Institution, and particularly the Orphan Houses, a godly sort of advertisement. It could scarcely be otherwise, for Müller and Craik are men of remarkable endowments, mentally and spiritually.

Nevertheless, it is not to be concluded that the large sums of money which come to Müller are obtained by "telling a story," which, while disclaiming the idea of a public appeal, does so appeal. The statements are plain and unvarnished: their peculiar attraction is a godly fragrance, for they are a sort of addition to the Acts of the Apostles; yet their interest is only for those who believe in prayer; they do not in any sense appeal to the ungodly. No reviewer of the day puts them in the category of literature that will last; nor is this surprising when we note the long lists which the report contains, column after column, of donations and articles sent in for the orphans. Yet the "Narrative" must needs live, by reason of its fascinating record of whole-souled trust in God. It is the glory of El-Shaddai that Müller has in mind.

Even when recounting, in the early pages of the "Narrative," the flaming wildness of his unregenerate days, he is magnifying the grace of God and hoping to win some wanderer home to Jesus Christ. "I judged," he says, " that in so doing, some who live at present in sin might see, through my example, the misery into which sin leads, even as it regards the present life and the happiness which is connected with the ways of God; and that they might also be encouraged through what God has done for me, to turn to Him. I made myself therefore a fool and degraded myself in the eyes of the inhabitants of Bristol, that you, my dear unconverted fellow-sinners, who may read this, may, with God's blessing, be made wise. The love of Christ has constrained me to speak about my former lies, thefts, fraud, etc., that you might be benefited. Do not think I *am* a fool, and have therefore told out my heart in my folly; but I have made myself a fool for the benefit of your souls."

In such sayings, we have Müller as he is, the true servant of God and a plain, outspoken man. He is no extraordinary being removed into a rarefied atmosphere, midway between earth and heaven, whence to look coldly down upon the sins and failures of poor humanity. It is the fashion sometimes to represent him as a kind of amalgam of Jerome and Simon Stylites and Lord Shaftesbury and William Blake, plus an unearthly quality which seems to remove him altogether from the category of men. Nay, he is a plain man : saved by grace, separated unto God and His work, but profoundly human ; a homely man sitting down to tea and toast with his kindly wife ; settling questions of administration ; puzzling over inept letters from superficial critics ; knowing full well the market price of coal and potatoes, the most advantageous ways of utilising half a sheep, and the most durable kinds of cloth for making little boys' coats and knickerbockers ; such is George Müller, servant of the Most High, apostle of Faith Triumphant.

The very house in which he lives, at Bristol, gives a kind of testimony, in its old-fashioned plainness, to the man who inhabits it. A picture of the place survives : no elegant villa in which a prosperous person, greedy of creature comforts may have a good time, but of the severest brick simplicity of ugly domestic architecture in the days of the Fourth William. It has a semi-underground front room which the most eloquent of house agents could scarcely designate a breakfast-parlour; there are two storeys above it. The gateway mortar betrays suspicions of crumbling. Truly, the most ordinary of dwellings—yet withal sufficient for one who, as he always loves to confess, is just a pilgrim and a stranger on the earth.

The modesty of the man appears when the time comes for publishing the first volume of the "Narrative." He lingers awhile in doubt, staring at the hapless volumes and half fearing that he has taken a wrong step; asking himself: "Is there not too much of George Müller in them?" True, the subject is "The Lord's Dealings with George Müller," but has he anywhere placed the accent on the mere recipient of Divine bounty, instead of in the mighty Giver?

Alone before God, he puts George Müller, so to speak, into the witness-box and cross-examines him. But George comes out unscathed, for the "Narrative" was framed and carried through in a spirit of fervent prayer. Faith puts the accent on God Himself. Never was a more precise, word-weighing writer than Müller. Not that he aimed at literary beauty; he did not aspire, like Bishop Burnet, to "polish his writings every day of his life"; nor was he one of those who, as Johnson says, "hope for eminence from the heresies of paradox."

He laboured, indeed, but it was to give the exact fact, to convey the absolute meaning within the least compass. Every sentence is well-balanced ; every paragraph is compact; the style is that of an alert and trained mind ; but the subject is not George Müller, it is the faithfulness of God. None can say that these terse stories of sweet deliverance swing to the side of glorifying Müller rather than glorifying God, " even in the estimation of a hair."

Easily misled by the eccentric exaggerations of Dickens, the world delights to describe a man of prayer as a Chadband or a Stiggins. Here, however, let the world see, if it will, the real man of prayer, almost morbidly timid of even the semblance of self-advertising. Faith triumphs ; he puts away the temptation to destroy the " Narrative " forthwith, but gives one away, as a definite act of committing himself to publication. Then he praises God for the honour He has bestowed upon His servant, in enabling him to lift up a standard of truth and witness for the Lord. The " Narrative," indeed, is its own witness. It is Müller's gage of defiance to unbelief. Not he it was who inspired the thought of the Orphan Houses : not he it was who raised the money : it was the Living God. George Müller opened his mouth wide, and God filled it with good things. The fearful and unbelieving, the " half-converted," whose obscure vision is merely of " men as trees walking," cannot understand ; but the record is clear and lovely to the eye of faith.

THE LIFE OF GEORGE MÜLLER

In the autumn of 1837, a house is taken for the new Home, but divers respectable folk in the neighbourhood, as fearful of a philanthropic institution as of a workhouse or a smallpox hospital, are, not unnaturally, grievously alarmed, and threaten legal proceedings; whereupon Müller, not wishing to embroil the landlord, cancels the agreement. He is at this time overdone with work and responsibility, and fain would get away from Bristol for a little rest, but what of the expense? Elijah's ravens, however, are a long-lived kind of bird; a letter arrives by one of them, enclosing an anonymous gift of £5 "for your personal use." The difficulty is solved; he visits Bath and Weston-super-Mare; the illness, however, is severer than he had thought, but in the midst of his weakness his cry is "Praise the Lord!" He is not far from a serious nervous breakdown, nor is this surprising when we remember the engrossing and multiplying character of his activities. "You do too much," his friends protest; but as he looks around and sees the vast majority of mankind doing so little, how shall he do less? Moreover, God will help him; he pauses amid his struggles to note "the kindness of the Lord" in this or that deliverance of the orphans, or in the gift, for example, of a hundred pairs of blankets for the poor.

As he lies ill, at Bristol, one sight is a splendid cordial for his fainting heart; it is the procession of young girls from the Orphan House, clean and well-clad, under the care of a Sister, marching to Bethesda.

This physical collapse is one of the trying periods of his life—shall he ever arise again and "do exploits"? His liver is inactive, his nerves in a lamentable state. Irritability sometimes masters him still—"irritability" —he sadly confesses—"towards my dear wife, and that almost immediately after I had been on my knees before God, praising Him for having given me such a wife."

Physicians urge him to go away again, for a change of air; he is reluctant to leave Bristol, but the same evening a letter arrives from a lady, fifty miles away, who gives him the same advice and adds to her counsels £15 to defray the expenses. Certainly, there are godly men and women who realise his value and the desirability of saving him, if possible, from complete collapse. He resolves to rest again, for his head troubles him terribly, and he is fearful of losing his mental balance; and the tendency to quickness of temper becomes so strong that he cries: "O Lord, mercifully keep Thy servant from openly dishonouring Thy name. Rather take me Home to Thyself."

There is much wrestling in prayer. One day, at Trowbridge, he feels the cold very much, whereupon, taking the poker, he stirs the fire, but is irritated because, on account of his feeble circulation, he remains in a chilled state. Like Jonah in the heat, so Müller in the frost. He is angry even with the coals; but the thought rises: this is Satan's plan to rob him of communion with God, wherefore he says: "I confessed my sin of irritability, and sought to have my conscience cleansed through the blood of Jesus. He had mercy upon me ; my peace was restored. I sought the Lord again in prayer and had uninterrupted communion with Him." And, that there may be no mistake as to his meaning, he adds : "I have purposely mentioned the above, in order to show how the most trivial causes may operate in suddenly robbing one of the enjoyment of most blessed communion with God." So, in the full delight of peace and trust, he continues in prayer for hours, and meditates with songs of praise, upon Psalm 66 : "We went through fire and through water : but Thou broughtest us out into a wealthy place." All this and much more he writes, prints, publishes—as a testimony and to God's glory ; here is the heart-cry of George Müller—of a soul separated unto Christ.

During this time of physical nervous suffering, he enjoys sweet seasons of communion : "My heart has been drawn out in prayer for many things, especially that the Lord would create in me a holy earnestness to win souls. For this I have been quickened by reading Whitefield's 'Life.' . . . The Lord is yet merciful to me. My soul has been led out in prayer this day [January 17, 1838], and that for a considerable time. I have read on my knees, with prayer and meditation, Psalm 68, verse 5 : 'a Father of the fatherless' has been a special blessing to me, with reference to the orphans. The truth which is contained in this, I never realised so much as to-day. By the help of God, this shall be my argument before Him, respecting the orphans, in the hour of need. He is their Father, and therefore has pledged Himself, as it were, to provide for them, and to care for them ; and I have only to remind Him of the need of these poor children, in order to have it supplied. My soul is still more enlarged respecting orphans. This word, 'a Father of the fatherless,' contains enough encouragement to cast thousands of orphans upon the loving heart of God."

After journeying on the Continent and making various brief stays also at divers places in England, Müller finds himself sufficiently recovered to return to Bristol; whereupon, at Gideon Chapel, May 8, 1838, he reads the 103rd Psalm, and thanks the Lord publicly for his affliction. Not, be it noted, for deliverance therefrom, but for the affliction itself, as a means of grace, in the school of God.

All this time, the Orphan work has been making its way. The story of its support is one of wonder, in such an infinite variety of ways are its needs supplied ; now with a gift of a shilling or two, now with a large donation ; now with a handful of jewellery or a silver teapot, for sale, and now with a cartload of vegetables. "Owe no man anything," continues to be one of Müller's mottoes, and the "Narrative" gives some delightful glimpses of its out-workings: for example:—

"November 21 [1838].—Never were we so reduced

in funds as to-day. There was not a single halfpenny in hand between the matrons of the three Houses. Nevertheless there was a good dinner, and, by managing so as to help one another with bread, etc., there was a prospect of getting over this day also; but for none of the Houses had we the prospect of being able to take in bread. When I left the brethren and sisters, at one o'clock, after prayer, I told them that we must wait for help and see how the Lord would deliver us at this time. I was sure of help, but we were indeed straitened.

"When I came to Kingsdown, I felt that I needed more exercise, being very cold; wherefore I went not the nearest way home, but round by Clarence Place. About twenty yards from my house, I met a brother who walked back with me, and who, after a little conversation, gave me £10 to be handed to the deacons towards providing poor saints with coals, blankets, and warm clothing; also £5 for the orphans and £5 for the other objects of the Scriptural Knowledge Institution. This brother had called twice while I was gone to the Orphan Houses, and had I now been one half-minute later, I should have missed him. But the Lord knew our need, and therefore allowed me to meet him."

Another day, there is sufficient provision for dinner, but not for tea. Never has the food store seemed so low. The case is spread before the Lord, in prayer. While the little company are praying, comes a knock at the door, and a sister goes out to answer it, the rest continuing to remind their Father in heaven of the orphans' need and of His Divine promises. At length they arise, Müller ejaculating: "God will surely help." While the sentence is yet unfinished, his glance falls on a letter that has been brought in, addressed to himself. It proves to be from his wife, and contains an enclosure, from a friend, with £10 for the orphans.

It is the intense realisation of the man that God will unfailingly do exactly what is best, that makes his faith shine as with the light of the sanctuary. Not a whimper sounds when the way is dark: what are clouds, but the hiding-place of the Most High? Where the ordinary man might be petulant, we can only think of Müller with a calm smile, awaiting God's provision. "Consider," he cries, "how *seasonably* the Lord sends supplies. Not once does He forget us. Not once is our need only *half* supplied. Not once do His supplies come too late. 'Oh, taste and see that the Lord is good!'"

On a certain Saturday, Müller remarks to a friend: "The salaries are due, the treacle casks are empty, all the provision stores are exhausted, clothing is needed, and worsted for the boys' knitting. It would be desirable to have £50." They manage very well, however, over the Sunday, but on the Monday nothing remains for the midday meal. Müller, notwithstanding, is resting in that assurance of faith which he describes as "being just as certain of having the money as though I actually had it in my pocket." Very soon a letter arrives from India—dispatched two months previously—containing a draft for £50. All is well. Flow afresh, O treacle-barrels; hurry, good bakers and butchers, for very soon the tablecloths will be laid!

Müller's name has come to be associated in the public mind with the raising of huge sums only. This is natural enough, and it is of course correct, not only that the sums raised were huge in total, but that certain single donations were for large amounts, yet to Müller there was no more marvel in fifty shillings—or, for that matter, in fifty farthings—than in five thousand sovereigns. The real, substantial fact being the answer to prayer, what matters it if that answer is a rich man's cheque or a poor woman's pound of sugar? The orphans are eating, so to speak, bread from heaven, whether in a vanful sent by some godly merchant or in a twopenny loaf left at the gate by Mrs. Brown, charwoman and saint. Müller has been speaking on: "I am poor and needy; yet the Lord thinketh upon me"; immediately afterwards there arrives a gift of half a crown. Does he pass the fact as too small for notice? No; the half-crown is "another proof that our Father cares for us."

Once more; there is nothing—except potatoes—to be prepared for dinner. In two hours and three-quarters dinner-time will have arrived. Müller prays and waits. Within a quarter-of-an-hour a large box is delivered at the door: it contains some lengths of dress material, sundry articles to be sold, and £12 in cash. Here is another illustration of the Lord's "timing" of gifts. Two and a half hours—just convenient space of time in which to fetch provisions and prepare the dinner.

Müller stands ever by the principles of Christian duty and probity; he will accept no donation under circumstances that his conscience refuses to approve. "But," some timid heart might have objected, "there is not enough money in hand to meet the needs of the day—is it not insulting Providence to send money away?" Nay; there is plenty in God's treasury; He is entirely independent of the proffered gifts of hypocrites. So it proves again and again. Marvel and matter-of-fact, prosaic needs and Divine provision, mingle beautifully in making up the daily experience, as regards the requirements of the Orphan Houses, of George Müller; nor is it to be thought, by the fact of stocks running low, that any need goes unsupplied—"They that seek the Lord shall not want any good thing."

Amid his numerous activities and heavy responsibilities, Müller's thoughts run many a time to the old home in Prussia; thoughts that are mournful, on account of the darkened minds of his relatives. Just before Christmas, 1838, he receives news of the death of his brother. "When I saw him in April of this year," says Müller, "he was living in open sin. I cannot learn that his end was different from his life, so that I have no comfort in his death. Of all the trials that can befall a believer, the death of an unconverted near relative seems to me one of the greatest. 'Shall not the Judge of all the earth do right?' must be the stay of the believer at such a time, and it is my stay now." At least will Müller adore once more the grace through which he was himself plucked out of the horrible pit many years before. At the same time he is deeply concerned for his father, who is living without God, and prays for him and yearns over his soul.

The melancholy fact, which is outstanding also in the life of many another servant of God, that Müller lacks the sympathy of his relatives after the flesh, has its contrasting encouragement, however, in the true help rendered him by many who by the tie of the New Birth are spiritually his brethren and sisters. These strengthen his hands and labour with him to keep the work true to its main object, the testimony of faith.

The growing reputation of the Orphan Houses inevitably attracts visitors from all parts, many of whom, however, having only the vaguest idea of Müller and his aims, leave with a new light on Christian philanthropy and Christian faith. "Of course," remarks a lady visitor to the godly matron of the Boys' House, "you cannot carry on these Institutions without a good stock of funds!" Two other visitors hear the comment, and one of them interjects the question, to the matron: "*Have* you a good stock?" The matron is of the true school of faith, and replies, in all simplicity : "Our funds are deposited in a 'Bank' which cannot break." There is something in her look, and in the emphasis of her words; a pearly moisture glistens in the eyes of the inquiring lady, and the second questioner, on departing, leaves £5 with one of the teachers. It is a timely gift, for Müller has paid out his last penny that afternoon, and is literally without means; now comes this £5 from—the Unbreakable Bank.

"When the yearly accounts are made up," inquires a patronising friend, "will the balance in hand be as large as it was last time?" In such materialistic phraseology, however naturally it may spring to the lips of a business man, Müller detects the language of unbelief, of a lack of confidence in the governing Providence of High Heaven. The affairs of an institution whose existence is based on the Divine promises are not to be spoken of in terms applicable to a trading corporation or characteristic of Budget night in the House of Commons. But it is good evidence of the growth of spiritual strength in his own soul, that, manifesting no trace of irritability, Müller meekly replies: "It will be as the Lord pleases"; and he adds the plain testimony regarding the welfare of the little ones in his care : "Had I thousands of pounds in hand, the orphans would have fared no better, for they have always had good nourishing food and necessary clothing." Truly it is so, for—the Bank of Heaven breaks not.

CHAPTER VI

The Ministry of the Word

WHILE the Orphan Houses of necessity occupy a large part of Müller's life at this time, the pastoral work does not suffer. Holding that an unvisited church is a feeble church, and yet realising the difficulty of grappling with multiplying responsibilities, he arranges with Craik to meet the membership in small groups, for Bible study and prayer. In all these duties he is most assiduous. Neither Müller nor Craik will be satisfied with a self-congratulatory people, who are proud in their correct doctrine, and make a fetish-phrase of "only believe." Not even Brethren are exempt from dangers of spiritual pride and spiritual coldness. Wherefore both Müller and Craik bring the people constantly to the Bible itself and to the ideal of a consecrated life.

Meantime, a matter of grave concern is near Müller's heart—the welfare of the Brethren Movement in its larger developments, and in the conservation of spiritual freedom and spiritual unity—without which, the very name of Brethren would come to have a significance merely satirical. The beginnings of serious division are being evidenced in controversies in which the spirit of the old Adam sometimes makes bitter the fountains of sweetness and light. To stand for a cherished view, with genuine conviction, is one thing; to lower the standard of Christian brotherliness by sour words and fiery attacks one upon the other is quite another. Müller is calm, looking to God; albeit his heart is torn when that which began in the Spirit threatens to end in the flesh.

To touch, however slightly, on these troubles is to move a little aside from the great testimony of faith with which Müller's career startles an unbelieving world and gloriously encourages the children of light. Nevertheless, the experiences of Müller, in these times of storm in the Forties, mark an important series of episodes in his career: in all of which this fact emerges, that he was determined to try all things, in all controversy, by the infallible standard of Holy Scripture.

It is well to understand the principles, at this anxious time, of the Bethesda and Gideon fellowships. Membership at Gideon is open to all believers, but full membership at Bethesda is confined to baptized believers only; the communion, however, being open. Upon the question of receiving the unbaptized, Müller consults, as usual, Robert C. Chapman, who puts the matter thus : " Unbaptized believers either come under the class of persons who ' walk disorderly '—and in that case we ought to withdraw from them (2 Thess. 3 : 6)—

or they do not. If a believer is 'walking disorderly' we are not merely to withdraw from him at the Lord's Table, but our behaviour ought to be decidedly different from what it would be were he *not* 'walking disorderly,' *on all occasions when* we meet him. Now, this is evidently not the case in the conduct of baptized believers towards their unbaptized fellow-believers. The Spirit does not suffer it to be so, but He witnesses that their not having been baptized does not necessarily imply that they are 'walking disorderly,' and hence there may be the most precious communion between baptized and unbaptized believers. The Spirit does not suffer us to refuse fellowship with them in prayer, in reading and searching the Scriptures, in social intercourse, and in the Lord's work; and yet this ought to be the case were they 'walking disorderly.'"

Müller ponders this, turns to the passage mentioned, and concludes the mind of the Lord to be this: "that we ought to *receive all whom* Christ has received (Rom. 15 : 7), irrespective of the measure of grace or knowledge unto which they have attained." Craik, inquiring independently, arrives at the same opinion. Next, an illustrative incident arises: a sister who has neither been baptized nor considers herself under an obligation to be, applies to be received into fellowship. The matter is prayerfully discussed with the applicant. Still she wishes to be received; still she is unconvinced regarding baptism: what, then, is to be done?

Müller places the facts before the Church and urges that the sister should be received; but conscientious difficulties are entertained by about a third of the fellowship, and a separation seems imminent. Happily, Müller's Scriptural arguments and sound sense prevail; only fourteen persons withdraw, and even of these the majority soon return. More than twenty years after, Müller, looking back, witnesses, with a thankful heart: "The receiving of all who love our Lord Jesus into full communion, irrespective of baptism, has never been a source of disunion among us."

Three years later, Müller and Craik are exercised regarding Gideon. Unbelievers sit among the saints at the Breaking of Bread; pews are regarded by some as private property—much to Müller's indignation, who holds that such claims are a violation of the rule that "all seats are free." His soul revolts at the very notion of special pews, which he considers, of necessity, set up a distinction between seats for the poor and seats for the well-to-do. "Are ye not all brethren?" Müller and Craik are much disturbed: finally it is decided to yield up Gideon; the clouds pass; the work at Bethesda goes forward.

Another important service, in which Müller again appears as a witness to Scriptural truth, is his visit to Germany, where, in 1843, he is instrumental in forming the first Assembly—which word always designates, in Brethren terminology, the Meetings of the Saints. He has long been concerned about the spiritual condition of Germany, and the visit of a German lady, whom he is enabled to lead to the Lord, deepens the impression. At length Müller feels that he must go; also that he should issue the "Narrative of the Lord's Dealings with George Müller," in German. True, he has no money for travelling, none for printing—but what are these details to Faith Triumphant? "When the Lord's time is come," says Müller, "He will blow away all obstacles, as chaff before the wind." A quarter of an hour after, he receives news that a large sum—over £700—is placed at his disposal for various objects, one of them being his journey to Germany.

Seemingly, all difficulties are removed, and he sets out for Stuttgart. A trial of faith awaits him, however, for upon arrival he receives the staggering news that the money which he had joyfully regarded as a token of God's will for him to visit the Fatherland, has been recalled. Does a querulous note escape him? Nay. His suffering is indeed poignant for a time, but he searches his heart, leans on the Lord, and declares: "'*All* things work together for good to them that love God.' This also does work for my good. I know it is the very best thing for me." In after days he looks back upon this fiery trial, saying: "I have again and again had reason to admire the goodness of the Lord, in having allowed this thing to be as it was, for it proved in the end in every way good for me. Our greatest trials often turn out our greatest blessings." Thus, then, he learns with peculiar zest the lesson of trusting God in all circumstances. He is completing his education in God's own school.

The Baptist Church at Stuttgart welcomes him, but he finds that the truth they hold is mixed with much error. It is evident that a sharp division must eventually arise. It comes when the elder who is the chief speaker in the church meetings indicates that they have a rule against taking the Lord's Supper with any person who would at any time take it either with "an unbaptized person" or "with one who is a member of a State Church." Müller stands, of course, for Believers' Baptism, but he will not lay an undue stress upon a *part* of truth.

After a discussion lasting six hours he is "rejected"; but several believers declare that they will stand by him—indeed, they do so, much to their own spiritual profit, since the leader they forsake declares that "the forgiveness of sins is received only through baptism" and that the "old man" (Rom. 6 : 6) *dies* through baptism, being, in fact, *drowned*! Moreover, Müller finds Universalism is prevalent, and that, according to some, the devils themselves shall finally be saved. Out of all this gloom of ignorance and fanaticism, Müller is enabled to rescue a company of those who are determined to hold by the Word. Seventeen believers meet in quiet at his lodgings, for the Breaking of Bread; thus does Müller witness the realisation of his hope, in the arising of a *living* Church, small indeed as to numbers, but based on Scriptural principles, which is to be a light to Germany.

No pains are spared to confirm the brethren in the way of truth. Under Müller's guidance, the little flock meet every Lord's Day : in the morning for the exposition of the Word, and in the afternoon for the Breaking of Bread. Further, two nights a week are also given to exposition and two to the simple reading of Scripture. Müller's notable combination of personal humility, which leads him to take the humblest place, and of confidence in God, inspiring him, whenever necessary, to fill the position of instructor, shines delightfully in these days among the Stuttgart folk. He finds the little company to be quite uninstructed regarding the presence and power of the Holy Spirit in the Church of Christ and their ministry one to another as of fellow-members in the Body of Christ. Accordingly, he spends much time in teaching them ; this done, desiring neither praise nor position, he takes his place "simply as a brother." He is ready to use the gift which is within him to help them as they may desire ; but in all things he urges powerfully upon them that they must rely upon God.

It is characteristic of the man, too, that he is by no means absorbed in this circle of his friends : his heart goes out to all men ; he walks out of the city and speaks to people, as he meets them in the fields, of the love of God in Christ Jesus ; wherever he can do so, among saints or sinners, he pleads for his Lord. As time passes, the numbers of the Assembly increase; the "Narrative" is duly published; Müller feels that his work in Germany is completed, and accordingly he turns homeward and is back in Bristol, March 6, 1844, to the delight of Bethesda and of the orphans.

At this time, John Nelson Darby and Benjamin Wills Newton are opposed upon weighty matters of doctrine and discipline. A discussion takes place at Plymouth, December 5, 1845 : no conclusion is arrived at. Points of difference multiply. Carnal Christians, wrapped in ease, may be engrossed in these divisions of the Brethren; for our own part, with a heart of love, let us neither, on the one hand, linger over things that sever, nor, on the other hand, ignore a record from which it may be that God would have us learn solemn and abiding lessons.

Müller and Craik, ardently pursuing their work and by no means rushing into battle, are, nevertheless, directly involved in the struggle, for John Nelson Darby declares that he "can go no more to Bethesda," since Bethesda does not formally condemn Newton's tracts.[1] Bethesda, however, is not "taking sides,"

---

[1] The points of difference may be given in the words of *The Principles of Open Brethren*. "Certain tracts issued by Mr. Newton were judged to contain error regarding the nature of the Lord Jesus Christ, and the question arose whether it was sufficient to exclude from fellowship those who held the erroneous teaching, or whether all who belonged to a gathering where the error was tolerated were to be put outside the pale, even if they themselves had not embraced it. One party, led by Mr. Darby, took the latter view. Others, in particular the Bethesda Church, in which Messrs. Müller and Craik ministered, refused to admit any who were convicted of holding the evil doctrine themselves, but did not ex-

is not in the least fond of controversy, but is simply awaiting the results of an examination of the tracts.

Has all this aught to do, vitally, with Faith Triumphant? Is not this an atmosphere in which the old ideals of love and brotherliness seem likely to fade and die? Let us hasten to the conclusion. In July, 1849, Darby calls upon Müller, but the latter, as it happens, is fixed for an important engagement, and could not possibly, at this time, devote more than ten minutes to conversation, amid pressing duties. Obviously it is impossible, in that brief space, to enter upon a discussion that must inevitably prove complex. This is the final meeting of the two; here they stand face to face. Their protagonist figures stand out as upon a great historic canvas. In some aspects we are reminded of the sharp sundering of Paul and Barnabas or of Wesley and Whitefield. So, John Nelson Darby and George Müller part, never to meet again upon earth.

Of the divisions which subsequently mark the history of the Brethren, let us at this time say nothing. Except this, that in recording days of sorrow we are not to be obsessed by a vain fear for the Ark of God, and rush, with the rashness and weakness of Uzzah, to uphold it. The Lord Himself will safeguard His

clude those who came from Mr. Newton's meeting. The exclusive party thereupon declined to have any further fellowship with members of the Bethesda Church or others like-minded. The latter soon came to receive the title of 'Open Brethren'." This just record needs to be read in the light of the fact that John Nelson Darby was a man of ardent character, full of energy. Let this suffice; let the clouds — long-lingering—pass for ever, and the day of brotherly confidence return!

own Truth, and cause even the wrath of man to praise Him. We have also to remember our duty to those who may come after. Our children's children—if the Lord tarry—may reasonably ask: "Was not that, after all, a subtle form of Unbelief which said: 'Do not inquire into the controversies of the Forties; let them rest in oblivion, and "universal darkness bury all"'? Should they not have handed down to us plain and reliable information—not sourly dogmatic, but meekly spiritual in tone yet lacking nothing of essential history?"

This would doubtless appear to be a reasonable position, involving present responsibility; but the task of the pioneer along such a path of historical inquiry and record can only be undertaken when the lava has thoroughly cooled. Moreover, it will always be necessary to differentiate between the record of fact, with all its sadness, and the solemn subject around which that record must inevitably gather.[1] The duty of the hour is rather to endeavour, in the spirit of Faith Triumphant, to heal old wounds, and by no means to

[1] In this connection, the wise words of Anthony Norris Groves (who in 1848-49 was frequently at Bethesda), uttered when first he learned of the controversy, should ever be remembered : " I always feel the very attempt to subject the one adorable Christ of God to a process of mental analysis, is, in its very operation, desecrating. It has engendered the worst of divisions in the Church, and will, I believe, ever do so ; however carefully, however *cautiously* pursued. When I look at Jesus as the Word represents Him, I see one whole aggregate of loveliness, suited to my every necessity, able and willing to love, succour, comfort, bless, redeem sanctify, and make accepted the vilest and most unworthy : this is all my joy and glory ; Jesus, descending, dying, ascending and returning to bless and take His own, is my all and in all."

reopen them. Records of disunity among the children of the Lord are themselves apt to prove divisive—so easily do men turn from the heavenly to the earthly; the "better way" is to recognise the ways in which the saints were essentially one.

Let us also recognise that, no matter how we view the bitter struggles of other days, the Brethren were at any rate united in this: they broke with the world and confessed that they were strangers and pilgrims on the earth. They have been loyal to the Bible, have created a new expository and doctrinal literature regarding it, have stood to its defence against a horde of foes, have loved it, honoured it, taught it; and they have given, despite all the mingling dross of human imperfection, a testimony to the truth, which, so far from dying down, may truly be said to increase in fervency and in volume; moreover, the missionaries of the Open Brethren are to be found, preaching, building, teaching, suffering in the sacred Name, from Vigo to Tokio, from Patagonia to the Arctic Circle.

Who shall say, moreover, after all, that any of Müller's days, albeit of spiritual struggle and spiritual anguish, were lost time? We cannot afford to lack a complete view of the man. It is good to remember that he could face the difficulties of the hour both within and without. Yet the great fact is that, all the time, he was organising a world-wide testimony of Faith Triumphant, through the various branches of the Scriptural Knowledge Institution; and was grappling solitarily, in a hard and unsympathetic time and while the outlook of Britain was dark and lowering, with the great problem of child-rescue.

This brings us back to our main thought. We might well have set Müller down as a saint, as a hero of faith, as a keen student, as an able theologian, as a precise thinker and a capable administrator, and he was all these; but here, in his heroic endeavours in child-rescue, we recognise also his true missionary spirit, as he seeks above all to demonstrate the power and willingness of the Living God, and, so-doing, stoops to the help of suffering childhood. There is no swerving, then, from the main purpose of his life. We are not to think of him as disturbed from his characteristic serenity and sunny quiet in God. Thus, he says [Janaury 20, 1847]: "How blessed to have the Living God to go to! Particularly precious is it to know Him in these days of widespread distress! Potatoes are too dear for food for the orphans. . . . The rice, which we have substituted instead of them, is twice as dear as usual; the oatmeal more than twice as dear, and the bread one-half dearer. But *the riches of God are as great as ever!* My soul is at peace."

And again [August 9, 1848]: "The Lord has been very kind to-day, and proved afresh that none who trust in Him shall be confounded. This evening, while I was walking in my little garden, lifting up my heart for further supplies for the work of God in my hands, there was given me a registered letter from

Liverpool, containing £20 for the orphans." And again he reiterates his chief aim : "To show that there is verily a God in heaven, whose ears are open to all who call upon Him in the name of the Lord Jesus, and who put their trust in Him. Cheerfully have I dedicated myself, with all my physical, mental, and spiritual energies, to this life of faith upon the Living God, for everything I need in connection with my own personal and family necessities, and in connection with the work of God in my hands, if but by any means, through it, multitudes of believers and unbelievers may be benefited."

The years have sped by. John Nelson Darby and George Müller have passed beyond the clash of human debate. We incline, remembering the great gifts and great zeal of each of these men of God, to unite them by a characteristic testimony in the Name of their Saviour—thinking, not of their severance, but of their fundamental unity in Him.

Let Darby speak first, of his Divine Lord. "The Man in the Glory" was a phrase often upon his lips; and he said: "Christ is my righteousness before God. God's righteousness has been displayed in putting the Man who bore my sins at God's right hand in glory. The Holy Ghost comes and says to me : 'You have no righteousness before God.' Then I try to grow more holy. Quite right in itself that I should long after holiness; but as a means to peace it will not do. But here in Christ I have a

THE MINISTRY OF THE WORD

Divine Righteousness that is fit to put me into the glory. In the cross of Christ it is not merely that my debt is paid, for that might be and yet I might have nothing as it were to live upon; but God has made me a joint heir with Christ, and now down here I live looking for Him to come and take me to Himself, to be for ever with Him in the glory where He is!"[1]

Next, still upon the glorious theme of Immanuel the Prince, let us hear George Müller: "'Who is this that cometh up from the wilderness, leaning upon her Beloved?' (Cant. 8 : 5). We are to look to the Lord Jesus. There is treasured up in Him inexhaustible fulness; and just as by prayer and faith we lay hold on the strength of the Lord, so shall we receive comfort according to our need, instruction in the hour of perplexity, help in the hour of depression, deliverance in the hour of difficulty. Lean upon the arm of that blessed One, and you will find it never grows weary. If you have never tried it, let an elder brother now beseech you to try it, and you will find how strong that arm is, how able and ready to carry you through. It will never, never tire. Oh, bright prospect, to have such a Friend for ever and ever!"[2]

The simplicity of George Müller's trust is a sweet lesson; what can hinder or permanently trouble this heir of glory, this pilgrim of the Lord? Thunder-clouds may loom overhead, but the path of faith glows with a

---

[1] *The Gospel of the Glory.*
[2] *The Redeemed in the Wilderness.*

line of light, and he declares : "Make but trial of the way and you will see how truly precious it is to wait upon the Lord for everything, even for the bread which perishes!" So real indeed, to the eye of faith, is the presence of the Good Shepherd, that, bethinking himself of the never-failing provision of breakfasts and dinners and teas, and boots and clothing, for the orphans, George Müller seems to see his Divine Friend going from cupboard to cupboard ; wherefore his cry is : "How kindly does the Lord inspect our stores!"

The general record is not of huge sums, but rather of small ones totalling to—sufficiency. Human weakness might unbelievingly ejaculate : "How insignificant the gifts ; after all, *will* God supply?" But George Müller, as ever, surveys the position from the side of Heavenly Ability, of Limitless Resource, and therefore holds that the very fact of needs being supplied little by little comes about "in order that both He Himself may often have the joy of our calling upon Him for the supplies, and that He may give unto us the joy of obtaining our supplies day by day in answer to prayer." Of which truth we behold a parable : the door of the Girls' Orphan House stands wide open ; a Christian passer-by rolls a half-crown into the passage. Faith keeps the door open and looks for the half-crowns ; and God sends the Christian passers-by.

CHAPTER VII

The Writing on the Window

YEAR after year the glorious record of Faith Triumphant goes on. When money is needed, money is there. "Mere coincidence," says unbelief; but the "coincidences" are innumerable, stretching over half a century. They occur in what men call "small" matters as well as "great." One evening there is insufficient money in hand — as we have seen, this frequently happens—for the needs of the ensuing day. Then, a kindly lady, who has undertaken the duty of disposing of articles sent in to be sold for the benefit of the orphans, brings in the required sum: she is by no means in good health, "but has it so laid on her heart to call that she cannot stay away."

Again, bread and milk are lacking for the orphans' tea—which should soon be prepared. There is no money in hand, although, of course, there is plenty in the Unbreakable Bank. Just then a visitor calls and places in the box—unperceived, as he thinks—a banknote. There it might have lain until the clearing of the box, later in the day, but one of the helpers has noted the action, and so the box is opened and the necessaries purchased.

We are not to marvel, then, that Müller, taking up one day a diamond ring that has been sent in to be sold, scratches upon his very window-pane : "Jehovah-Jireh"—"the Lord will provide." These same words have refreshed his soul for many a year, and when, out of some one's poverty, a little gift of one shilling is placed in the box at Bethesda, wrapped around with paper on which is written "Jehovah-Jireh," his heart swells with gratitude ; he must needs scratch the words on the glass in front of him. "This way of living," he delightedly records, "brings the Lord remarkably near. He is, as it were, morning by morning inspecting our stores, that He may send help." One morning the exchequer balance is $2\frac{1}{2}$d. In two of the Orphan Houses every loaf has been cut up for use, and there is nothing provided for dinner. At eleven o'clock a letter arrives from Barnstaple, enclosing £5. 10s., and dinner is forthcoming.

Let us not imagine Müller as a rather nervous person, "all wires," waiting anxiously just inside the door for daily miracles *via* postmen or visitors. Such a position would be merely a travesty of faith. Contrarily : with a quiet soul and a wide outlook, he waits God's time ; is never excited ; rests confidently. This attitude of faith is evidenced by the perfect naturalness with which he turns from questions of potatoes and milk and treacle, and the sale of a silver coffee-pot, to the visitation of the sick and dying, or the elucidation, for the encouragement of the saints, of some point of high doctrine. He has no such distorted idea of himself as to imagine that the orphans will go dinnerless, simply because duty calls him away from the Orphan Houses. Not he, but the Lord, is their Deliverer and their Shepherd.

Müller is also busy giving counsels to believers; these counsels are entirely faithful; warm, also, with sympathy; having the characteristic freshness and spirit of teaching drawn direct from the Bible. They are no dry iteration of truths given to the self-satisfied circle of a religious Mutual Admiration Society. Realising the necessity of a firm foundation, and knowing how easily people come to trust to a false hope—resting upon artistic tastes or personal amiability or a little mild patronage of a church, rather than upon the Atonement alone—he deals, in answer to a sister who is distressed by the lack of assurance of salvation, with the way to obtain certain knowledge of the forgiveness of sins. Differentiating between "feeling forgiven" and having a heart knowledge of forgiveness, he puts his points in the form of Question and Answer :—

Q. "How may I obtain the knowledge that I am born again, or that my sins are forgiven, or that I shall 'not perish, but have everlasting life'?" A. "Not by my feelings, not by a dream, not by my own experience being like or unlike this one's or that one's; but this matter is to be settled, as are all other matters, entirely by the revealed Word of God, which is the only standard for believers. The questions to be put to ourselves are : Do I walk in utter carelessness? Do I trust in my own exertions for salvation? Do I expect forgiveness for my sins on account of 'living a better life in future'? Or do I depend only upon this, that Jesus died upon the cross to save sinners and that He fulfilled the Law of God, to make sinners righteous?

"If the latter is the case, my sins are forgiven, whether I feel it or not. I have already forgiveness. I shall not have it merely when I die, or when the Lord Jesus comes again; but I have it now, and that for all my sins. I must not wait to *feel* that my sins are forgiven, in order to be at peace, and in order to be happy; but I must take God at His word. I must believe that what He says is true, and He says that whosoever believeth in the Lord Jesus shall receive remission of sins."

A characteristic "Müllerism," too, is his word on Election : *Q.* "How may I know that I am one of the Elect? I often read in the Scriptures about Election, and often hear about it; how may I know that *I* am a chosen one, that *I* am predestinated to be conformed to the image of the Son of God?" *A.* "It is written : 'As many as were ordained (*i.e.* appointed) to eternal life believed' (Acts 13: 48). The question therefore simply is : Do I believe on the Lord Jesus? Do I take Him to be the One whom God declares Him to be, *i.e.* His beloved Son, in whom He is well pleased ? If so, I am a believer, and I never should have believed, except I had been appointed by God to eternal life— except I had been made by God to be a vessel of mercy. Therefore the matter is a very simple one : if I believe in the Lord Jesus, I am a chosen one—I have been appointed to eternal life."

Nor does Müller fail to apply the teaching of the Bible to his own heart. His main concern, he declares, is to have his soul " happy in the Lord," not of course in the narrow and selfish sense of honied enjoyment of spiritual truths, but in the rest of faith, the glad ac- ceptance of the Divine will, that he may more perfectly glorify God. It is quite easy, he sees, to benefit saint or sinner, to seek to win souls, and generally to behave as a child of God should, and yet not to be " happy in the Lord." Accordingly, while at Nailsworth—March 20 to May 7, 1841—preparing the second part of the " Narrative " for the press, and ministering the Word, he resolves to change his method. For ten years he has regularly given himself to prayer, after dressing, in the morning, up till breakfast-time. But now, he will first read from the Bible and meditate thereon, " that thus my heart might be comforted, encouraged, warned, reproved, instructed ; and that thus, whilst meditating, my heart might be brought into communion with the Lord." Accordingly, he meditates upon the New Testament, from the beginning onwards, early in the morning, purely for the well-being of his own soul, as an inspiration to prayer. He is thus led out to intercession or thanksgiving, supplication or praise, so that "my inner man almost invariably is nourished and strengthened, and by breakfast-time, with rare exceptions, I am in a peaceful if not happy state of heart."

Pursuing this method, he goes outdoors, walks quietly in the fields, rests awhile upon a stile, all the while reading and meditating. He carries a Bible and a large-type Testament. This practice of "field-walking," while meditating and praying, he maintains nearly eight years, until, in February, 1849, a weakness in the right foot compels him to desist; but he suggests, of course, no necessary difference between meditating outdoors and meditating indoors : the point is, to apprehend that the necessary food for the soul is, not prayer, but the Word, wherein God Himself instructs, humbles, reproves : *then* prayer follows, the "fountains of the great deep" being broken up. This spiritual truth is strongly urged by Müller upon fellow-believers.

Under his former plan he would spend much time collecting his wandering thoughts, but now, his heart being brought at once into experimental fellowship with God, he speaks to his Father and Friend—"vile though I am and unworthy of it"—about the things which He has brought before His servant in His own Word. Other seasons for the Bible and intercession are at family prayer, in the morning, when lengthy portions of Scripture are read ; and in the course of the day as opportunity suggests and the Spirit prompts.

Another point on which both Müller and Craik feel strongly is one which touches the central idea of the Brethren. They have all along declined to receive any salary, but have approved the putting-up of a box, at Bethesda, to receive the ministry in temporal things of those to whom they ministered spiritually. With the passing of the years, however, circumstances have greatly altered. The work at Bethesda has grown wonderfully. Other brethren, godly and qualified, are now able likewise to minister the Word ; and it may please the Lord, therefore, to call and qualify others. The names of Müller and Craik being affixed to the boxes, the impression may be imparted that these two are assuming an office, and must be looked on as being exclusively " the ministers "—as if, as Müller says, " we were seeking to keep our place in the church by some outward title, rather than just filling it up in obedience to the Lord, and quietly leaving it with His Spirit to produce subjection to us on the part of the saints." Thus, they decline—in all love and while still desiring to serve the saints earnestly and faithfully— to receive any more offerings in the accustomed way. This is their position, from July 7, 1841, to the end. If people give, they must please do so without any intermediary in the way of labelled box that seems to exalt two brethren above their fellows. " Jehovah-Jireh ! " The Lord will provide.

More precious, sometimes, than the gifts received, are the words which accompany them. Thus, when there is not a penny in hand for the necessities of the day, a little paper packet is brought in : it contains ten shillings, and on the paper is written : *" Your Heavenly Father* knoweth that ye have need of *these* things. Trust in the Lord." "This," declares Müller, sweetly enjoying the message, "is of more value than many bank-notes." But the packet is only an earnest of more help to follow. Within five minutes comes a sum of £10, sent by an Irish sister through a London banker. Once more—"Jehovah-Jireh."

In a time of abundant resources, Müller thanks God, not so much for the plenty itself, as for God's gracious kindness ; and when a particular period of plenty ends in a time of waiting, he is equally grateful that God does not *at once* allow sharp trials to come. Which is to say, in essence, that George Müller, strong in faith, knows full well that all things work together for good to them that love God. The quiet of trust prevails.

For example, on a certain Saturday, November 13, 1841, Müller empties a money-box and finds therein— one shilling. At this time, there are a hundred persons, all told, to be provided for. Here were a subject for a Nineteenth-Century painter. Not yet were the Pre-Raphaelites ; but what a subject for any of them in George Müller and his shilling, as he goes out on a cold November morning to meet all the financial calls, and provide all the food and clothing and wages which may be necessary for his family of just one hundred. Holman Hunt perhaps would have made something of a nimbus about his head; Millais might have made him strong, with vital force flashing from his eyes as he strode out into the grim, commonplace streets. Actually, here is a middle-aged, gentlemanly man, calm and precise, with a little smile playing round the corners of his mouth. What worries burden him? None. Do not anxieties tear his heart and make him old before his time? Nay. He is not thinking of the shilling, but of God, and enters in his diary: "Is it not precious, under such circumstances, to have the living God as a Father to go to, who is ever able and ever willing to help as it may be really needed?"

Yea, and to this privilege every one who believes in the Lord Jesus has a title, for, as Müller reminds himself and them, there is Gal. 3 : 26—"Ye are all the children of God by faith in Christ Jesus." So he goes his way, with the shilling. Coal stocks are low in the Orphan Houses; the store of potatoes and treacle is meagre; has no other money come in? Not another penny. Stay, there is a silver watch: only yesterday it became the property of the Institution; let it be sold. This just carries them through. Next morning comes five pounds—not a huge sum, but enough to manage upon.

Thus does God supply every need, not necessarily in ways that would meet the ideas of authors apant for dramatic situations, but, somehow or other, the children are fed and no bill remains unpaid. Sometimes the tide comes in with a roar like the bore on Severn or Trent; sometimes it swells gently to a flood. In either case, the poetry of faith and the prose of domestic detail march harmoniously together. None dares say that Gal. 3 : 26 goes not well with : "A sister sent a gammon and some peas. . . . One of the workers was able to provide a dinner in the Girls' Orphan House, out of his own means. . . . One of the workers gave five shillings; eleven shillings came in by the sale of articles, and sixpence was in the box : little as this was, yet we were able to procure with it all that was really needful."

On a certain Saturday morning, there is not even a shilling in hand; nay, not a farthing : all the boxes are empty. How would our Victorian limners depict this deeper trouble? It is no trouble, however, to Müller. "Jehovah-Jireh!" It shall not be said of God the Provider, as Elijah spake ironically of the Sun-god, "He is on a journey, or peradventure he sleepeth, and must be awaked!" Looking to the Lord, Müller is equable and undisturbed ; prays that "the Lord will be pleased to send us supplies early in the morning, otherwise there will not be sufficient for dinner." Quietly enough he goes to the Orphan Houses, to wait the result.

Here, indeed, were an opportunity for sensational journalism, if only the era of the cheap newspaper were come. Imagine, thrust back upon Ashley Down, a

THE WRITING ON THE WINDOW

modern correspondent, alert, full-armed with camera, eager for a "scoop," wiring a picturesque "story" to Fleet Street: "Philanthropist Müller's Sad Straits. Hopeless Outlook for Orphans. Reported Closing Down. Local Councillors' Strong Views," and the like. Yet, hold thyself in rein a moment, O gifted correspondent, for—Jehovah-Jireh! Having reminded the Lord of the necessity of an early answer, Müller mildly chronicles, a little later on: "Accordingly, about ten o'clock, a parcel came from Clapham." Here, indeed, is a godly use of a plain adverb— "accordingly"—in harmony with the need, in immediate answer to the petition, this parcel arrives. Truly, there is much virtue in an "accordingly." Not that the parcel contains wedges of gold: busy hands open it, and the yield is just an assortment of children's clothing, an old silver thimble, and a half-franc piece. Stay, here is also a little packet of money—eleven shillings. Is this all? No, Müller takes it as being also "a token for good that He would send what else might be needed." And—let Gal. 3 : 26 still be borne in mind—He does send: there is received £2. 1s. 3d., and the next day £5. 19s. 7d. Once more, all is well.

Inevitably, in these sayings and doings of Müller, there rings out a continual challenge to unbelief. Indeed, we remember that the whole aim is to demonstrate that God lives, and answers prayer. An illustration of this challenge appears at the end of

1841. It has been Müller's custom to make a statement regarding the progress and needs of the work at some public meeting, the plan, like that of the publication of the Report, being adopted for the encouragement of the saints, in the path of faith. It occurs to Müller, however, that the holding of such meetings and the publication of a Report, at a moment when the Orphan Fund is exhausted, would savour of a desire to work upon the sympathetic feelings of the people of God instead of leaning wholly upon Him. Wherefore, he postpones the meeting and the publication, asking himself: "What better proof could we give of our depending upon the Living God alone, and not upon public meetings and printed Reports, than that, in the midst of our deep poverty, instead of being glad for the time to have come when we could make known our circumstances, we still went on quietly for some time longer without saying anything?"

Calmly as Müller faces the position, he knows full well that God's plan is not necessarily to rain down sovereigns from heaven. "Nature," he declares, "will always be tried in God's ways, for God's ways lead always into trial so far as sight and sense are concerned." At which plain statement of the opposition of faith to sight Unbelief will cry, "Now we have him: like the Clerk of Chatham before Jack Cade, 'he hath confessed.' George Müller talks of 'deep poverty' and admits 'trial.'" Truly he does; but it is the trial of *faith*. In answer to the question, "Lacked ye anything?" he still answers, as of yore: "Nothing." The "trial" is simply God saying: "Now will I prove whether you look to Me or to your subscribers and donors." After all, the point to demonstrate is, whether these hundred orphans will be cared for by Him who marks the fall of a sparrow, or whether they will not.

This four months of delayed Report, then, is a crucial time, Müller's foundation principle, of trust in God being, as men say, "at stake"—the term, however, being in itself ridiculous, God being the Father of His children. Humanly it is a solemn season for Müller. Yet it is glorious to mark how God speaks through the stillness, to incline men to give. Sometimes, faith sees its triumph in the beautiful timeliness or appropriateness of a gift, unknown to the giver. Thus, a visitor calls, hastily looks over the Orphan Houses, and is speedily gone. Before leaving, he places in the box sufficient money, as it proves, to pay for the orphans' tea. "Had he stayed long and. conversed much, as might have been the case," remarks Müller, "his donation would not have been in time."

Sometimes, again, faith's triumph is not so much in the circumstances of a visit as in the fact of the visit itself. On the morning of February 9, 1842, Müller goes to the Orphan Houses, after prayer, "to see whether the Lord has sent in anything." Yes, He has sent just two minutes before, and in a way that is beautiful to the children of faith. Once more, it is: "Before they call, I will answer." While Müller is meditating before the Lord, a certain Christian man is starting out from home, on the way to his place of business. On goes the Christian brother half a mile or so, when suddenly his pace slackens; a strong impression has come upon him that he must give to the Orphan Houses. He halts; is undecided; reflects: "It is scarcely worth while going back home, to fetch the money, after coming this distance." So he walks on. Mark the two men; yonder is Müller praying; here is the business man hurrying forward; neither knows anything of the other's doings. Prayer prevails. The business man stops short again—must needs do so—and, turning back, fetches three sovereigns and takes them to the Orphan House. Breakfast, O children, breakfast! "Jehovah-Jireh!"

Faith triumphant is likewise faith patient. It is in the Lord's own way that He will provide. Early in the morning of March 17, 1842, money is needed for the milk. At eight o'clock the milkman will arrive, but, on the principle of "no debt," there will be no order given unless the money is there to pay *instanter*. Müller, starting for the Orphan Houses just before seven o'clock, lifts up his soul to God, his prayer being, in effect: "Wilt Thou be pleased to pity us, even as a father pitieth his children, not laying on us more than we can bear. Remember, O Lord, the consequences, in reference both to believers and unbelievers, if we should have to give up the work for want of means; for this Thou wilt not permit it to come to nought. Yet I confess before Thee that I am not worthy that Thou shouldest continue to use me in this work any longer." As he prays, he walks on, and is presently within a couple of minutes' walk of the Orphan Houses when—he meets a Christian brother who is going to business thus early. A few words of greeting are exchanged and the two men part.

"Jehovah-Jireh!" Müller, going on, is only a few yards from his destination; suddenly he is overtaken by the Christian brother, who has turned and run after him, and now hands him a sovereign, "for the orphans." "Jehovah-Jireh!" There shall be milk. Here comes the milkman; listen to the clattering of the cans! In the happy moment of answered prayer, Müller assures himself that "it is worth while being poor, and being greatly tried in faith, for the sake of having such precious proofs of the loving interest which our kind Father takes in everything concerning us. It is also worth being poor and greatly tried in faith, if but thereby the hearts of the children of God may be comforted and their faith strengthened; and if but those who do not know God, and who may read or hear of His dealings with us, should be led thereby to see that faith in God is more than a mere notion, and that there is indeed reality in Christianity."

The milkman, indeed, is a frequent figure in the Müller record of faith. On a certain morning, no money comes in. Plenty of food is there for breakfast and dinner, but no milk for tea—indeed, in one of the

Orphan Houses, no bread. At three o'clock in the afternoon—no funds. At that time Müller has to go out with a friend, but is back within a quarter of an hour or so. Several persons are waiting to see him, among them a sister whom he particularly desires to speak to, on church affairs. They are talking for a quarter of an hour; then the sister leaves, but, before going, she hands Müller £10 for the orphans. Just a few minutes later, the milkman comes jingling up to the Orphan Houses; a messenger from Müller speeds to meet him, and arrives first, with the money: also, there is time to buy bread. "Language cannot express the real joy in God which I had," said Müller of this deliverance. "I was free from excitement. The circumstance did not unfit me for a single moment to attend to my other engagements. I was not in the least surprised, because, by grace, my soul had been waiting on God for deliverance."

While Müller is thus praying and believing and receiving for the orphans, how does the principle of faith work in his own family circle? The answer is: as at the Orphan Houses, so with the Müllers themselves. Will not God, who has given His Son for their redemption, with Him richly give them all things?

They lack nothing. "This afternoon," says Müller, "when we had no money at all of our own, a brother gave us three shillings for ourselves"; and: "During this week we have had several times not one single penny for ourselves; yet during this week also, we had all that was needed in the way of nourishing food, etc., and we have threepence left." Blessed balance of three bronze coins. Lowly but positive proof that the provision of God is ample. "Having food and raiment" is the apostolic injunction, "let us therewith be content." The children of faith require no Heliogabalus' banquet. "Jehovah-Jireh!" Once, indeed, dinner has to be postponed half-an-hour, but it is duly ready, and Müller holds it to be worth while to have waited, otherwise he might not have experienced exactly the meaning of Phil. 4 : 12 : "I know both how to be abased, and I know how to abound : everywhere and in all things I am instructed both to be full and to be hungry, both to abound and to suffer need."

Each penny brought by kindly souls to the orphans is as beautiful to Müller as if it were a sack of gold. Eightpence is lacking to make up the payment for dinner : a careful examination reveals that sevenpence can be gathered ; somebody then reveals that "something was put in the box" the previous night, and the box being emptied, the "something" proves to be—one penny. Thus the cost of the dinner is exactly made up, and Müller's comment is : "Even the gift of this one penny was thus evidently under the ordering of our kind Father, who not in anger, but for the trial of our faith, keeps us so poor." A little later, there comes a gift of £100. It is joyfully received, but Müller is neither surprised nor elated; as with a penny, so with a bag of sovereigns—again he asks: are not both from God?

While the story of Müller's answers to prayer goes round, men first raise their hands in incredulity; then, finding the facts to be indisputable, they declare that the exercise of faith in such a way is obviously a peculiar gift that no ordinary person could expect to possess. Such a notion is denounced by Müller himself as a device of Satan. Although every believer is not called to establish an Orphan House, yet every one is called upon to trust Him fully; all are to cast their burdens at His feet, and live a life of simple faith in Him.

Further, he strenuously protests against the notion that his faith has only to do with money-raising. By the grace of God he desires that his faith shall extend to his entire concerns, whether temporal or spiritual; yea, and chiefly to the affairs of the Kingdom of God. Not that he has attained, in his own view, to great faith, or that he desires to have his name bandied about among religious chatterboxes, as that of a religious prodigy.

Yet he has sage counsels to give, regarding faith and its strengthening: they may be crystallised, and logically stated, thus: To read and meditate upon the Word of God is to become more and more acquainted with the nature and character of God, learning that He is not only All-powerful and All-wise, but is kind, good, merciful, and faithful. Thus we shall come to rest first of all upon His *ability* to help us, and then upon His *willingness* to do so. To grow in faith we must first of all maintain a good conscience, for how shall we possibly exercise faith in God while we are habitually detracting from His glory? A guilty conscience and a strong faith cannot be co-existent. Again, faith may be strengthened through its trial; wherefore, let us not shrink from such trial, but embrace it cheerfully, so shall we see the hand of God outstretched to deliver. Finally, let that subtle temptation be resisted, to work out a "deliverance" of *our own*: on the contrary, with hope and patience, let us "give time" to God to work out *His* deliverance in His own way, and thus shall we enjoy the delight of Faith Triumphant.

But: "Why not take the bread on credit? Seeing the Orphan Houses are the work of the Lord, may you not trust Him to provide the means to pay at the end of the quarter?" Here is a fairly inevitable question; but Müller has thought this point out very carefully. His reply is: "Not only will God supply, but He will do so at the very time when needed: why trust God at the end of a quarter and not trust Him *now*? Moreover, to lean upon credit is by no means to be strengthened in faith; beyond which the Word says: 'Owe no man anything.' But the chief reason is, that to take food upon credit is to deny the fundamental object of the Orphan Houses, to show before the whole world and the whole Church of Christ, that even in these last evil days the Living God is ever ready to help, succour, comfort, and answer the prayers of those who trust in Him. We need not go away from Him to our fellow-men or to the ways of the world."

In such experiences of faith, as he engages in incessant activities and records a thousand proofs of God's faithfulness, do the years pass with George Müller. It could scarcely be expected that an unbelieving world would allow him, in his open demonstration of the entire reliability of God's promises, to go altogether free from the arrows of slander. The very stories of Divine deliverance and faithfulness suggested to the ungodly the idea that "these poor orphans suffer." This is the world's spurious philanthropy—not to make any real endeavour to succour the suffering, for that would take up too much of the time claimed by the frivolities of fashion and the indulgences of ease, but to offer a show of sympathy which has no reality and therefore no practical result. Such foolish attacks Müller answers plainly. Rather than any orphan should suffer, he would close the Houses altogether.

Indeed, *should* an orphan suffer, he would no longer have any purpose to serve in keeping the Houses open, for the fact itself would be a demonstration of the failure of his great aim—to show that through the faithfulness of God the orphans should have their every need supplied. It is not surprising that the world should miss this central fact of Müller's testimony. His faith, as we see, is tried, but the orphans know no need. That the money for dinner arrived only an hour before dinner-time cannot in the least militate against the main fact that when the dinner-bell rings, dinner is ready.

So, "Jehovah-Jireh" is a good phrase for Müller to scratch upon the window-pane. History, or at least legend, is not without some singular records of inscriptions cut upon panes or into walls. Above all, there is the romantic story of great Raleigh scratching upon the window: "Fain would I climb, but that I fear to fall," and of great Elizabeth replying with: "If thy heart fail thee, do not climb at all." Great Raleigh, stout-hearted, and valiant, and gifted, climbs, but his climbing brings him little. Look upon his gallant head, brought upon the scaffold by the most paltry of monarchs, and then cry, with the Psalmist: "Put not your trust in princes." Look now upon this plain man of the Victorian day scratching "Jehovah-Jireh" upon the window; see the results of his faith in a long God-honouring concourse of boys and girls delivered from woe and misery, and then admit that it is well to trust in the Living God. Wherefore, let us sing anew the glories of the Faithful One, and joy in this— that "Jehovah-Jireh" will hold, for the saints of the Lord, while the world lasts, and until faith is dissolved in sight.

CHAPTER VIII

"Arise and Build"

MÜLLER, as we have seen, will never apply the adjectives "great" and "little" to the work of God. Who shall say, in the mighty plans of Heaven, that this or that is great or small, important or of scant account? Such differentiation were rank blasphemy to George Müller. To him the great matter is doing the will of God, whether in renting a humble cottage or building premises that are huge. It is the attitude of soul that matters. To a servant of God, living in His light and dedicated to His service, nothing is trivial. The projection into the sphere of Divine government, of human contrasts and notions, is absurd. Yet there is also the manward outlook as well as the Godward; hence the testimony of faith becomes increasingly powerful in its influence upon men, as it speaks of the accomplishment of great things. The time comes for Müller to march forward. Towards the end of 1845 he sees, as in a vision, that he must arise and build.

Hitherto, the orphans have been living in the Houses in Wilson Street, Bristol. The arrangement is eminently suitable in the day of commencements ; it is modest and simple, according to the mind of the Lord, as the Divine blessing testifies. But there are pressing reasons for removal. The noise made at play by the large family of healthy youngsters does not appeal to quiet neighbours, nor are the conditions ideal for a growing work. It will be well for the young people to be nearer to green fields and to have opportunity for open-air industries.

Accordingly, Müller ruminates, prays, makes known his thoughts to his friends. Land and buildings to accommodate, say, three hundred children, and to include space for vegetable gardens, will cost no less than £10,000. True, Müller is a plain man without financial resources, but the sum "is not large to the Lord." To venture it means entering upon a difficult path, but the Leadership is good. "I was not discouraged," says Müller, "but trusted in the Living God." So intimate and precious, indeed, are his seasons of communion and prayer, that he seems to be "talking over" the whole arrangements with his Friend ; which, in fact, he is doing. The assurance is given him that a new Orphan House shall be : the realisation is as vivid as if the building were already in being.

Consultation with Robert C. Chapman brings much encouragement. "Build," says the saint from Barnstaple, "always asking God to show you the plan, that all may be according to His mind." Other friends are also consulted. Müller himself continues quietly waiting upon God. On the thirty-sixth day of his watching, he receives a donation of £1000. This is by far the largest single gift he has received. Three days later he receives, through his sister-in-law, an offer, from a Christian architect, to prepare plans and superintend building operations—free of charge. Clearly God is answering. Was not the prayer for a plan? Now, a plan is offered by one of His children.

The great matter is to wait patiently. No circulars are issued; no appeal is made. If conversation leads naturally to the subject of his hopes and proposals, Müller is ready to speak of them, but he thrusts the subject upon nobody, his trust being in God, not in man. Humanly the time seems scarcely of the happiest, for a mania for speculative building has sent up site values. However, there is certain land on Ashley Down which seems particularly desirable and is reported available, and inquiries are instituted regarding it.

Herein is the hand of God wonderfully made manifest. Müller, endeavouring to interview the owner, goes to that gentleman's house—only to be told, however: "He is at business." Next, a call is made, therefore, at the business establishment—only to find: "He has left for home." "Shall I follow him up?" Müller cogitates. "Nay, is not this the hand of God? Is not *He* intending to manage the affair? I will not force matters, but let patience have her perfect work." A heart of unbelief would have summed up the experience: "Two journeys for nothing!" But Müller goes home content to leave the conclusion with Him who does all things well.

Exactly what report the owner's domestic gives, regarding Müller's call, does not appear; but, whether detailed or brief, it is amply sufficient to arouse deep thought, for, early in the morning, he lies awake, being unable either to sleep or to think of anything but George Müller and the land. For two hours this landlord thus debates with himself. Finally he resolves that if Müller really needs the land and applies for it, he shall have it, and that the price shall be reduced to £120 per acre, from £200. This conclusion arrived at, he can sleep soundly. A few hours after, Müller calls, makes the application, hears the story of the interrupted slumbers and the reduction in price, and, crying: "How good is the Lord," buys nearly seven acres. In Müller's diary, we read: "Observe"—he uses these pet words, "observe," "pause," or "consider"—whenever stating something specially providential in the way of Divine movements or arrangements—"observe the hand of God in my not finding the owner at home last evening. *The Lord* meant to speak to His servant *first*, about this matter, and to lead him *fully* to decide, before I had seen him. Thus does God work for those who wait for Him."

Although, however, the land is thus secured, Müller is fixedly determined not to commence building until *all* the needed money is in hand—which plan he holds to be according to the mind of God. On the watch-tower of faith, he is looking out, eagerly but not excitedly, for answers to prayer. If the money should come within a week, well; if in a year, or ten years, equally well. Of one thing he is persuaded—the bare acres of Ashley Down shall see God's palace of childhood erected in His own time. Four months pass: there is over £2700 in hand—not much more than a quarter of the required total, but what of this? Shall not the will of God be done in waiting as in receiving?

Here let it be solemnly writ: George Müller is not to be regarded as a fascinating conjurer, who exercises a certain intangible power called faith, working somewhat like unto wireless telegraphy, whereupon, hey presto! here is an Orphan House descending like an Aladdin's palace, from mid-air, upon Ashley Down. God's ways are not our ways, and Müller, after all, is a man. His faith is tried as by fire; he honestly declares: "My faith and patience have been exceedingly tried"; nevertheless faith tried may still be, in fact, actually is, Faith Triumphant—faith purged from admixture of human petulance and flesh-confidence, faith that shines serene despite all whirling thunder-clouds.[1]

[1] Müller's experiences in regard to the patience, or "final perseverance," of faith will awake memories and reminiscences in many hearts. A characteristic story on these lines is that of Mr. D. M. Heydrick, city missionary at Boston, Mass. Mr. Heydrick once undertook the responsibility of paying for certain seating, ordered for a Mission by a person who had subsequently severed his connection with the work. "Give me a month and I will pay," said Mr. Heydrick to the seat-manufacturer.

"ARISE AND BUILD"

Even after the owner has agreed to sell the land, various unexpected obstacles to taking possession have to be encountered, but Müller rests in the assurance of faith. Even were the land taken from him, he feels that it would only be permitted in order that the kindness of God should be shown in the gift of a still finer site! All *must* be well; what are difficulties to the Living God? Finally, the conveyance is made out and the land secured. Just at the same time comes a donation of £2050 (of which £2000 is for the building, and the remainder for "present necessities") as if in demonstration of the watchful care of God, for, during the time the money was not absolutely needed, no great amount was sent, but, now that it is required, this large sum comes—a lovely stimulus to faith. So sweet is the realisation of his Heavenly Father hearing and being very near, that Müller can only "sit before God, and admire Him."

Thus refreshed in the contemplation of God, the

Then he prayed earnestly for the money—three hundred dollars. At the end of the month, he had received no money towards the debt, but went to the manufacturer, sorrowful at heart, to ask for an extension of time. "Certainly," said the man, "but I thought the Lord always helped you to keep your promises! How do you explain it?" "I cannot," was the simple reply, "God has never before disappointed me. Good-bye." "Good-bye," replied the other; "but stay, a man I met in the street to-day was asking after you, and when I mentioned that you were to call at my office to-day, he asked me to give you this letter; I had almost forgotten it." Mr. Heydrick opened the letter and read : "Use this in the Lord's cause." Enclosed therewith were six fifty-dollar bills. "There is your money," said Mr. Heydrick, "exactly three hundred dollars. Please give me a receipt. God has not disappointed me—blessed be His name for ever."

man of prayer gives himself again to intercession. The news of his high hopes stirs the saints far and near: old jewellery is cleaned and sold; long-hoarded treasure parted with; mementoes of tender association yielded up—as witnesses the following letter, received by Müller, Nov. 14, 1846 :—

"The contents of the accompanying casket being in my unconverted days a wedding gift from a very dear husband, have, as you may suppose, been hitherto preserved as beyond price. But since God, in His great mercy, revealed to my soul His exceeding riches in Christ, and gave to it more (Oh, how much more!) than He has taken away, they seemed as the Babylonish garment or wedge of gold, which ought not to be in the Israelite's possession. I therefore give up what the flesh would fain keep, and still prize; but which the spirit rejects, as unworthy a follower of Jesus. Accept then, dear brother, those toys, once the pride of life, and the food of folly; and use them in the building of the Orphan House in which I feel it a privilege to lay one stone."

The casket enclosed a gold chain, with ear-rings and a brooch, one of the "sets" of the Victorian fashion. The gift was precious to Müller as "a proof of the continued readiness of my Heavenly Father to help me in this work"; but doubly welcome on account of the circumstances under which it was given, and the state of mind in which the anonymous donor had devoted these mementoes of affection.

"ARISE AND BUILD"

The months pass; there are many necessities to meet—poor saints must be helped and the stock of tracts replenished; at the end of 1846 comes a donation of £1000, of which £800 goes to the building fund. Early next year, as the season approaches when building operations may be commenced, he pleads with fresh earnestness that God will give all that is needed. He still talks with the Lord as friend to Friend. For "fourteen months and three weeks" have these prayers ascended; but yet again are the arguments set forth why, to the glory of his great Helper, a new Orphan House should be erected. Finally, on January 25, 1847, he rises from his knees in full confidence not only that God *can*, but *will* send the means—"and that soon!" The answer is at hand.

So simple is Müller's language, so lacking in dramatic force, that it is possible for the fact to elude the reader that this is the story of a man wrestling with God as Jacob at Peniel, and prevailing. No eye for a tableau has George Müller. Yet, O unbelieving world, mark this plain man, of rather feeble physique, who comes gently out of his little room, with a quiet smile playing upon his benign countenance. Think you such a mild brother is of the Elijah type, and has power with high Heaven? "Heaven is a *myth*?" Well, let us come to grips on this. This feeble Anglo-Prussian, of somewhat singular accent, declares that God, who has given him some thousands of pounds sterling, will speedily give him some thousands more. Doubtless, this would make a choice morsel of humour for a hunt supper or a garden party? Tell it, O merry trifler of this world, as a spicelet of human eccentricity, but—forget not that the much money already in the bank is good solid evidence for George Müller.

But wait, keep thine eyes on yonder clock of Müller's, and, if the task be not too exacting, wait just sixty minutes, and then mark that a messenger arrives, bearing somewhat for this same praying man who asserts that he is soon to receive large help from God.

What hast thou, O messenger? "Two thousand pounds sterling, for the Orphan House!" Is it a marvel to thee, gallant Colonel Fitz-Dazzler and gay Lady Waltz-around? What thinkest thou now of Faith Triumphant? The answer has come; whatsoever Anglo-German mixture of accents attached to the praying man's simple sentences, the prayer of faith is amply justified. Moreover, all the time, of what small personal income he may receive, Müller is always giving. "Put money in thy purse," is the world's sage counsel, by honest Iago. "Cast it abroad, to God's glory," is Müller's. "By all means *get*," says the world. "By all means *give*," says Müller, "for—God gave His Son."

Listen to him, too, as he muses upon the gifts of God; does he lament "the falling-off of support and the urgent need to obtain new annual subscribers"? Nay, there is no word uttered that suggests the placing of dependence upon men in any way whatsoever.

"ARISE AND BUILD"

There is, so to speak, one Subscriber only, the Lord Himself, who sends in many ways and at divers times. Hence Müller ejaculates : "How great is the blessing which the soul obtains by trusting in God and by waiting patiently. Is it not manifest how precious it is to carry on His work in this way, even with regard to the obtaining of means?" See him refer to his diary, compare and check figures and dates, and then write : "From December 10, 1845, to January 25, 1847, being thirteen months and a half, I have received, solely in answer to prayer, £9285."

Little by little, through the early months of 1847, the total creeps up. In June comes a donation of £1000, for the building. The £10,000, then, is in hand. It is time to put in the foundations; on July 5, the work is commenced; on August 19, the foundation-stone is laid.

Let us look around and see whether this is what men would call the "psychological moment" for launching a great scheme. On the contrary, a more unlikely season for carrying through a great philanthropic plan could scarcely be imagined. Europe is ablaze with revolutionary excitement. A universal upheaval seems imminent. Only a few weeks of 1848 have passed when Paris becomes a city of insurrection and barricades : Louis-Philippe and his queen are in full flight for England, being smuggled out of France, by the British Consul at Havre, as "Mr. and Mrs. Smith." The spirit of Paris is working in every capital in Europe. The old order of things, as solemnly confirmed by emperors and kings, after the fall of Napoleon, is shaken to its foundations. Austria herself is in such straits that Metternich—mighty Metternich, type of Things-that-were—also finds a resting-place in England, and the Emperor prudently retires for a season to the Tyrol, "for the benefit of his health." Italy is in the first and sad days of the struggle which is to end in freedom and unity. But these events are after all merely the outcroppings of a great movement among the peoples which seems determined to root up the last remains of Feudalism.

What of Britain? The reduction of employment consequent on the introduction of machinery; the changes in industrial conditions caused by the discovery of coal and iron, whereby "rural England" is largely transformed into "workshop England," the cornfield giving place to the clanging smithy, the factory, and the cotton-mill; the high price of bread; the ignorance and misery of the poor; these are among the causes which contribute to bring the country to the verge of a cataclysm. Disraeli, after careful observation, thus describes an industrial district :—

"As you advanced, leaving behind you long lines of little dingy tenements, with infants lying about the road, you expected every moment to emerge into some streets, and encounter buildings bearing some correspondence, in their size and comfort, to the considerable population swarming around you. Nothing of the kind. There were no public buildings of any sort; no churches, chapels, town-hall, institute. At every fourth or fifth house, alleys seldom above a yard wide, and streaming with filth, opened out of the street. Here, during the days of business, the sound of the hammer and file never ceased, amid gutters of abomination, and piles of foulness, and stagnant pools of filth; reservoirs of leprosy and plague whose exhalations were sufficient to fill the country with fever and pestilence."

The apprentices in this district, Disraeli adds, " are worked sixteen and even twenty hours a day; they are fed on carrion, and they sleep in lofts and cellars"; yet one optimistic "filer" bears witness regarding his master: "I never had horse-flesh the whole time I was with him. Never had no sick cow except when meat was very dear. Sometimes he would give us a treat of fish, when it had been four or five days in town, not sold. No, there was never no want for anything at meals, except time to eat them in."[1]

[1] In *Sybil*. Recurring to the subject, in 1870, Disraeli (preface to *Lothair*) touched frankly upon the relations of organised Christianity to the people at the time when *Sybil* was written: "There were few great things left in England, and the Church [of England] was one. Nor do I doubt that if, a quarter-of-a-century ago, there had risen a churchman equal to the occasion, the position of ecclesiastical affairs in this country would have been very different from that which they now occupy. But these great matters fell into the hands of monks and schoolmen, and the secession of Dr. Newman dealt a blow to the Church of England from which it still reels." Disraeli did not take the Brethren and George Müller into account, yet it is important as well as interesting to note that he recognised the need and the opportunity for a powerful testimony on the side of Evangelical truth.

THE LIFE OF GEORGE MÜLLER

Amid such a whirl, with thousands clamouring for food, with incendiary fires reddening the midnight skies, and with incipient insurrections threatened or actually breaking out here and there like eruptive boils, the political aspirations of the labouring classes find expression, as a hopeful way of pioneering towards the realisation of their social ideals, in "Chartism," which is to say on seven points of parliamentary change embodied in the famous "Charter." About two months after the outbreak in Paris, a huge demonstration is organised by Chartists ; half a million people are to assemble on Kennington Common—the old meeting-place where Whitefield used to preach—and march to the Houses of Parliament, to present a petition. The question is in everybody's mouth : "Will the wild scenes and street battles of the French capital be repeated around Westminster ? " London has not been so mightily astir since the Gordon riots, indeed, since the days when Charles I. burst into Parliament to seize the five members. Wellington takes command of the troops, and prepares to face any revolutionary onset with such a "whiff of grapeshot" as that with which Citizen Bonaparte blew away the Men of the Sections on the 13th Vendémiaire of Year 4 of the Republic. Happily, Wellington has no need of grapeshot or Lifeguards' swords. Chartism's great army dies down into a curious conglomerate crowd— for the most part peaceable enough.[1] Social legisla-

[1] " SIR,—The Cabinet have had the assistance of the Duke of Welling-

tion ultimately takes the place of revolution. Shaftesbury proves more potent than Wellington. Britain is delivered from Civil War—but the condition of the people is awful indeed.

Through such dark times, the erection of the Orphan House goes steadily on, Müller being steadfastly devoted to his great ideal of demonstrating to all the world that " God is, and that He is a rewarder of them that diligently seek Him." In the very fact that the whole matter is simply one of God and His servant, George Müller, lies a fresh proof of Divine wisdom ; it is easy to imagine a committee of dignitaries protesting against " the distinct unwisdom of Mr. Müller, however well-meaning that gentleman may be, in insisting on his vast scheme in these days of unparalleled social unrest." Doubtless, an " advisory council " of commercial men would " urgently point out to Mr. Müller that British investments at home

ton in framing their plans for to-morrow. Colonel Rowan [Chief Commissioner of Police] advised that the procession . . . should be allowed to come as far as the bridge . . . and there should be stopped. He thinks this is the only way to avoid a fight. If, however, the Chartists fire and draw their swords and use their daggers, the military are to be called out. I have no doubt of their easy triumph over a London mob. But any loss of life will cause a deep and rankling resentment."—Lord John Russell to Prince Albert, April 9, 1848.

" Lord John Russell presents his humble duty to your Majesty, and has the honour to state that the Kennington Common Meeting has proved a complete failure. About 12,000 or 15,000 persons met in good order. . . . The last accounts gave the numbers as about 5000, rapidly dispersing. The mob was in good humour. . . . Lord John Russell trusts your Majesty has profited by the sea-air."—Lord John Russell to Queen Victoria, April 10, 1848. [The Court had removed from Buckingham Palace to Osborne, I.W.]

and abroad were never in so precarious a condition, and that in view of the general unsettlement of affairs he will be well-advised to postpone his operations till a more opportune season." Müller, however, is dependent on nobody but the Living God—who is sufficient even in so wind-swept an age.

Let it not be forgotten that, while the plan for the New Orphan House is afoot, the old Orphan Houses in Wilson Street are being maintained. Here, too, there are trials of faith, as in past days, but triumphs of faith also. Indeed, the story is of trial and triumph all the way through. Thus, Müller says (Feb. 2, 1848): "This morning I only had one farthing left, like the handful of meal in the barrel, when, on my usual walk before breakfast I felt myself led out of my usual track, in a direction in which I had not gone for some months. In stepping over a stile I said to myself: 'Perhaps God has a reason even in this.' About five minutes afterwards I met a Christian gentleman who gave me two sovereigns for the orphans, and then I knew why I had been led this way. Thus the farthing has been already multiplied. This afternoon I received still further from a brother £1. 1s.; also a letter from Portsea containing £1. 10s. The letter from Portsea contained these words: 'Please accept it as another token of the Lord's watchful care for you and yours.'"

Does this life of faith prove wearying? Müller shrewdly suspects that he is suspected of growing a little tired of trusting in God. It seems, to some, "too good to be true," this idea of implicit reliance on the resources of Heaven and on the word of Him who cannot lie. So, for the reassurance of such, the plain statement is made in the "Narrative": "Should the reader say that he thinks 'I must find this a very trying life,' and that I must be tired of it, I beg to state, that he is entirely mistaken. I do *not* find the life in connection with this work a trying life, but a very happy one. It is impossible to describe the abundance of peace and heavenly joy that often has flowed into my soul by means of the fresh answers which I have obtained from God, after waiting upon Him for help and blessing; and the longer I have had to wait upon Him, or the greater my need was, the greater the enjoyment when at last the answer came—which has often been in a very remarkable way, in order to make the hand of God the more manifest. The longer I go on in this service, the greater the trials of one kind or another become; but, at the same time, the happier I am in this my service, and the more assured that I am engaged as the Lord would have me to be. How then could I be tired of carrying on the work of God on such principles as I do?"

In August, 1848, the New Orphan House is nearing completion, the building is up and the roof almost finished. Funds will now be wanted for furnishing. Shall the gentry be circularised? Nay, such a notion is not in Müller's mind. That is not Müller's way. God, who has sent the money for the erection, will also supply the means for furnishing.[1] Now comes a renewal of urgent pleadings before the Lord, pleading His promises. A gift of £500 is an encouragement, an earnest. The days creep on. At length Müller computes that within six weeks from February 12, 1849, the Orphan House will be ready.

Going carefully through the rooms, scanning, measuring, planning, he sees that, while exercising all economy, the expenditure for furnishing must of necessity be large, wherefore he entreats the Lord that the means may be sent in. Eleven hundred and ninety-five days have passed since he commenced to ask for the money for this building. The plan is reaching fruition—will his Heavenly Father, so good, so kind, forsake him at this supreme moment ? Nay : he will give himself to prayer once again : indeed is on the point of doing so, when a brother in the Lord calls, and, after a few minutes' conversation, gives £2000, to be used in the work just as Müller pleases. Once

---

[1] "Müller's way," of simply looking to God for all needed supplies was never a vague sentiment : it was a fundamental principle. Thus, upon one occasion, two persons, collecting, from house to house, for a chapel debt, called on him and he urged them that to ask promiscuously from one and all involved asking the enemies of the Lord for pecuniary assistance. The two collectors answered : "The gold and silver are the Lord's" ; whereupon Müller replied : "*Because* the gold and the silver are the Lord's, therefore we, His children, need not go to His enemies for the support of His work." Although his contention was not received, it received, at the moment, a striking illustration. Müller had absolutely no funds in hand, but at that moment, as if in support of his pleadings, a postman delivered a letter containing post-office orders for £10 : other monies also arrived, so that "whilst those two persons were with me, £12. 15s. 5d. had come in."

more—"Before they call, I will answer." "Thus," says Müller, "the Lord shows that He can and will not only give *as much as is absolutely needed* for His work, but also that He can and will give *abundantly*. It is impossible to describe the real joy I had in God, when I received this sum. I was calm, not in the least excited, able to go on immediately with the other work that came upon me at once after I had received the donation; but inexpressible was the delight which I had in God, who had thus given me the full answer to my thousands of prayers, during these eleven hundred and ninety-five days."

Nevertheless, we are not quite at the end of this pilgrimage of faith. Although the building is all but ready, and the furnishing is being completed, there will be required, prior to the opening, extensive stores—provisions, soap, haberdashery, and so forth; likewise some thousands of yards of material for clothing. There will be three hundred orphans to provide for, instead of a hundred and twenty as hitherto, and therefore the stocks will have to be proportionately larger. Surely, at this final moment, there will be no blockage. A donation of £300 is the crowning providence. All that remains to be done, in this fascinating record of the raining-down of heavenly manna, is to prepare a plain statement of income and expenditure.

Always careful and precise, Müller has his statement ready. Money has continued to come in, so that the figures are: total received, £15,784. 18s. 10d.;

total expended, £15,008. 4s. 6¼d. Therefore, when all outgoings have been defrayed, for the land and its conveyance, for the enrolment of the trust-deeds in Chancery, for the building and its furnishing and preparation for use, there remains a balance in hand of £776. 14s. 3¾d. Thus the balance-sheet testifies, to an age absorbed in material concerns, of the faithfulness of God; testifies to the carnal mind: "See, O blind, and hear, O deaf, here is a matter of £15,000 given to a comparatively obscure man, in a provincial city, without one farthing of the money being solicited, but in direct answer to his pleadings before God"; testifies, moreover, to a further matter—albeit trifling in comparison—of over £700 left, to demonstrate the fulfilment of the Scriptural phrase, "good measure, pressed down, running over." And, if the blind see not and the deaf hear not, at least let the children of light, the Church of the Firstborn, rejoice in this Nineteenth - Century testimony to the power and graciousness of God, and cry: "He hath done marvellous things: His right hand, and His holy arm, hath gotten Him the victory!"

CHAPTER IX

Still Building

THE New Orphan House being opened, here, assuredly, is a life occupation sufficient in extent even for so energetic a pioneer and so skilful an administrator as George Müller. Were it God's will, he were supremely content therewith, but there comes to him another and larger vision of receiving and maintaining by faith a grand total of a thousand children. To achieve this will mean erecting another and a yet larger Orphan House, to accommodate seven hundred little ones. The cost will probably be £35,000.

This fresh thought is ever before him. To any but the man of Faith Triumphant, this might indeed seem a tremendous task; a burden too heavy to be undertaken by a mild-mannered gentleman, of clock-work habits, like George Müller. Easy would it be to settle down quietly, training and teaching the children, in school or cabbage-field, and above all tenderly drawing them into the Way Everlasting. However, God will have him go forward: the Voice declares:

"This is the way, walk ye in it." Not that Müller needs thunders, or admonitions: he knows full well that the path of communion is the path of obedience. He will move as swiftly or as slowly as God pleases, having no spark of desire to assert his own personality ; but the thought of those wasted years of youth is still with him, and under this calm exterior there burns a holy flame of aspiration that he may now be permitted to accomplish yet mightier things.

Nor can such a man look unmoved upon the condition of poor children in this dark day. O Britain, " stony-hearted step-mother," what of these thousands of miserable, starving, ophthalmia-blighted youngsters of workhouse and slum? Verily, this seems the hardest, coldest time for boys and girls the land has ever known. Here and there, truly, a wail of sorrow is heard. Elizabeth Barrett Browning weeps, writes, pleads. Her piteous appeal will be quoted by philanthropists of a later generation, and the day will come when dismal little slummers shall be helped by her throbbing verse to make friends with daisy-spangled fields and running brooks and green waves breaking upon the sands—yea, the day when garden villages and training farms shall receive the feeble, white-faced child of neglect, as into an earthly Eden. But such halcyon days are not yet. In these drab and dismal early-Victorian times, the heart moan of the poetess holds an infinite deal of terrible meaning. In the prisons, alone, of England there are six thousand orphans—a fact which speaks with sufficient significance of the conditions under which neglected or deserted children normally exist.

The slums of Britain are as antechambers of the pit. The typical phrase in this day of Müller's is "a rookery"; which is to say, a nest of ghastly little lanes and filthy courts, crammed with families whose characteristics are criminality or abject misery; where Law is set at defiance and cleanliness and sanitation are things undreamed of.

Happy is the alley which, in these days of back-street squalor, boasts a pump unpoisoned by sewage—although men are not greatly concerned as to water's purity, seldom using it as a beverage, but only for cooking and washing; and, for that matter, why wash? Happy, too, is the rookery tenement in which the filth and the various odours are not such as to send a stray wanderer from civilisation and St. James' reeling back in horror. The "two-and-seventy different stenches" which Coleridge enumerated at Cologne, were probably not so emphatic as those of St. Giles' or St. Luke's, in the Metropolis. After years, with their slum clearances, shall reveal the innermost of some of these wretched hovels, with their artfully-designed, iron-sheeted hiding-places, and trap-doors that have afforded a swift retreat from Peel's newly-formed and enthusiastic police force, as from the Bow Street runners of old: darker still, moving panels, affording a way to river or tidal ditch, shall hint of foul and mysterious crimes. Some of these "rookeries" have sprung up on the old gardens at the rear of city houses. One terrible district is meaningly designated "Jack Ketch's warren"—Ketch being the public hangman. The knowledge of such conditions, and the absence of any very earnest movement by the State or the Churches, may well fan the flame of holy aspiration in George Müller.

Other mighty men there are who realise the shame of child-neglect. Shaftesbury, with sorrow and indignation tearing at his heart, not only denounces and exposes abuses, but sets to work to stop them for ever, so far as legislation and the awakening of a new sense of public responsibility can do : and he prays that the unhappy little ones may not only be rescued from human tyranny, but converted to God. He "rides out," as befits a Christian champion, to deliver the boy and girl slaves of factory and mine. He takes the Prince Consort into London's chief rookery of St. Giles', on a tour of inspection, whereat the startled beggars and thieves swarm out of their filthy "kitchens," into the streets, to cheer.

Another important factor is the humanitarian influence of Dickens, with his vivid exposures of child-misery, child-criminality, and child-exploitation ;[1] moreover, of Bumbledom and the callousness

---

[1] Compare Dickens' (*Christmas Carol*) sarcasm : "Are there no prisons ? Are there no workhouses ?" with Müller's : "The moral state of the poor-houses greatly influences me to go forward. . . . By God's help I will do what I can to keep poor orphans from prison."

of poor-law administration.[1] Again, Kingsley
describes the fever-ridden attics and consumption-
breeding workshops wherein tailors and sempstresses
toil for a miserable wage; and of the semi-starvation of
the agricultural labourers and their children. Such
lightning flashes and thunder rumblings have at length
the effect of awakening Britannia. She yawns, rubs
her eyes, looks around, sees—what? That, whereas she
kept of yore a keen look-out lest Villeneuve should
suddenly appear in the Thames, she has now to face
enemies that are within, enemies more difficult to meet
than would be Ney and the Old Guard marching
across Hyde Park or Murat charging down Piccadilly.
Enemies within? Yea; poverty, filth, disease, sullen discontent, whether aggregated in cities or lurking beneath
the shadow of chestnut blooms in country hamlets—
the misery of the ill-fed, ill-clad, ill-housed poor.

It is well, then, that George Müller will by no
means settle down into a comparatively quiet life. Lest
exaggeration be suspected, let his own simple words be
given. He says (December 26, 1850): "There are

---

[1] It is, of course, not suggested that Dickens is to be classed, with
Müller and Shaftesbury, as being of evangelistic spirit. His odd fancy
for depicting Evangelical preachers as vulgar and hypocritical persons
showed how little he was in touch with the message of saving grace;
and if it be retorted that "he was only exposing the unreal," we cannot
but reply that, this being so, he was disproportionately fond of such
exposing; and his ridicule of such godly ministers as Thomas Binney
and Joshua Harrison, for a simple prayer at the funeral of the famous
William Hone, does not help the case. Nevertheless, we must needs
recognise Charles Dickens' pathetic comradeship with the starved child
and the slum cripple.

vast multitudes of orphans to be provided for."[1] This is the time of the coining of the phrase "street arab." Hordes of children, unowned by parent, uncared for, perhaps escaped from apprenticeship or pauper-schools or factory slavery, wander at large, sleeping in out-houses or stables, or in any odd corner where an intelligent young Ishmaelite, nimble of foot as of hand, may find a hiding-place, unarrested by constable or by "old daddy watchman." These are the tribes which produce the professional criminal, developing from the young pickpocket and the boy filcher from tradesmen's stalls into the brutal burglar. Pretty little Willie Sikes, the slender, fatherless, blue-eyed boy who haunts barges by Thames' side or dwells in an empty barrel in Covent Garden Market and exists by "pinching," becomes Bill Sikes the cracksman, and a recruit for Newgate.

Knowing full well these awful conditions, George Müller sits silent before the Lord, like one of the old

[1] Dr. Barnardo's evidence, sixteen years later, demonstrates the correctness of Müller. In 1866, Dr. Barnardo was directed by a homeless lad named Jim Jarvis—whose description of himself was: "Got no father; got no friends; don't live nowhere:"—to one of the midnight haunts of the "arabs." This able guide, on "a dreadful winter night," climbed walls, threaded a way through a wilderness of outhouses, and finally, scaling some sheds, showed Dr. Barnardo a company of poor boys "sleeping in all postures, in the gutters of the iron roof, clad in thin rags, with not a shred more to cover them, exposed under the open sky to all winds and weathers." "Shall I wake 'em?" asked Jim Jarvis. "No, no," replied the awe-stricken visitor. "Well, shall I show you another 'lay,' sir?" But Dr. Barnardo—at that time a young medical student—had seen enough for one night. He afterwards declared: "That dread night of discovery determined my subsequent career."

prophets lamenting the woes of the land. He is resolved to do just what is God's will, and not to be betrayed by human emotion into any mistaken action. In the course of his Scripture-reading he is at this time in the Book of Proverbs, and finds strength for his soul in three particular passages: "Trust in the Lord with all thine heart; and lean not unto thine own understanding. In all thy ways acknowledge Him, and He shall direct thy paths" (3 : 5, 6); "The integrity of the upright shall guide them; but the perverseness of fools shall destroy them" (11 : 3); and "Commit thy works unto the Lord, and thy thoughts shall be established" (16 : 3). Seeking God's honour and the benefit of the orphans, he is soon assured that the Lord would have him go forward; and the matter is weighed and settled with a characteristic combination of faith and common sense, in a sort of balance-sheet giving "Reasons for and against establishing another Orphan House, for seven hundred orphans": whereof the "Questions and Answers" run :—

(1) *Q.* "Should I be going beyond my measure *spiritually*?" (And the apostolic reminder is brought in, that "man is not to think of himself more highly than he ought to think.") *A.* "If the Lord were to leave me to myself, even a tenth part of my present trials would overwhelm me; but He is pleased to sustain; and I look, too, for an increase of faith with every fresh difficulty."

(2) *Q.* "Would it not be going beyond my measure

naturally ? " A. " By husbanding strength, by orderly ways and regular habits, and by using all possible help, I get through a vast amount of work. My correspondence is about 3000 letters a year; I attend to it all without a secretary. In addition, the entire management devolves upon me. Then, with the help of a secretary, a clerk, and a school-inspector, I could clearly accomplish yet more."

(3) Q. "There must be a limit to your work." A. " True, but the Lord has helped me hitherto, and now my mind is drawn out just as it was when I first started, when it was enlarged, and further enlarged, and when I decided to build. I cannot say as yet that the Lord has brought me to the limit."

(4) Q. " Is it not 'tempting God' to think of building another Orphan House, for seven hundred more orphans?" A. " 'Tempting God' means, to limit Him in any of His attributes. By His grace, I do not wish to limit His power or His willingness to give to me, His poor, humble servant, all the means to build."

(5) Q. " Surely you will not get the means for building and furnishing so large an Orphan House; and, even if you did, how will you, at the same time, get the means of carrying on the work which already exists?" A. " Looking at the matter *naturally*, this is a weighty objection. The New Orphan House, with its three hundred orphans, cost about £15,000 to build and fit up and furnish—although the style of build-

ing is simple, and the land was comparatively cheap. A building to accommodate seven hundred orphans, with ground for growing vegetables, will not cost less than £35,000. Despite the fact that help has been given liberally, there is no prospect of receiving the large sum I should need; especially as £6000 to £7000 is required for maintaining the work already existing, and people giving to a Building Fund might give less for upkeep. Nevertheless, God has the power to give me this £35,000, and much more, and the large sums needed for current expenses also. Indeed, I delight in the greatness of the difficulty, for I desire to be most fully assured at the outset, that I go forward only according to the Lord's bidding. If so, He will give me the means; if not, I shall not have them."

(6) *Q.* "Suppose you were even to succeed in getting this large Orphan House built, how will you be able to provide for seven hundred more orphans?" *A.* "There is much weight in this objection, *naturally*, and I am too much a man of calm, quiet, cool calculation not to feel its force. But I am not discouraged, *spiritually.* Supposing that, at the outset, I had acted according to 'natural reason' instead of trusting in the Living God! I might have said : 'Here are two charity schools started: let them suffice.' But I looked not to natural fallen reason, I trusted not in a circle of Christian friends, but in the Living God. The result has been that there have been, since 1834, ten thousand souls in the Day-schools, Sunday-schools,

and Adult-schools; several hundred orphans have been brought up; many thousand copies of the Bible have been circulated, and hundreds of thousands of tracts, while forty Gospel preachers, at home or abroad, have been assisted for several years, and the New Orphan House has been built and is flourishing. How blessed is it, therefore, to trust, not in circumstances or friends, but in God alone!"

(7) Q. "But, supposing you were able by prayer to obtain all that is needed, and to maintain such an Institution during your lifetime, what would become of it after your death?" A. "My business is with all my might to serve my own generation; in doing so I shall best serve the next. Supposing this objection to be a sound one, I ought never to have commenced the work at all, and thus all the destitute children whom the Lord has allowed me to take care of, during the past fifteen years, would not have been taken up by me. Let every one take heed lest, in caring about what will become of the next generation, he forgets to serve his own."

(8) Q. "You will be in danger of being 'lifted up.'" A. "I am even now in danger of it, but hitherto the Lord has kept me humble. I do not see that this fear ought to keep me from going forward, but that I have rather to beseech the Lord that He would be pleased to give me a lowly mind, and never suffer me to rob Him of the glory which is due to Him alone."

Such arguments against have doubtless risen in the

mind in the case of many an ardent worker; they are part, too, of the obvious stock-in-trade of the pessimist and the dour critic desirous above all things of blocking or discounting any earnest endeavour in the interests of the Kingdom of God. Müller's answers to himself were answers, also, to the unbelievers and "carnal Christians" of his own day. But he does not stay retorting upon objections; he takes up the positive side, giving reasons *for* :—

(1) "The many applications for the admission of destitute orphans are a call from God to do all in my power to provide a home and a Scriptural education for a still greater number.

(2) "The moral state of the poor-houses greatly influences me.

(3) "All the Orphan Houses already existing are insufficient to admit even the most deserving and distressing cases. By God's help I will do what I can to keep poor orphans from prison.

(4) "The great and uninterrupted help which the Lord has given me for more than fifteen years, is a great reason for going forward.

(5) "The *experience* I have had in the work. I have been the sole director, under God, from its smallest commencement.

(6) "The spiritual benefit of still more orphans. I long to be more extensively used than hitherto, in the salvation of their souls through faith in the Lord Jesus.

(7) "When I began the orphan work it was for the definite and especial purpose that, by means of it, the unconverted might see, through the answers to prayer that I received, that there is verily reality in the things of God; and that the children of God might have their faith strengthened, and be encouraged in all simplicity to deal with God under every circumstance, and trust in Him at all times. If this would be answered in a measure by the state in which the orphan work has been in former times—and more so since the erection of the New Orphan House—it would be still more so, by the blessing of God, by my going forward in it to a far greater degree than ever before.

(8) "I am peaceful and happy, spiritually, in the prospect of enlarging the work. This, after all the heart-searching I have had, and the daily prayer to be kept from delusion and mistake, and the betaking myself to the Word of God, would not be the case, I judge, had not the Lord purposed to condescend to use me more than ever in this service."

The matter thus settled in his own mind, Müller, while certain that the way will be opened, keeps the matter private; finally, he tells his wife, and then places the whole story of his leadings and reflections before "a prayerful, judicious, and cautious man of God." This brother gives encouragement and half a sovereign, the first donation towards the second New Orphan House. A week or two later, the plan is made public. Very little is received, and the tempter suggests: "After all, are you not mistaken?" To which Müller replies by casting himself before God in prayer, crying: "Lord, wilt Thou be pleased to refresh my spirit by sending some large donation?" In answer there comes a cheering gift of £500. Müller is living on faith's watch-tower, looking out for more and more. Delays are nought but trials of faith, and that trial accomplished, God will send help. Long seasons he spends upon his knees, wrestling in prayer.

All this time, of course, the already existing New Orphan House has to be supported, as well as the other branches of the Scriptural Knowledge Institution; so, when a sum comes in to be used according to Müller's discretion, part is allocated to the Building Fund, part to the maintenance of the orphans, and so forth. Out of a donation of nearly £1000, he apportions £600 to the new building. The printed "Annual Report," containing an account of the fresh proposal to build, makes its way—as Müller's reports usually do—to all parts of the world: £70 is sent from a stranger—a believer—at Madras; £50 from another at Melbourne. It will take many such to make up the total sum required, but the accomplishment shall surely come.

For the means to build the New Orphan House No. 1 there were two years and three months to wait, continuing instant in prayer, before receiving the full answer. But what of that? Who shall dictate to the Living God as to the times when He shall send? Faith, not to degenerate into a mere attempt to snatch, must undergo its trial. And is it not made clear, a thousand times, that "all things work together for good to them that love God"? Almost daily, some answer to prayer is given. Some, indeed, are what men call small, but they are God's reminders that prayer is heard, and are therefore precious, witnessing that He listens to the supplications that go up from Ashley Down, for the godly workers, being themselves sent thither of God in answer to prayer, are united in spirit with their leader—who, wrestling for yet larger sums, and eagerly waiting for the witness of God's faithfulness, receives the promise of £8100, as the joint donation of several Christians. Of this, he purposes to place £6000 to the Building Fund. The promise is refreshing, but Müller is not startled at the magnitude of a donation: why should he be? Is he not expecting great things from God?

If the gifts that are received for the Lord's work are themselves refreshing, so, too, is the spirit of the givers. Here are no ambitious souls anxious to figure at the head of a philanthropic list, or to make a mighty donation the stepping-stone to a peerage. These are the gifts of the saints. Here is a Christian brother calling on Müller, sitting down, quietly producing a small packet, and unfolding the same: there are bank notes for £110: the Christian brother desires to lay them at the feet of Jesus, and, when he has done so, the whole property remaining to him is less than the donation given. That friend, too, who wrote from Madras, sent his £70 as "a mite cast into the Lord's treasury towards building the Orphan House . . . may the God of Jacob, that has fed me all my life long unto this day, accept of it, as an acknowledgment of the thousandth part of the mercies I have received at His hands." Truly, there is much grace to be found among the saints. At the end of the year 1854, Müller reports £13,670. 11s. 7¾d. in hand. Much more than double this sum will he need; and the donations given for the specific purpose, or placed thereto, in the succeeding year, amount to about £3500.

There are many orphans waiting admission; wherefore Müller thinks it well to inquire about suitable land. Indeed, he has long had in mind two fields —adjoining the land on which the New Orphan House No. 2 was later built—hoping to purchase them. Inquiry, however, reveals that under the will of the late owner, the fields cannot, at this time, be sold. Whereat Müller strives with Müller: natural Müller is woebegone and says: "*What* a strange disappointment"; but spiritual Müller retorts, by the grace of God: "The Lord has something better to give thee, George; be of good courage, trust and fear not."

Speedily the wisdom of God in His dealings on this matter is revealed. Müller has himself gradually become convinced that instead of building a House for seven hundred orphans, the better way would be to have two Houses each to hold about three hundred and fifty. Now, by the side of the New Orphan House No. 1 there is clearly room for a second House, and to build there will not only save the cost of ground but will make for ease and simplicity in the management and administration. The change in plan, which thus arises out of what seemed a disappointment, is promptly decided upon; wells are sunk and the building contract settled, in which connection comes one more beautiful assurance of God's loving-kindness. There will be about three hundred large windows in the New House: in the other building, the glass required was contracted for, in the usual way, but in the new contract the glass is not specified, and will therefore be an extra. Now comes an unsolicited offer of all the *glass* that will be required. "A mere coincidence," says Unbelief: "No doubt the ordering of our Heavenly Father," says George Müller.

It is well to recognise that many of the people who give large help to George Müller are sagacious business men; they are truly converted, but are not in the least likely to be led away either by fanaticism or sentimentality. These men thus give to the Christian causes, in particular identified with Müller's name, for three main reasons: (1) Müller is transparently sincere and unselfish; (2) he is an excellent "business man," a wise and careful administrator; (3) more especially, they gladly find themselves at one with him in "laying up treasure in heaven," and are entirely frank in saying so.

STILL BUILDING

Müller touches frequently upon this subject of the duty of the business man. For example, a friend writes him: "Beloved Sir, I enclose you £10, as *the fruit from seed sown.* Last year, I consecrated a certain portion of my year's income to the Lord's service, and sent you in anticipation of it, and the result is that I have nearly £100 to devote to Him during the present year." Herein, large questions are opened. The intention of the donor is excellent; so, too, is his spirit. Yet there is the danger that a man may "ring-fence" a certain business operation and declare that God shall have all the profits thereof while all the rest—the bulk of his gain in trading—is reserved for himself. Proportionate giving is good; the devotion of the fruits of some special endeavour is good; but no man is to label *this* income as God's, and *that* as his own; the only true Christian position is that of entire dedication. "What hast thou that thou didst not receive?"

Further, no man is to rest satisfied with giving a donation or a percentage of profit, if at the same time he neglects to give, of what God calls him to do, in Christian service. Accordingly, Müller, with his customary lucidity and spiritual perception, makes the point clear. There *is* such a thing as "sowing and reaping," for "he that soweth sparingly shall reap also sparingly; and he which soweth bountifully shall reap also bountifully." But there are different ways of sowing. Teaching the children the

Way of Life; visiting the people and speaking comforting words of the love of God and the Gospel message; distributing to the poor in the name of the Lord Jesus; and using money for His honour and glory. The recompense may appear in this present life—almost invariably it does—but even if for purposes of His own the Lord did not allow such reaping here on earth, there will be the harvest in the world to come. The Müller view, then, with regard to consecrating a "portion," may be expressed in his contrasting saying: "I fear that while admitting the general claim on 'all,' we shorten the actual claim on 'everything.' We are not under law? True; but that is not to make our obedience less complete, or our giving less bountiful; rather, is it not, that after all claims of law are settled, the new nature finds its joy in doing *more than the law requires?*" Rejoicing in which idea he cries: "Let us abound in the work of the Lord more and more."

On through the two years or so between the commencement of New Orphan House No. 2, and its completion, money comes in, now in tricklings, now in a mighty rush—as though some warm breath of the Spirit had melted the glaciers in the experience of some who had ample means but were cold at heart; or as though some beloved child of God, on coming into the possession of earthly treasure had run to pour it at the Redeemer's feet. One day, he receives ten shillings from one of the orphans now out in domestic service : the gift is precious, for it represents the careful savings of a poor girl. Nine years before, in the Orphan House in Wilson Street, this little orphan received the light of life ; now her ambition is to "put a corner stone in the wall" of New Orphan House No. 2, and her only regret is that she has "no more to bestow upon such a noble work."

Another day, when the new building is approaching completion, Müller returns home after—careful man that he is—personally testing the efficiency of the gas apparatus and burners—and finds awaiting him a cheque for £1000 from a brother in the Lord who desires to spend the whole of his large income for the Lord, laying up no treasure on earth and spending very little on his own necessities. This wise brother, with a touch of gentle humour, says that he "considers it profitable to invest a little in the Orphan Houses." Doubtless ; but for the benefit of critical apprehensiveness Müller assures his friends : "The donor has not received any interest from me, nor will he have any from me, on this £1000 ; and yet, I doubt not, this investment will be profitable to him. In such cases I have found that the Lord, even in this life, has taken notice of such deeds, and given ample repayment, often tenfold, twentyfold, yea, in not a few instances even a hundredfold, according to that word : 'Give and it shall be given unto you ; good measure, pressed down, and shaken together, and running over, shall men give into your bosom.'"

THE LIFE OF GEORGE MÜLLER

At length, November 12, 1857, New Orphan House No. 2, for four hundred orphans, is opened. Day by day for nearly seven years has Müller been praying for this. Now that the accomplishment comes, he flashes forth again in his Report with a characteristic "Pause, esteemed reader!" We know what this trumpet-call means. Müller is going to exult, not in a personal triumph, not in a public glorification of himself, but in the confounding of unbelief and natural reasoning; in the triumph of faith. When New Orphan House No. 1 was commenced, the taunt of Unbelief was: "How absurd to think of taking three hundred orphans instead of a hundred and twenty, and building a new Institution, when you have already to wait upon your God, day by day, for supplies even for the hundred and twenty you already have!" Yet the Lord sent all that was needed—"good measure, pressed down, and shaken together." So he goes steadily on to the fulfilment of his great hope of receiving a thousand orphans in all; God will stand by him, and Faith be triumphant still.

CHAPTER X

The Orphan Houses Completed

FEELING that the time has come for pursuing the building operations, Müller still prays that Divine help may be given. Orphan House No. 1 accommodates three hundred orphans; Orphan House No. 2, four hundred, so that a third House, for three hundred more, would complete the scheme for housing a thousand. A highly suitable piece of land, separated from the Houses only by a road, is purchased, and so ample is its size that Müller decides to build for four hundred orphans instead of three hundred. Next, consultations with the architects demonstrate that, with but little further expense, four hundred and fifty might be provided for. Why not? The number of destitute children pleading for admission is very great, so there can be no question regarding the need. And there are two other reasons that urge a forward step. One is, the greatness of the Lord's blessing upon the work; the other that Müller, being now fifty-three years of age, realises deeply: "I have but one life to spend for God on earth, and that that one life is a brief one." Wherefore the original plan, to have, ultimately, a thousand orphans, is enlarged; there are to be eleven hundred and fifty. The development will call for £6000 to £7000 more, for land and buildings, and £1800 a year more for maintenance. "But," declares Müller, sounding a Pauline note, "none of these difficulties discouraged me."

The money comes in. New Orphan House No. 3 is commenced July 11, 1859. Thousands of times, year after year, is the need spread before the Lord. Finally, the buildings are completed and paid for: the opening takes place March 12, 1862.

Here, it would seem, we might certainly leave Müller with his great vision realised, in charge of eleven hundred and fifty orphans, having also the other activities of the Scriptural Knowledge Institution resting upon him. Not indeed in semi-retirement can he spend the last of his days, for he is in the forefront of the battle, yet kindly friends think he might, with a band of earnest helpers around him, "take things a little easier"! But, George Müller take things easier? Nay, his spirit is already stirring for fresh advances. He cannot forget the hosts of uncared-for children. Ten years before, he hoped to see a thousand orphans sheltered; *now*, he thinks of *two* thousand. This will mean the erection of, say, still two more Orphan Houses, accommodating, in all, eight hundred and fifty children. The scheme is great indeed, but, being God-given, it has to be carried through.

THE ORPHAN HOUSES COMPLETED

Fresh cases are being brought before Müller almost daily, sometimes three or four at a time, although the stipulation still holds that every child received must be destitute, and bereaved of both parents. Hitherto it has been thought best to consider, more especially, the needs of girls, as requiring more sheltering care. Moreover, while boys need to be apprenticed, when fourteen years old, girls may be kept until they are eighteen, useful employment being found for them; and to retain them has this further and inestimable advantage, that to have the care of them at this age is to influence them spiritually just when, as experience shows, they are readiest to give personal heed to the call of God. Certainly, many of the orphans are converted prior to attaining the age of fourteen; but, even so, to keep them longer under Christian teaching is very desirable. Much has been done for girls; now is an opportunity to do more for boys.

True, there are other Orphan Institutions in Britain, but they are entirely inadequate to the need; there are workhouses, but, at this time, although later years bring a great change, "vice abounds in them, on account of the kind of inmates who, generally speaking, are found there." How can the struggling poor endure the idea that their orphan relatives, bereft of father and mother, shall "go to the Union"? Ugh! the idea is repellent. The workhouse garb, workhouse skilly, workhouse joylessness, of mid-Victorian days are repellent indeed—melancholy is it that the name of the kindly queen should have such association!

Beyond even these considerations is the further great fact that Müller has now been so long engaged in befriending orphans, that he can see the effects of the Ashley Down teaching in hundreds of young lives. The poor, half-starved, ill-clad children of poverty who, but for George Müller and Faith Triumphant, had fallen into the clutches of the thief-trainer, or some other of the army of villains who batten on vice, are bright, blithe, industrious young people, many of them servants of the Lord. "The germ," says Müller, "was planted by the Lord, and He caused it to grow and increase. The gift which He had been pleased to impart, for such service, was used, at first, while the work was small; for I began with thirty orphans. Afterwards were added thirty-six more, and then, after a year, again thirty more, and finally, after the lapse of several years, thirty more. Thus, for above thirteen years, the number of orphans under my care never exceeded a hundred and twenty-six; but it grew to three hundred with the opening of Orphan House No. 1, and with the opening of No. 2 to seven hundred; and now, with God's blessing, it will shortly be eleven hundred and fifty."

"Fie!" says Unbelief, "here is George Müller boasting!" Stay, let the man of faith finish: "There is not the least honour due to me for all this, as God called me for the work, fitted me for it, has sustained me in it, and caused my experience to grow with the work." Nevertheless, he realises the responsibility laid upon him; no slothful servant is he to wrap up his talent and lounge away the golden hours of existence, crammed as they are with splendid opportunity; he will accordingly make use of his gift and experience and march still further ahead.

Here, then, is the saint, the humble servant of God, at war with evil. While Parliamentarians are scarcely awake to the elementary duties of the State or the value of child-life as a national asset, here is a giant grappling with the evils that beset the land; and doing so, be it observed, without a word of support from secular reformers, or an ounce of sympathy from the utilitarian; never moving in what the world calls "the limelight," but maintained wholly and solely by faith in the Living God. George, too, has experimental knowledge of the ways and thoughts of the poor. Not without acquiring stores of experience has he lived in humble, shabby-genteel dwellings; and when kindly old ladies left a quarter-pound of tea or small boys carried up the steps a gooseberry pie "from father, for **Mr.** George Müller," the experience was valuable in more senses than one. It taught faith; it also taught the pathos and homeliness of "the short and simple annals of the poor." Not without ripening of wisdom, either, has he toiled in and out the homes of the people, and interviewed the relatives of poor children and chatted with the boys and girls of the Orphan Houses. If he were to "state a case" for us, for the need for extension, it might be somewhat of the "human document" order, as :—

John Smith, bricklayer, dies of consumption. Mrs. John Smith is emaciated and feeble, having denied herself food and clothing for the sake of her husband and children, in addition to taking in "a bit o' washing for the villa folk," to keep things together. John Smith is buried by the parish. Mrs. Smith collapses ; survives her husband a fortnight ; dies also, moaning : "my children, my children !" and is also buried by the parish.

After the funeral, a family council is held regarding the children. "I doant see what can be done for 'em," groans Aunt Betsy; "they'll all hev to go to t' Union; why dost say, 'Zekiel?" Uncle 'Zekiel, who is taking a slice of turnip, is the family Solon. "Never to *that* 'ere place, Betsy," says he. "Never," echo the rest, "not if *we* knows it." "Ay, lad," says Grandma Smith, "I knows what ets loike—a-cussin' an' swearin' an' snuffin' all day long, an' as for t' food, 'tis shocken'."

The company are at their wits' end. Grandma Smith gets out the tea-things. 'Zekiel has brought a loaf; Aunt Sue a bit of tea ; somebody else a trifle of sugar ; there is some dripping in the cupboard. Over the tea-table they agree that none of them can take either of the children, having neither resources nor house-room. "There be on'y one 'ope," is 'Zekiel's verdict ; "we mun try Master George Mooller."

THE ORPHAN HOUSES COMPLETED

In such ways do the boys and girls come to Ashley Down. The Orphan Houses are quickly filled. Through poverty, neglect, and ignorance, how many little ones there are who, despite the efforts of every church and every philanthropist, despite the kindly aid of clergymen and ministers and schoolmasters, and godly ladies in country or city, pine away to an early death! In the churchyards and cemeteries, how many *little* graves! Alas! O tiny green hillocks, all too slowly proceeds this weary business of awakening Britannia: but here at least is one answer—of a man of God—to this cry of suffering children: "By the help of God," says George Müller, "I will seek yet further to be the orphans' friend."

So, then, he is speedily moving ahead again, sunny and kindly, and—confident in the Lord. Things go well. Prior to the time of the great enlargement, in 1850, the expenditure of the Scriptural Knowledge Institution was about £6000 a year; the enlargement meant that £15,000 a year would be required. "Natural reason regarded £15,000 a year as preposterous," says Müller, "it 'never could be raised'; yet, without a single regular annual subscriber, without one collector, in fact without asking anybody, the money has come in." "Natural reason" being, then, routed and faith triumphing, shall not God still further help His servant? Can He not as easily send the further £50,000 required for further premises, and the further £20,000 a year for current expenses? True, "natural reason" is prodigiously staggered at the magnitude of the task of raising £35,000 a year for maintenance. If Unbelief is not weary of cross-examining, it may ask, with a touch of acid sarcasm : "What are your prospects?" Well, as hitherto, they are solely in God.

After considering all difficulties, Müller puts them aside, by the grace of God. As the work was commenced, so it shall go on; in faith. To consider the extension proposals, naturally, is to be overwhelmed, but he is looking solely to the Lord for helpers, lands, means, and everything else needed. Above all reasons for going forward is the determination still to seek the original object—"the glory of God, by giving a practical demonstration as to what could be accomplished through the instrumentality of prayer and faith, in order thus to benefit the Church of God at large, and to lead a careless world to see the reality of the things of God, by showing them that the Living God is still the *Living* God."

That such demonstration, given in the Orphan Houses already existing, is not in vain, appears by the number of visitors. Tens of thousands have been to Ashley Down, marvelling, to behold the actual stone and mortar and the actual orphans, which are "really there," in answer to prayer, witnessing to God's faithfulness. Yea, and if the visitors have eyes to see, they may know that these godly helpers who take care of the children are as wonderful an answer to prayer, as sovereigns or bales of cloth or cartloads of cabbages. Müller may plant, but there must be an Apollos to water. One? Nay, many.

With affairs of magnitude to administer, Müller must needs leave the actual shepherding of the lambs more or less to his assistants—rather, his co-operators in the work of the Living God. One awkward governess, one sour and irritable master, may destroy or mar the usefulness of a whole institution. One evil or "cranky" spirit will blight the home life, poison the very springs of true and lasting success. Of what use would it be for George Müller to receive orphans if selfish helpers were to bend the little twigs of life earthwards, and worldly-minded ones declare, by their love being set on material things, that the high and glorious hopes of George Müller are only the crazy notions of an eccentric mystic? Numerous offers are there from would-be helpers who think, perhaps, that there is a special glory in being " at Müller's," and that Ashley Down invests them with a sort of halo of sanctity; from people, albeit with admirably-reading references, who fancy that such an abode of peace will supply an excellent opportunity of living at ease. From such, God has sent deliverance; unity prevails; those who have charge of the boys and girls are likeminded with the founder, glad to tread the Christian path of self-denial, and being absorbed in the good work. In providing helpers, as in providing means, God is faithful.

Regarding the spiritual results, the testimony of faith is : "Multitudes of sinners have been converted; multitudes of the children of God in all parts of the world have been benefited." Thus declares Müller himself. Wherefore, to labour on, to enlarge and develop the work, will bring greater glory to the name of the Lord; and this is the great object, as ever. The praise of the world is nought; "that HE may be looked at, magnified, admired, trusted in, relied on at all times, is my aim in this service, and particularly so in this intended enlargement."

Now has Müller launched out once again in the venture of faith; now sail the argosies of prayer which are to bring home golden cargoes of help for the orphans of Britain. Let it not be thought an easy matter. The answers to prayer do not come simply because George Müller has drawn up a schedule of outlay and decided to move forward. There will be solemn hours before the Lord, many an outpouring of the soul in the midnight watches, many a wrestling with temptation, many a tender talk as of friend with Friend, with the Adorable One who is his All-in-all : "thousands and tens of thousands of prayers may have to ascend to God before the full answer may be obtained; much exercise of faith and patience will be required; but, in the end, it will again be seen, that His servant, who trusts in Him, has not been confounded." With his mind in peace, then, again he marches on. From the point of view of orphan-need, the step is pressing; fresh and distressing applications pour in; it is not possible to entertain a twentieth part of the number.

This decision is arrived at in May, 1861. Now ensues a series of experiences parallel to those of the years that have gone before, in the matter of praying, waiting, receiving.

Yet, in recording his activities, emphasis must be laid upon the essential quality of his life, the saintly fragrance, the walk with God. At the root of every action is the thought of doing God's will. "Wherever you go," said Robert Murray M'Cheyne, "carry a *savour* of Christ. His name is like ointment poured forth; it is like the vine flourishing, and the pomegranate budding. Let the smell of your garments be as a field which the Lord hath blessed. And carry a *sound* of Christ wherever you go. Not a step without the sound of the Gospel bell." Here is a picture of Müller's inner life and outward, as he seeks to follow his Lord. The fragrance of the pomegranate, lovely both in flower and fruit, and the sweet sound of the golden bell—"a golden bell and a pomegranate, a golden bell and a pomegranate, upon the hem of the robe round about." And every trial of faith is like the winds of heaven blowing upon the soul: "Awake, O north wind; and come, thou south; blow upon my garden, that the spices thereof may flow out. Let my Beloved come into His garden, and eat His pleasant fruits."

THE LIFE OF GEORGE MÜLLER

Inspiring as the story of answered prayer always is, yet, if we would understand it fully, as it is told in the life experiences of Müller, we miss the beauty of it if we miss the thought of Müller alone with God in the sanctuary of intercession. There it is, while he searches his heart and talks in sacred joy with his Heavenly Friend, that we understand the inner meaning. It is heart-thrilling to see what answers to prayer God gives him—his whole life speaks to us of faith; but the lesson is but half learned, the story is but a "cake not turned," if we do not see that all is founded upon his seasons of prayer. Some of these are long indeed. He wrestles with God, abases himself, points to the precious blood. Here we are upon sacred ground. To look upon those holy scenes between Müller and his God, to reproduce them in the mind aright, we need to partake of that same spirit. It is impossible to draw aside the solemn curtain with a rough, irreverent hand, and yet think to comprehend the holy happenings within. The language of the "breezy writer" cannot apply to George Müller on his knees, with the open Bible before him, praying on in the night silence, bearing up before the Lord the needs of this poor world and the sorrows of Britain's orphans; remembering, too, the unevangelised masses of heathendom, whether abroad or at home; and the labours of men and women of God everywhere, who are making known the Good News of Redemption. In such moments, when the oracles of

God flash with light, and his soul is stirred to prayers and tears, we are near indeed to the fountain of his inspiration. That he challenged unbelief, that he was the apostle of Faith Triumphant, that he brought a new spirit of confident hope to his time, we know; but in knowing this let us not noisily march by, forgetting the very kernel of all—his hours with God. It may be said: "but his whole life was a prayer; he lived in the atmosphere of prayer, he illustrated the apostolic word which bids us 'pray without ceasing.'" This did he; but, nevertheless, these "set" seasons, these consecrated hours, these holy interviews, are, if his life be rightly studied, the foundation of his practical experiences and the strength of his Christian service.

Of these seasons, Müller does not tell us all. Indeed, how could he? He can but describe, in his own characteristic way, for our profit, some special inspiration, some beautiful thought of what Christ is to him. For example (November 4, 1862): "There came in the course of my reading, through the Holy Scriptures, Isaiah 26 : 4 : 'Trust ye in the Lord for ever: for in the Lord Jehovah is everlasting strength.' I laid aside my Bible, fell on my knees and prayed thus : 'I believe that there is everlasting strength in the Lord Jehovah, and I do trust in Him; help me, O Lord, for ever to trust in Thee. Be pleased to give me more means this day, and much this week, though only so little now has come in.'" Praying thus, he is answered. In the course of the week £457 is received. Let not the swift transition from the holy place of prayer to coin of the realm be deemed abrupt, and destructive of the spirit of pleading with God: Müller did not take it so, but as a renewed demonstration that: "Jehovah again proved that in Him *is* everlasting strength, and that He *is* worthy to be trusted." Wherefore this man of prayer appeals to the believer: "Seek but in the same way to trust in the Lord, if you are not in the habit of doing so already, and you will find, as I have found thousands of times, how blessed it is."

Somewhat earlier in 1862, Müller is having one of his "long seasons of prayer for all the various objects of the Institution, and a variety of subjects in connection with them, as also for individuals for whom I daily pray." The Building Fund is inevitably mentioned, and God is petitioned to send help for it. About half an hour afterwards he receives a letter, containing a cheque for £2000, which the donor asks Müller to accept, "with my best love and the expression of my heartfelt thankfulness to God for the privilege of being a fellow-helper in the work of caring for orphans." A simple letter is this, but it casts an infinite deal of light upon the spirit which Müller inspires in others, in the ministry of faith; those who give to the Orphan Houses are those who are constrained of God, and who therefore deem it a high privilege to give to Him of that which they have received from Him. Three days afterwards, out of £2000 placed at his disposal, Müller places £800 to the Building Fund; a fortnight after, out of £2500 thus placed, the Building Fund gets £1000. Within a year, from May 26, 1861, he has received in all (let us be as precise as this precise and business-like George Müller) £6598. 11s. 5½d.

Now comes a slackening in the rate of income, hence in July, 1863, he remarks : " At this rate, it would be a very long time before I should be able to take active measures towards the contemplated enlarge-ment. But I am not discouraged." A similar thought is expressed six months later, when the computation is made that, at the prevailing rate of receipt, about seventeen years must elapse before the whole £50,000 required for the Building Fund will be in hand ! No mournful note, however, is this; for " God can give in a short time not only larger sums, but even by one donation the whole amount required." The full answer will come, in God's time. In the following month, February 1864, there comes for the Building Fund, £2815. Onward goes the man of faith, renew-ing his requests, pleading the promises, eagerly looking for answers. By May 26, he has in hand £19,321. 7s. 1½d. towards the £50,000.

Clearly, it is not necessary to wait for the whole sum and then erect *two* houses. When £25,000 is in hand, *one* may be proceeded with; which means that a commencement will be made when a further £5700 or thereabouts is received. The saints still look to Ashley Down from all parts of the world, and their letters are ofttimes precious. Here is one from a Christian, who has just lost his sister; he desires to dispose of the money she has left, in a way that, if still living, she would approve. He sends £1000 to the Building Fund. A few weeks after, "a donor, who desires neither his name nor residence to be known," sends £5000. Much more than the £25,000 now being in hand, it is time to build. Where is "natural reasoning" now? What sage comment can Unbelief make? Faith is justified. Müller's heart is overflowing with delight. He is not surprised at the magnitude of the last donation, for "that bountiful heart, which spared not the Lord Jesus," will still give bountifully; to see any particular marvel in a large sum coming would, after all, be an expression of unbelief, as though we were astonished to find the Living God *really* the Living God. Nay, but Müller sees, in being set free to build, the answer to thousands of prayers, and another potent demonstration, before all the world, of the power of God.

Where shall the building be erected? Where is suitable land? There is a beautiful piece yonder of eighteen acres, separated only by a road from New Orphan House No. 3. How can New Orphan House No. 4 be erected anywhere else? Has not the prayer gone up hundreds of times from Müller's innermost soul: "Oh that for Jesus' sake Thou wouldst count me worthy to erect on this ground two more Orphan Houses!" Prayer has, so to speak, put a girdle of faith round these eighteen acres; they are bespoken for God's service. True, Müller might have bought them years before, but that would have been contrary to the principle not to begin until the whole money should be in hand.

Now, at length, the way appears clear: he visits the agents, to be met, however, with the news that the land is let, on a partially expired agreement which will not terminate for two years and a half. Müller had wanted it in six months—which is to say, as soon as lawyers could prepare the conveyance and builders their specifications. The intelligence might seem discomfiting to some, but not to him, for he fully expects to have an offer of suitable compensation duly accepted by the tenant. And if one asks George Müller the ground of this confidence that all will be well, he mildly replies : " the Living God."

This obstacle of the agreement is by no means the only one. It is as though the powers of men were determined to keep Müller out. The owner asks £7000 purchase money—more than it is actually worth; and the Bristol Waterworks Company, the story runs, are about to secure parliamentary powers to construct a reservoir on this very site. What more can be said ? Are all the prayers of God's servant to count for nought ? Is he to give way, in rout, and say with Napoleon, on seeing the Old Guard hurled back at Waterloo : " All is over"? Not so. Just where "human reason" would conclude Müller to be defeated and mournful, we come once again upon that unfailing sign of triumph, the inevitable: "Pause, esteemed reader"!

"Pause"! Müller has come to this point of decision regarding the land, by the leadings of the Spirit. There are hundreds of orphans waiting admission. The donation of £5000 has made the commencing possible. Will God allow a seemingly devastating blow to crush the whole scheme as a Nasmyth hammer would crush an acorn? The "carnal" Christian might hypochondriacally mourn: "Hopeless, dear sir, hopeless; hie thee home to tea, and rest content." But listen to Müller: "Thus have I found it hundreds of times since I have known the Lord. The difficulties which He is pleased to allow to arise are only allowed, under such circumstances, for the exercise of our faith and patience; and more prayer, more patience, and the exercise of faith, will remove the difficulties. Now, as I knew the Lord, these difficulties were no insurmountable difficulties to me, for I put my trust in Him, according to that word: 'The Lord also will be a refuge for the oppressed, a refuge in times of trouble. And they that know Thy Name will put their trust in Thee; for Thou, Lord, hast not forsaken them that seek Thee.'"

Faith again lays hold of the promise. Müller goes out to make a few calls, the first being at the Water Company's office. "No, Mr. Müller," say the kindly committee, "only a small portion of the land will be wanted; not enough to interfere with your plans; and we will not take even that if we can avoid doing so." Excellent! *Exit* Difficulty No. 1.

Next comes an interview with the tenant of the land—and of the house which stands on part of it. A man of somewhat slow mind, perhaps, is the tenant; but by no means awkward or perverse, for, after taking time to consider the matter, he declares that, the land being required for such a purpose, he will by no means stand in the way. Nevertheless, considerable money having been laid out upon the house and land, reasonable compensation, he thinks, should in fairness be given him. This is exactly what Müller desires, so that the only remaining difficulty is the owner himself. *Exit* Difficulty No. 2. Faith and works go together; yet there are long seasons of prayer, day by day; likewise, friendly discussions with the owner. Ultimately, the price drops from £7000 to £5500; Müller agrees, and the land is forthwith conveyed to the trustees. Thus do the difficulties vanish; thus does the Lord undertake for His own! "Pause, esteemed reader" —and rejoice in Faith Triumphant.

Not yet, however, is the battle completely won. The present intention is, we remember, to build New Orphan House No. 4. But an examination of the plans demonstrates that serious disadvantages and considerable increase of cost would result from building one House only. Wherefore, after all, it will be best to wait. Of the total £50,000 required, there is £30,000 in hand, so that, allowing £10,000 to be the cost of fittings and furnishings, a further £10,000 will be enough to pay for the actual buildings. "Only about £10,000," says George Müller, in the superb simplicity of faith.

"Only"! ejaculates "human reason"; but Müller knows full well that the Lord has His own precious saints upon the earth who hold to the principles of apostolic giving and apostolic self-denial, and are touched with apostolic zeal and fervour. These are the people whom God can use. Note one of them, a missionary, of whom Müller says: "Here is a missionary, labouring for years under many difficulties, trials, privations, and hardships, in order to preach the unsearchable riches of Christ to poor benighted idolaters, himself having been repeatedly reduced to his last piece of money. Now, all at once he is put in possession (through receiving a legacy) of many hundreds of pounds, and, instead of spending it on himself, or keeping it laid up in the bank or otherwise on interest, the love of Christ constrains him to spend it, and gladly too, for the Lord"! The sum sent by this zealous brother is £500; of which £250 is placed to the Building Fund and £250 to Missions to the heathen.

Money comes in steadily; yet, when the contractors' tenders are examined, so largely have materials advanced in price and wages increased since the first calculation was made, five years before, that the difference amounts to £8000. What is to be done? There is a temptation to argue: "The work is so manifestly of the Lord, that no fear need be entertained in building; let us build at once, for God will surely send the needed help." To which subtle thought Müller replies: "When God's time has come, God will give, to the last shilling needed, but to begin building before He does send it would be equal to saying: 'God has not money enough to pay for His own work'; and I should be acting not in faith but presumptuously."

Now, the contractors have sent in separate tenders for New Orphan Houses Nos. 4 and 5. There is ample money to pay for No. 4: an agreement is made that No. 4 shall be commenced. Also, that the contract for No. 5 may likewise be accepted by the succeeding first of January, 1867. It is now May 3, 1866. To warrant the signing of the contract on the day fixed will mean that £7000 must be received within the seven months. The sum is duly received; on December 31, 1866, the contract is signed; the building is commenced; a little over a year later, the total amount required for fitting and furnishing the two Houses is in hand. For six years and eight months has Müller been praying for this.

Now are seen the final victories, in these building operations of George Müller, in the exercise of Faith Triumphant. New Orphan House No. 4 is opened on November 5, 1868; New Orphan House No. 5 on January 6, 1870. When every expense is met for building, Müller foreshadows in faith that there will be a balance over, deducing this from the evidence of his own experience regarding the Orphan Houses already built, and—from the character of God: "This is just like the ways of God. When He orders something to be done for the glory of His Name, He is both able and willing to find the needed individuals for the work and the means required. Thus, when the Tabernacle in the Wilderness was to be erected, He not only fitted men for the work, but He also touched the hearts of the Israelites to bring the necessary materials and gold, silver, and precious stones; and all these things were not only brought, but in such abundance that a proclamation had to be made in the camp, that no more articles should be brought, because there was more than enough."

Here, once again, is God's measure: "good measure, pressed down, and running over." "Who is a God like unto Thee?" The Houses are up; are filled with orphans. Here is simply the fulfilment of the three plain conditions laid down by Müller himself —which conditions, or maxims, let all servants of God ponder: (1) Be sure that the work in which you desire to engage is *God's* work. (2) Be sure you are the person to be engaged in this work. (3) Be sure that God's time has come when the work should be done. Such are Müller's maxims: the spiritual mind shall understand, and agree.

Here endeth the building of George Müller. Yet, there remains for him a long span of labour in the Lord. He is sixty-four years of age. The principles upon which his life-work has been founded grow increasingly dear to him. The expenditure is vast, but all needs are met. Seldom is any glimpse of statistics seen, for the counting of heads is not Müller's way. It is required in stewards, not that their operations should necessarily be upon an enormous scale, but that they should be found faithful. Let a man do the will of God, and his ways shall be pleasing in His sight, whether he has been given ten talents to administer or but one. Only by an occasional word of Müller's do we gain an idea of the responsibilites resting upon him. Thus, in July, 1874, he computes that the Scriptural Knowledge Institution requires an income of £44,000 a year; that there are 2100 orphans to be supported, and a hundred schools, with a total of about 9000 scholars; there are likewise 189 missionaries to be assisted; and four millions of tracts and tens of thousands of copies of the Holy Scriptures are sent out in the course of a year.

Seeking only to do God's will, Müller is not careful to consider whether this or that action will be considered as an advance or a retreat; he is ready to learn any lesson that Divine wisdom desires to teach.

Thus, as the years go by, the Day-schools come to absorb a disproportionately large amount of the general income, which is to say, that many donors leave Müller to decide to what department of the Scriptural Knowledge Institution and in what proportions the gifts shall be allocated; and the Day-schools require more and more. The situation is somewhat delicate: in the day of State provision of education, no surprise can be felt if donations specifically for Day-schools fall off, and that Müller has therefore to use for this object more and more of the general funds entrusted to him. But he does not feel free to proceed on these lines. The Scriptural Knowledge Institution, by the grace of God, shall never go into debt. In 1882, there are seventy-two Day-schools supported; and, after the position has been examined, it is decided to close twenty-three of them. Thus a good conscience is preserved; if the money does not come in, for a specified department, that department must be reduced: but such a step is no failure of Divine provision or of faith: the Day-schools have been of untold value; Christian philanthropy has been working far in advance of the State.

In the public eye, of necessity, it is with the Orphan Houses that the name of George Müller is chiefly associated; and the maintenance of the institutions is as great a marvel as their origin. The more the crowd wonders, the greater pleasure have the children of light in contributing, for they realise that their gifts make a testimony to God and His faithfulness. Their offerings are made in faith, and are an incentive to faith in others. In many instances the stories of the gifts have themselves a singular interest; indeed, the records constitute in themselves a literature of faith that has a true apostolic touch, so rich is the joy which the donors have in giving.

The word "donor" is apt to suggest the offering of gifts of a princely magnitude, but the majority of the children of faith are humble folk. Thus, a man in lowly circumstances, growing old, finds it necessary to leave the service in which he has been engaged, and he settles down to live upon the little savings he has put by. It will be a keen struggle, but, come what may, he is resolved to send a sovereign to George Müller, as in the past years. At the expiration of twelve months, this humble Christian surprisedly receives, from his former employer, a handsome gift, whereupon he doubles his annual gift to the work, saying: "What shall I render unto Him for all His benefits?"

While, however, a peculiar fragrance attaches to the offerings of those who, like the widow casting her "two mites" into the treasury, give out of their poverty, yet the contributions of brethren of large means likewise breathe a beautiful spirit of hope for the prosperity of the New Orphan Houses. But the givers, whether poor or wealthy, unite in recognising that the faith of George Müller has resulted in a revival of interest in the suffering and neglected, in Missions to the heathen, in the knowledge of the Book of books, and especially in systematic Christian giving.

The very stones of Ashley Down Orphan Houses are as so many testimonies to the faithfulness of God; the clatter of the milk-cart down the road, the home-coming of sacks of potatoes and cart-loads of cabbages, the cheerful song of praise from a thousand blithe young hearts in the evening hour—all these things are a testimony to the world. Who, then, would not help support the Orphan Houses? So, the funds continue, as from the first, to be sufficient, and George Müller, alert and business-like as ever, although inevitably entering upon the sundown days of life, toils abundantly, finds himself loved and revered the wide world over, walks humbly with God, and is a father to the fatherless.

It may be natural to exclaim: "Müller's records are very similar one to another: a lack of supplies; a season of prayer: an answer from God; a shout of thanksgiving: then it begins again." This is undoubtedly so: there is such similarity, but Müller does not find it tedious; on the contrary, the repetition of such experiences of his own need and of God's faithfulness is the very warp and woof of his testimony. The natural man might well find long years of such experiences a little wearisome; so did not George Müller. It was not that he prayed now and then and had wonderful answers; he lived in the atmosphere of prayer. "As the apple-tree among the trees of the wood, so is My Beloved among the sons : I sat down under His shadow with great delight, and His fruit was sweet to my taste." The "apples of Canaan" were his food; he was sustained by the Bread of Life, and drank of the stream of Divine peace : how should such a man find monotony in the bounties of the Lord ?

Trials of faith there are, as hitherto, but, as Müller truly says : "This Institution has been from the beginning like the burning bush, and yet it is not consumed." On the other hand, wonderful encouragements come. A lady whom Müller has never seen, her name, indeed, being entirely unknown to him, bequeathes a legacy of £4100 ; and, including this sum, there is received within a little more than three months, over £18,400. These amounts are certainly large, but Müller's affairs are all on a scale worthy of their Divine Inspirer. "Not unto us, O Lord, not unto us !" The work is God's, and George Müller merely as dust before Him. Were it otherwise, the outlook, despite large donations and legacies, would sometimes be gloomy indeed : the income varies ; the outgo, up to a point, is fixed, so far as the orphans are concerned. Times of financial depression may have their reaction upon the income of philanthropy, but the heart which trusts in God is kept in perfect peace. The Unbreakable Bank is still the source of supply. Thus, the balance in hand, May 26, 1885, is sufficient to last only six days, at an average rate of expenditure. There is a balance of a certain legacy locked up in Chancery: for six years Müller has prayed that it might be released from the octopus grip of the courts; but he has always believed that it would be received in God's time—the best time of all. Just at the time of special need it comes —a matter, to be precise, of £11,034. 6s. Truly, God is George Müller's " Infinitely Rich Treasurer."

The printed " Narratives," issued year by year, indubitably serve to create a new atmosphere of faith throughout the world. The plainly-put, matter-of-fact and yet thrilling record is read with delight by the children of God, who joyfully take up the favourite phrase, of "laying up treasure in heaven." A certain business man declares, in sending a gift: " This makes the thirty-fourth year since I first read your ' Narrative,' which decided me to give up a certain portion of my income every year. I think I must have given away about £3000 to various objects. My example has been followed by several friends." Remembering this simple testimony, and noting the world-wide circulation of the " Narrative," we begin to gain some idea of the enormous influence for good wielded by George Müller.

Advocates of philanthropic causes are sometimes heard to remark mournfully: " Mr. Chairman, ' Reports' are of no use; people only throw them into the waste-paper basket." This is scarcely the language of faith; it might be well for philanthropy for such speakers to consider the case of George Müller's "Reports." These plain productions typify simplicity. Yet the saints delight in them. Never can it be alleged that the reader is carried away by brilliant flights of rhetoric, superb gifts of description, or tear-compelling pathos. The pitiful stories pigeon-holed at Ashley Down are enough to melt the hardest heart, but the only stories Müller tells regarding the orphans bear upon their spiritual welfare. He is not seeking to win the ungodly wealthy under pleas of seeking the material prosperity of the orphans, nor is he holding a revolver to the head of frivolous Society, saying: "Hand me money, or I will leave these children to grow up to head a red revolution which shall smite you to the earth!" There is nothing of either the sombreness of Rembrandt or the gorgeousness of Rubens about these pen-pictures from Ashley Down. On the contrary, the style — never forgetting, however, the atmosphere of faith—is more that of the "household interiors" of the Dutch School, with the suggestion of spotless cleanliness and domestic simplicity, always bathed in light.

There are items innumerable: donations and legacies; gifts of food and clothing; thank-offerings for special deliverances; jewellery and antiques sent to be sold; percentages on sales of goods—"a penny for every dozen eggs, and threepence for every couple of fowls"; business profits—"ten per cent. on profits, from one who has had to contend with a grasping, money-loving disposition"; half a sovereign "sent by the widow of an officer, whose husband fell in the Crimean War: this half-sovereign was found in his purse, and had hitherto been treasured up by the lady, who now thought it would be better spent for the orphans"; "one barrel of currants and five boxes of raisins for the Christmas puddings for the orphans." And amid such entries are Müller's own reflections on the dealings of the Most High with his own soul, and his flashes of holy joy at "the kindness of God."

One donor quite frankly admits that in former days he found the "Narrative" to be "very dry stuff"; the sweet gifts that came from God had no interest to him. "Dry stuff! Iteration of trivialities! Columns of chronicles!" This is just the carnal mind. What, we wonder, did it say to Paul when, by the space of three years, he ceased not to warn every one, night and day, with tears? It considers the lovely treasures of Scriptures as dull; it gives no heed to the message of Redemption itself; nor is there reason to marvel, since the carnal mind is not subject to the law of God, neither indeed can be. This "dry stuff" donor had himself, as an orphan, enjoyed the benefits of the Institution; however, a transformation being wrought in his soul, the items which had appeared so "sawdusty" became full of vital interest, by reason of their testimony to the faithfulness of God. The gift of barrels of currants; "£10 for sale of ferns"; "the proceeds of the sale of a little jewellery"; and "the proceeds of a thousand cocoanuts, £5, in remembrance of a visit to the Orphan Houses"—such matter-of-fact items are lit with the glory of another world to the eye of faith.

As in the matter of the Day-schools, so in regard to Bible distribution, there comes a lessening of gifts, but this cannot in the least touch Müller's confidence, since he knows full well that, with the multiplication and progress of Societies devoted definitely to the printing and circulation of the Bible, his own special department in that kind of work may show less income. Taking an all-round view, he sees that the dissemination of the written Word grows enormously throughout the world; and he is determined, on his own part, to keep clear of debt.

As for the New Orphan Houses, they lack nothing. The years speed by; the seventies give place to the eighties and the eighties to the nineties; still, all is well. It is urged, indeed, by some: "This is no work of faith: you publish a 'Report,' a 'Narrative'—call it what you will." To which the obvious reply is that Müller is in honour bound to publish an account of his stewardship, and that, moreover, to do so is to bear that witness against unbelief and "human reasoning" which it is the fundamental idea of Müller to give. The "Report," the "Narrative," is a plain hauling up of Unbelief to the bar of Faith. It is a challenge to proof, ungainsayable and unanswerable, of God's faithfulness. But its publication does not mean that any but the people of God are going to give. Moreover, what a howl of complaint would go up, from non-contributing-Unbelief, were no "Report" forthcoming!

Of necessity, in its essential character, the "Report" divides its readers: the children of God will love it and the unregenerate will find it "dry stuff." And as the "Reports" that go out, shall there not be remembered the prayers innumerable of George Müller that accompany them? Mark the way in which he speaks not only of prayer, as such, but *prayers*. It is not easy to recall many of the sons of men who speak quite naturally of "thousands of prayers"; but we see Müller primarily as a man of prayer—of Faith Triumphant in prayers: prayers poured out in solitude before God, prayers by day and by night, prayers as he goes in and out the New Orphan Houses, prayers as he gathers with the children. Truly these prayers of his are many; yet he still has those "special times," those long seasons in which, hour after hour, he pours out his soul, weeps and intercedes and pleads the sacred cause of the orphans, and the need for the witness of faith.

Wherefore, as a man of prayer he is a man of trust. If men desire him to alter his plans and "conform a little" to the world in his methods, his answer is clear and firm: "*God* has not altered. To *His* honour and glory I founded the Institution. *Him* I declared to be the Patron, and He has never failed me. On Him, and Him alone, have I relied." Age brings him no sourness, but a deepened and mellowed trust. In a time of special shortage, the thought comes to him that it may be God's will for him to sell some of the land which was purchased years before. This is done; more than £10,000 is realised, and the burden is removed; all things work together for good, in the kind providence of his Father in heaven.

All the time, the training of the orphans goes on with zeal and thoroughness. One of the dangers of philanthropy is that of becoming absorbed in the multiplication of agencies and in the raising of funds, rather than seeking the upbuilding of Christian character. If spiritual ideals become obscured, even an admirable administration may degenerate into a cold officialism, " simple Bible teaching " become fossilised into a sort of ritualism, and the objects of help be regarded as living pleas for financial assistance rather than potential witnesses to the power of saving grace.

Alive to the position, Müller spends many an evening with the helpers and the children; wrestles in prayer for them, urges them to seek daily manna from the Lord. Orphans and helpers alike revere Müller as their father and friend. There are in all parts of the world men and women who have been sheltered and trained at Ashley Down, and who owe practically all they have and are to him. The light kindled by God sheds its beams far and near, and many an institution is founded upon the principles set forth by George Müller. An impulse of faith goes forth towards all the world. In the Assemblies of the Brethren his life, his example, and his teaching exercise a deep and formative influence, reacting upon the spiritual life of Christians throughout the land, and inspiring many a young believer to tread the happy and blessed path of surrender and obedience to Christ,[1] and to cry : " How great is Thy goodness, which Thou hast laid up for them that fear Thee; which Thou hast wrought for them that trust in Thee before the sons of men ! "

Müller's Record, then, is not to be treated merely as an entertaining story. It is too solemn, too earnest. We " cannot skip the prayers," in a hurry to "get to the answers," or ignore faith's trial while relishing faith's victory. " Trial," indeed, is not a fascinating word; but it is interwoven with " triumph." For practically ten years, 1838 to 1849, Müller declares

---

[1] Among such was James Hudson Taylor, afterwards founder of the China Inland Mission, and attending (in 1851, aged nineteen) the Hull Meeting of the Brethren. Dr. and Mrs. Howard Taylor say : " Their quiet gatherings on Sunday morning were specially suited to help young Hudson Taylor. He was hungry for the Word of God, and their preaching was for the most part a thoughtful exposition of its truths. He needed a fresh vision of eternal things, and the presence of Christ was often so real on these occasions that it was like heaven on earth to be among them. They set before him an example of faith in temporal as well as spiritual things that passed his utmost thought. For this Meeting was in close touch with George Müller, of Bristol, whose work was even then assuming remarkable proportions. He had already hundreds of orphan children under his care, and was looking to the Lord for the means to support a thousand. He sustained in whole or part many missionaries, and was engaged in circulating the Scriptures far and wide. All this extensive work carried on by a penniless man through faith in God alone, with no appeals for help or guarantee of stated income, was a wonderful testimony to the power of ' effectual, fervent prayer.' As such it made a profound impression upon Hudson Taylor."—*Hudson Taylor in Early Years* (Morgan & Scott).

that he had to look to God not merely for daily supplies, but from meal to meal; and in the last thirteen years of his life also he had severe trials to face. But at the same time, despite the increase of his obligations, his soul still soared as on eagles' wings; his testimony was, in 1874: "I am comforted by the knowledge that God is aware of all this, and that, if this way be for the glory of His Name, and for the good of His Church and the unconverted world, I am, by His grace, willing to go this way, and do it to the end of my course. But God, our Infinitely Rich Treasurer, remains to us. It is this which gives me peace. God who has raised up this work through me, God who has led me to enlarge it, God who has supported this work for more than forty years, will still help, and will not suffer me to be confounded, because I rely upon Him. I commit the whole work to Him, and He will provide me with what I need, in the future also, though I know not whence the means are to come." Here is the explanation. George Müller is on such "terms" with the Lord his God, that he is strengthened, as well as taught, by the Spirit. He plucks the grapes of Eshcol, and is refreshed: wherefore "his fruit shall shake like Lebanon"—in the orchards of faith, that are watered by a thousand limpid streams of Divine blessing.

CHAPTER XI

The Müller Circle; and the Preaching Tours

THE social relationships of Müller with his wife and daughter and his Bristol intimates were fragrant with "odours from the King's garden." His chief helper in the orphan work was his wife: she was a lady of sterling worth, mental gifts, and intense devotion to Christ. The educational ideals of her day, regarding women, were poor and narrow, but her large fund of common sense and her godly aspirations early enabled her to rise superior to the level of the Society damsel. To be merely a conventional "superior person" with a few piano pieces in her music-case, a few water-colour drawings in her portfolio, and a fund of small talk for the entertainment of visitors was far from being the ambition of this zealous saint.

The sister of Anthony Norris Groves and wife of George Müller, one with them in their glorious hope of a return of the people of God to apostolic zeal and simplicity, was not likely, indeed, to sink her womanhood to the level of a drawing-room tattler. She was something of an astronomer, much of an arithmetician. The accounts of the Institution came under her shrewd examination, and an incorrect invoice would stand small chance of escaping detection under such eagle scrutiny. Yet it was as a housewife that she chiefly shone, and truly there was scope for such capacity in the mothering of a thousand children, many of whom, but for the Orphan Houses might have had no other shelter than that of a cart or a doorway; a warm corner near some coke oven in the north, or under a tarpaulin on a barge of Thames or Severn. An expert needlewoman, and a safe judge of cottons and woollens, she added to the precision of a business-woman the tenderness of a Christian soul seeking to do the will of God and to win the " Ye have done it unto Me " of the Day of Account. Moreover, there was that touch of pathos upon her sayings and doings which came from the experience of laying in the same grave at the same time her father and her little fifteen-months-old son. To supervise the household arrangements was a delight to her; in the direction of cooking and serving, in the management either of sick-rooms or play-grounds, dormitories or schools, she was invaluable. Her days, like those of her husband, were full of activity; full also—and primarily—of hope in God.

Following such a life, Müller and his wife, although possibly occupied upon the same building, would meet only at meal-times, but when they thus came together once more it was always with joy. Indeed, it was a frequent remark of Müller's : "My darling, I never saw you at any time since you became my wife without being delighted to see you." This tender regard, which sprang into being at their first meeting, easily bore the stress of life's trials, so that, when they had passed through four decades together, still he would ask : "My darling, do you think there is a happier couple in the world than we ? " The objection has sometimes been heard, that the position of Brethren regarding the ministry of women leads to the depreciation of women into a position of inferiority which is sometimes a little galling to them in the domestic circle. This objection, however, is emphatically negatived at Ashley Down, and in innumerable homes elsewhere.

At any rate from the Christian standpoint, the Müller circle was one of the chief of the time, albeit it had of necessity nothing in common with the coteries of fashionable and political and literary life. Müller was not simply an administrator of capacity, a preacher of insight, and a Bible teacher. Taking a large, human view, he must be confessed to be a man of extraordinary talents ; much more, he was an apostolic man, and stood for the primitive Christian *ecclesia* and the primitive Christian aims : for nothing less.

"One thing I do." We cannot imagine Müller at ease in Lady Jersey's drawing-room, or looking in at a Pall Mall club to discuss the prospects of Turkey with Palmerston or the Corn Laws with

THE MÜLLER CIRCLE

Lord George Bentinck. Nevertheless, he was one of the chief figures of our national life. Obedient to the heavenly vision, he set out solitarily upon an embassy to the waifs of Britain, and, by sheer force of the undisputed and indisputable triumphs of faith, drew to himself the lively interest of the people of God, and the respect if not the veneration of the civilised world. Such recognition was nothing to Müller : he never sought the approval of men; nevertheless, if we are to possess a true idea of what Müller was and did, it is important to note how the world regarded him. Further, there was nothing of the cold doctrinaire about him. He held the great doctrines of the Christian Faith ; much more, as a new creature, it was not so much Christian truth that he proclaimed as Christ Himself, in whom is truth, and who is Truth. Anthony Norris Groves once said of counsels given to a friend : "I tell him not to lay too much stress on the question of Baptism or the Lord's Return, or unpaid ministry ; they all have their place : but the important thing is Jesus Christ and Him crucified ; the grace, the fulness and freeness of the Gospel." Müller himself might well have said it.

Lydia Müller, gracious and sweet, was another member of the circle. Perhaps in all the stores of her father's correspondence there is no letter more precious to his heart than the one which he received from her when she was a girl of only thirteen years ; in the course of this tender little epistle we read : "Dearest

Father and Mother, I wished to tell you that I was now happy, but I have not liked to, and I thought I could tell you better in writing than by speaking . . . I know that the work of God in my heart was very gradual. I can now say : 'Thanks be unto God for His unspeakable Gift.' Please dear Father and Mother to pray for me, that I may be kept from dishonouring God, and that I may be more and more thankful to Him for the gift of His Son."

Lydia grows in grace and usefulness, ministers to the orphans, carries in her hands the threads of many administrative duties; but she does not marry until she is in her fortieth year, when she accepts James Wright, who has been Müller's chief assistant since April, 1859.

The presence of James Wright at the Orphan Houses means much in the work of consolidation and organisation. Many characteristics have commended him to Müller. Brought up among the Society of Friends, he was educated at a Friends' school, where he acquired habits of order, quietness, and attention to detail. His father was in business at Bristol, where James was attracted to Bethesda, and became a member. He afterwards removed to London, where his worth as a spiritual leader was witnessed to by the Brethren at Paragon Road, Hackney; his business capabilities were sufficiently demonstrated by an offer, from the firm employing him, of a partnership; his conscientiousness appeared from his declining the partnership, since it would involve borrowing money to support his position, and he would on no account go into debt. His duties at the Orphan Houses are defined by Müller in a letter which also gives glimpses of the ways of life in the Scriptural Knowledge Institution :—

"I desire your help for certain parts of my correspondence. The books and tracts which are issued gratuitously or by sale, are read first. I find increasingly that I have neither time nor strength for this, and yet I do not feel happy that that should be sanctioned by me which I do not know. I desire you, therefore, to read instead of me . . . This would greatly allow of an increase of good books and good tracts.

"I desire your help in advising and counselling the teachers, both in the Orphan Houses and Dayschools, and, as far as time allows, and as you gain their confidence, to lend them in every way you can a helping hand. Also, if you feel equal to it, and happy in doing it, now and then, examining the children; but at all events, to correct the written examinations, which I might from time to time give to the children, would be desirable.

"The three masters of the boys, in turn, take family prayers at the two Orphan Houses, at half-past eight in the morning, and half-past five in the afternoon; here also would you have to give your share. You have an opportunity to speak for about ten to

fifteen minutes, if you like, or you may read a portion
of the Holy Scriptures.

"In addition to these four specific parts of work,
you would be my assistant in general as to oversight,
counsel, correspondence, accounts, seeing persons for
me, etc."[1]

Henry Craik, simple-hearted, deeply learned, with
his "stand-up" hair, and—following some exhausting
bit of study—his fits of depression and his wrestlings
in prayer; his able expositions of Scripture, and scorn
of the glories of the world, is another leading member
of the circle. "Behold"—yet again—"how these
Christians love one another." Craik and Müller labour
together in a partnership of pastoral duty for nearly
thirty-six years, with never a cloud upon their friendship. Anthony Norris Groves, on returning from the
foreign field, bruised and broken in health, rejoins the
fragrant company. There is his sister Lydia, also—
the "dear Aunt Lydia" of Lydia Müller. And there
is close friendship between all of them and Robert C.
Chapman, student of the Word, servant of the Lord,
saintly counsellor, expositor and hymn-writer.

Here, then, is the Müller circle, quiet, sweet, and
sane, exercising, albeit without a spark of excitement,
a delightful influence whose sweetness is wafted to the
ends of the earth. Müller, always active, always
waiting upon God, passes the years in an atmosphere
of faith and hope and consecration. People write to

[1] *James Wright of Bristol.* By Dr. A. T. Pierson.

him from all parts of the world, as to a personal friend, seeking his counsel, encouraging him with gifts, assuring him of their prayers. He is an apostle of Faith Triumphant to all nations.

The years go by; the shadows deepen; the inevitable farewells have to be said. Müller's father dies, March 30, 1840. "During no period did I pray more earnestly for him, than in the last year of his life," says Müller, "but it did not please the Lord to let me *see* the answer." Anthony Norris Groves becomes obviously weaker; he lives in Müller's house, lies panting and suffering, but shows his affection by such ejaculations as "Precious George; dearest George," and praises God for being enabled, in physical extremity, to rest among beloved relatives. After keen suffering, he goes Home, May 20, 1853.

"I sought repeatedly," wrote Müller to Mrs. Groves, describing the end, "as he was able to bear it, with a few words of the Word of God, and a few lines of appropriate hymns, to encourage him in God, and my soul was up to the Lord all day long, that the Lord would deliver him. About half-an-hour before he 'fell asleep' I once more prayed aloud with him, that the Lord would be pleased to sustain him to the end. He was quite quiet and at the end said: 'Precious Jesus.' Being now greatly worn and having before me a heavy day's work and not thinking his end near even now, I left him with a brother who had come to stay with him, and his three sisters, to go to rest a little. Shortly after, I was called up. His happy spirit had taken its flight. He had said once more: 'Precious Jesus.'" Groves himself, writing to his wife, a little while before, said of Müller: "Dear, dear George is such a faithful and true brother, and will be such to you."

The loss of Groves is keenly felt by Müller; and it might well be so, for his was a rare spirit. "I could not help regarding him," said Dr. Alexander Duff, who knew and honoured him, "as one of the most loving and lovable of Christian men, while the singular fervency of his spirit made it quite contagious; diffusing all around the savour of an unearthly sanctity and self-consuming devotedness. Oh that a double portion of his spirit would descend upon all our drowsy churches throughout Christendom!"

Another heavy blow is the passing away, January 22, 1866, of Henry Craik. "I see what the Lord is doing with me," was his remark to Lord Congleton, "He is taking up the weakest one, who dreaded suffering, to give him triumph over all, in Christ Jesus." In such a spirit, while a Christian brother repeated aloud the lovely comfort of the Shepherd Psalm— "Yea, though I walk through the valley of the shadow of death, I will fear no evil, for Thou art with me "— this man of God quietly slipped into the presence of the King. Müller, who has "leaned" on Craik during the long years of their joint labours in the Lord, contributes the Introduction to a Biography of his long-time friend, which sheds light on their long partnership. " Our natural constitution of mind and temperament were very different, and yet we had to work together ; whilst about 2500 believers were received into fellowship in the Church meeting at Bethesda and Salem chapels, among whom we laboured. Mr. Craik was eminently a man of prayer, and a man given to the study of the Word of God. Such prayerfulness regarding the Holy Scriptures, such—truly— digging into the Word as for hid treasures, such meditations over the Word, as he was given to, I never knew surpassed. Among all the thousands of believers I know, there is none whose judgment on any part of truth I should have more esteemed than that of my departed friend.

" On Christmas Day, 1865, sitting a longer time than usual at his bedside, all at once I remembered what he had so often spoken to me about, and then told him, that the strength of the Lord was manifested in his constitutional shrinking from pain and suffering. He saw it. And verily the Lord greatly sustained His suffering servant, and did so to the end. Without complaining he passed through his sufferings, though praying and longing to be delivered out of them. And at last he was delivered. Peacefully leaning upon Jesus, he fell asleep."

Not easily can this long and beautiful friendship be severed, even for a time, until the shadows flee away. In the spirit of tender sorrow, and yet of soaring hope,

Müller adds : "His poor friend, who writes this, remains. As yet the Lord allows me to serve Him on earth. Pray, Christian reader, that whether this time be long or short, I may be enabled to spend it truly to the honour of God."

Müller's next severance is from his devoted wife. After a married life of thirty-nine years and four months, she "falls asleep" in the Lord, February 6, 1870, aged seventy-three. Ten years before, she had suffered for many months from a severe rheumatic attack, affecting the left shoulder and arm ; a return of the malady, coupled with an enfeebled action of the heart, brought down the earthly tabernacle. Even upon her dying bed her thought was for the work of God and the welfare of the orphans ; she continued, almost to her last hour, to give directions to the matrons. She had expressed an anticipation that God would allow her to live to see the opening of the final Orphan House, and that anticipation was fulfilled. Orphan House No. 5 was opened, as we have noted, January 6, 1870 ; and Mrs. Müller was privileged to see over a hundred children welcomed under its roof before, just a month later, she passed to her rest. "Her value to me and the blessing God made her to me," Müller testifies, "is beyond description" ; and he writes : "She was God's own gift, exquisitely suited to me even in natural temperament. Thousands of times I said to her : 'My darling, God Himself singled you out for me.'" Müller himself conducts the funeral service and preaches the funeral sermon—from Ps. 119 : 68 : " Thou art good and doest good."

The marriage of Lydia Müller and James Wright takes place the following year. Müller, left lonely, then decides, in the fear of God, that it is best for him to be married again. On November 30, 1871, he is united to Miss Susannah Grace Sangar, an elderly lady whom he has known for more than twenty-five years.

As we have seen, when first he came to England, it was to be a missionary to the Jews. Events led him into a different sphere of Christian service ; nevertheless, he is a missionary at heart, crying : " Woe is me if I preach not the Gospel." Through all the years he has carried this thought of a great crusade—largely inspired, without doubt, by the wonderful record of Whitefield's itinerations on two continents. " I saw it clearly," Müller declares, " that I should spend the evening of my life preaching in other towns and cities and other countries, as I had been for forty-three years preaching in Bristol." True, there has been, and still is, a splendid field among the orphans, but the fire burns, the Spirit of God impels him ; go he must. The New Orphan Houses are safe under the godly and judicious administration of James Wright. Mrs. Müller has been extremely ill, suffering from fever and delirium : on recovering, she is taken to the seaside, and, growing stronger, is ready to accompany her husband in his journeys. She is a capable correspondent and is able to give him that care which, at his age, is increasingly necessary for the conservation of his strength.

Thus, in his seventieth year, when most men think it time to withdraw from active life, this beloved servant of God is actually beginning a new career, and is led by the Spirit to undertake Gospel journeys to the ends of the earth. In March, 1875, he commences a series of tours—which ultimately extend, with intervals spent at Bristol, to May, 1892.

The aim of these preaching tours is sevenfold. (1) To preach Christ, simply and plainly, emphasising the doctrine of justification by faith. (2) To bring the children of God into that clear knowledge of their standing in God by which they shall realise that they *are* regenerated, pardoned, justified, accepted in the Beloved and shall enjoy real peace and joy in the Lord. (3) To bring Christians back to the Holy Scriptures, trying everything by the Word, and becoming, for love of its message, daily readers thereof. (4) To remove sectarianism and promote brotherly love among Christians. (5) To strengthen the faith of believers, that they may enjoy the blessedness of real confidence, and avoid the miseries of distrust. (6) To promote separation from the world, and heavenly-mindedness. (7) To give Dispensational teaching and lead the Church of God to look for the Return of the Lord.

Such is the programme which this hoary saint draws up: such, rather, are the glorious aims which kindle his soul : aged seventy ; having already crowded an enormous amount of service into his life ; bearing still upon his shoulders the financial and administrational responsibility of the New Orphan Houses—albeit the latter part is now practically delegated to James Wright—he will "ride abroad" in the name of the Lord.

The first of the journeys, March to July, 1875, covers a few of the chief cities of England and includes visits to Brighton, Sunderland, and Newcastle, and to Mildmay Conference; also a meeting of fifteen hundred Christian workers at the " Edinburgh Castle " in East London—a building which had been a public-house and " sing-song " of a low type, but was now a thriving centre of evangelistic effort, having been " captured " by Dr. Barnardo. Then, after a few weeks at Bristol, a second tour is commenced.

To appreciate rightly the value of these tours, it is necessary to understand the " atmosphere " of the time. That atmosphere was one of spiritual Revival. Days of drought had long prevailed. True, the Ulster Revival of 1859–60, following the marvellous movement of 1857–58 in the United States, had wrought wonders, and the labours of such men as Joseph Denham Smith —particularly in Dublin—and Reginald Radcliffe, Brownlow North, James Turner, Richard Weaver, and Henry Moorhouse, in various parts of the United Kingdom, had brought a warm breath of Divine blessing to many parts of the land. Yet there had been no great movement, in England and Scotland, comparable in extent to the Eighteenth-Century Revival under Wesley and Whitefield.

In June, 1873, two little-known Americans, Dwight L. Moody and Ira D. Sankey, landed at Liverpool, and commenced to hold meetings, beginning at York. Moody had been invited over by three Christian laymen who appreciated his extraordinary gift, but all three had died, and Moody, in a predicament, said to his "singing partner": "God seems to have closed the door. We will not open any ourselves. If He opens the door we will go in; otherwise we will return to America." Then, in one of his pockets, he discovered an unopened letter received before leaving New York. It was from the Young Men's Christian Association Secretary, at York, expressing a general hope that "if you ever come to England you will come and speak at the Association." "This door is only ajar," was Moody's comment, "but we will consider the letter as God's hand leading to York." To York they went, and despite the difficulties of the position, the directness, force, and unconventionality of the visitors had an immediate effect; Moody's graphic appeals and pathetic stories and Sankey's beautiful singing captured the attention of the crowd; invitations to great centres of population came pouring in; and the visit to Britain was prolonged for more than two years—till August, 1875.

The effects were astonishing; they proved solid and permanent. The attendances were enormous; in

THE PREACHING TOURS

London alone they aggregated over two-and-a-half-millions. The Metropolis had not been so stirred, as a whole, since the day when Whitefield preached in Moorfields, and Wesley at "the Foundery." The same could be said of the great cities of the North and the Midlands, while in Scotland the whole country seemed aroused. Thousands were converted to God and a splendid impetus given to the Christian cause. A new spirit of evangelism was awakened, of which the conspicuous feature was the multiplication of missionary efforts among the poor. The number of men and women who at this time set to work in a plain, unconventional way to win souls for Christ was very large. Now came George Müller to encourage and bless and instruct. Again, on the fringe of every great evangelistic movement are to be found many who, despite every appeal and every argument, reject the Spirit's pleadings, but, when the movement has seemingly passed, are ready to repent with tears if only another word be spoken to them. Now came George Müller to speak that word.

Going north, he preaches in a number of towns in Scotland. At Dundee, he occupies M'Cheyne's old pulpit at St. Peter's, and addresses about three thousand people in the Kinnaird Hall : in all he speaks seventeen times in fifteen days. The news of his presence in a town—and he goes quietly from place to place, seeking no advertisement, but accepting as many invitations as he is able—at once creates a stir. All Christian people delight to welcome him. At Glasgow, thousands hear him. The impression he makes is well expressed by a brother who writes to *The Christian*: "His speech is truly in power. His very presence is a sermon. It makes one magnify God for all the great things He has wrought through His child. At the same time we are humbled as we contrast the dwarf-like stature of our own faith with the giant growth which that of this beloved brother—and father—in Christ has attained."

All Scotland is open to him, but he cannot stay, having accepted an invitation to Dublin—where he speaks, by request, to a gathering of four hundred ministers, at the annual Christian Convention, and then to a great audience in a public meeting.

Numerous meetings in England follow. In the huge building at Liverpool which had been erected for Moody and Sankey, he addresses six or seven thousand people. In this vast audience sits a bronzed, weather-beaten man, now the captain of a merchant vessel, who in other days was an inmate of the Orphan House. How can such a man, still unconverted, sit in peace while his old benefactor, grey and obviously ageing, delivers once again, as in the long ago, the blessed message of eternal life? The scarred captain listens, weeps, apprehends spiritually the motive of Müller's life, and steers straight for the haven of soul-rest.

Müller goes on to York, Carlisle, Annan—the scene of the wonderful awakening under Edward Payson

Hammond—and to Edinburgh, where he holds fifty-three meetings during his six weeks' stay. In the Scottish capital, as elsewhere, he speaks to ministers, giving them his views and unfolding the experiences of his long life. Simple as his words are, they are searching in their thoroughness. A minister, he urges, "should be truly converted, lead a happy, spiritual life, be familiar with the Bible for himself, be very humble, be instant in prayer, give an impression of reality and thorough earnestness in his preaching; also, he should seek God's guidance in the selection of his subjects of discourse, should deal much in exposition, should speak the truth of God in the most simple language, should live daily in the fear of God, and should hold frequent inquirers' meetings."

Other places are visited for preaching services, notably Crathie Free Church, near Balmoral; and Inverness—where the leading ministers and commercial men express their delight with the meetings, whereupon Müller replies: "I have undertaken this task in a great measure to supplement or follow up the great work which my friend Mr. Moody has already done in Scotland. Regarding Christian work generally, I believe that during the last eighteen years there have been more converts than during any other period of the history of the Christian Church, the apostolic age included. While more evangelists may be prayed for, pastors and teachers of young converts are especially required; in this duty let us engage—but let us remember, as regards those who are required in such work, that quality is better than quantity."

Returning to Bristol, July 5, he is soon quietly at work again among the orphans, and prepares his thirty-seventh annual Report. Clearly, the preaching tour has done him no harm, for he declares that, notwithstanding the exacting character of his engagements he has been in good health and is as well able to labour, physically and mentally, as he was fifty years before.

Nor has his absence made any difference to the principles upon which the Orphan Houses are conducted ; for he declares : "With every year almost, the institution has been further and further enlarged, so that the work is now great and the expenses are considerable every year ; but our Heavenly Father, simply in answer to prayer, without personal application on our part to any one, has always supplied us with the means, and though often brought low in funds, we have always closed the year with a balance in hand. We never went in debt —and this was another of the principles on which the Institution was established, for we judged that, if we did the Lord's work, in the Lord's way, and that His time was come for doing this work, and we honoured Him by looking to Him alone for the means, He would surely help us." The Scriptural Knowledge Institution is supporting, apart from missionary efforts abroad, 75 Day-schools and 29 Sunday-schools, having nearly 10,000 regular scholars. The income was £45,000, upon which Müller comments : "If this is added to the total income for all purposes during the previous years, it will be seen that we have received altogether, simply in answer to prayer and the exercise of faith, without applying to any one for anything, above £710,000 sterling."

Müller is no mere curious sight-seer : his business lies all in the Kingdom of God. The amount of work he gets through in these preaching tours, the number of meetings he holds, the spiritual energy with which he breaks through conventions and holds just such gatherings as he judges will conduce to the welfare and extension of his Lord's Kingdom—these things are truly astonishing. Busy, however, as he has been, numerous as his activities have proved, these two tours are in a sense comparatively small matters compared with what is to come ; yet they are of high value to the Christian community at large, for George Müller, walking with God all these years, speaks in the ripe wisdom of one who, from the lofty peaks of faith, seems to catch the foregleams that herald the Coming of the Son of Man, and views all things in the light of that stupendous fact.

CHAPTER XII

The Preaching Tours—*Concluded*

THE third tour lasts ten months, August 1876–June 1877, and is devoted to the continent of Europe, chiefly in Switzerland and Germany. For the first time in thirty-one years he speaks, at Berne, in German. Mrs. Müller writes to *The Christian*, October 4, 1876: "During the whole of our stay, Mr. Müller held meetings twice on the Lord's Day, and every evening during the week, which were crowded to the utmost. On one of the week evenings, he addressed about eight hundred Christian workers. Christians were greatly strengthened and encouraged, while sinners were awakened and converted. We commend ourselves to the prayers of all readers, and earnestly request them to remember us day by day before the Lord. This is the special object of my writing, as I know many thousands of Christians take the deepest interest in the labours of my dear husband. His particular aim is to lead Christians increasingly to the Holy Scriptures, in order that they may seek to conform their ways to them; and also to promote brotherly love and union among Christians, as well as in the greatest simplicity to set forth the truths of the Gospel to the unconverted. In all these particulars his labours have been greatly blessed. Though he is now in his seventy-second year, he is remarkably well, is able to work as much as at any former time in his life, and generally preaches eight or ten times every week."

After remarkable meetings at Zurich, some time is spent in Germany. Scores of towns are visited, with a constant record of crowded churches or halls— not that Müller makes the least stir about himself, but that his name and career, associated with Faith Triumphant, are familiar to the people : doubtless, too, there is a desire, touched with patriotic enthusiasm, to encourage a son of the Fatherland whose character, as a servant of Christ, is held in universal esteem. Rich and poor are alike interested. At Stuttgart, the Queen of Würtemberg sends for him and asks for particulars of the Orphan Houses : at Darmstadt he is invited, with much respect, to tell the story of his life and work, in the house of the Court preacher; a princess and other great ladies form part of the company.

With what emotion he enters Halle ·may be imagined. He finds himself back in the familiar scenes of his student days. Yonder are haunts where sin once held him in grip. But let the dead past be left in its silence. Down this street he used to wander arm-in-arm with " Beta," pondering the great questions of God and eternity, trembling at heart and faintly trusting. There is the house of Wagner, the believing tradesman, whose kindly words of old seem to ring again in the ear: "Come as often as you please; house and heart are open to you." How the memories crowd in; of the lodgings where he decided to burn the translation of the French novel; of his repentant tears when he realised: "I had given up the work of the Lord, I may say the Lord Himself, for the sake of a girl."

Half a century has slipped away since then; yet, spanning over from 1826 to 1876 is not so difficult a matter after all, for his preaching place, now, is the great hall of Francke's Orphanage—where, also, he gives an address on Prayer, making particular reference to Francke's life and labours, and their inspirational effect upon his own life. At Halle, too, he calls upon Tholuck—perhaps the one solitary being who can recall the George Müller of long ago—Tholuck, the godly professor who, at a critical period in Müller's life, went to Halle, shining for God amid the darkness of unbelief, and was used of God to help and bless many a student; particularly to confirm Müller in trusting God as the Kind Provider for every want of His children.

To trace Müller's footsteps through the remainder of the tour is to chronicle a list of important cities in Germany and Holland where people thronged to hear him. Crossing the Channel again, he reaches Mildmay in time to speak once more at the Conference. There

he declares, in the course of a brief personal reference :
" I have joyfully dedicated myself to go from country
to country, to preach the Word." This is in the spirit
of the simple, practical address he has just given on
the words : " Be ye transformed by the renewing of
your minds," wherein he has said :—

" As sure as anyone walks in the way of consecration, he will be less and less conformed to the world
and more and more transformed, more and more like
Jesus. Though it be but little, in comparison with
what it might be and what it ought to be, still, there
will be more and more conformity to the image of our
precious, adorable Lord. And He is worthy—that
blessed One who laid down His life for us—that we
should seek to live for Him. Let us aim at this. We
are here in order to be 'strengthened with might by
the Spirit, in the inner man'; not to be amused, not
to have certain things brought before our minds and
after all to remain in the state in which we were
before ; but that we may obtain spiritual strength.
The Lord delights to give us blessing ; it is the very
joy of His heart. A little of all these things I have
known, in my own soul, for the past forty-eight years
particularly, and therefore I can recommend them. It
is a blessed thing, even for this life, to walk in the
ways of the Lord. What He looks for is that our
whole heart—not a part of it—should be given to Him.
' My son, give Me thine heart.' Not 'a little of thy
money '; but 'give ME *thine heart.*' When the heart

is given, the purse, the profession, the business are given also. All we have and all we are belong to the Lord."

Returning to Bristol, his mind is already fixed on responding to a joint letter sent by Christian brethren in the United States, urging him to visit their country. Accordingly, he sails from Liverpool, August 23, 1877, for Quebec, and thence proceeds to New York.

The "Narrative" has circulated in the States as well as in Britain; moreover, Müller's reputation has extended to a remarkable extent among the people who perhaps have never even heard of his writings. To the saints, his visit with its sweet expression of the joy of faith and of confidence in "the kindness of God," comes like an invigorating sea-breeze in a hot summer. He preaches in the North, both in English and German; going south to Baltimore and other cities, is engaged night after night with immense audiences; suffers not from any sense of self-importance, but is as ready to give a tract and speak a word to some humble person in train or boat as to speak to a crowd.

During this American tour he visits Newburyport, where Whitefield died, and preaches from the pulpit just over the spot where the dust of the man of God lay.[1] The story of Whitefield's zeal and fervour

---

[1] Familiar as the tragic and pathetic story of Whitefield's end may be, it seems peculiarly appropriate to recall it. Müller could not have stood by the vault and looked upon the dust without thinking of it. Whitefield set out, Saturday, September 29, 1770, from Portsmouth, N.H., intend-

and of the astonishing results of his preaching has been one of the chief factors in Müller's own experience. In his personal notes on the tour, Müller makes no reference to the visit, but the thoughts that were in his mind may be gathered from the account given by his wife, who records that, like many other visitors, they were shown the vault in which the coffin lay—" but when the lid was removed, the skull and a few bones only could be seen of the celebrated man whose voice once reached the ears of tens of thousands, and whose eloquent appeals in years gone by made careless, unconverted sinners tremble."

They read, too, the memorial inscription, which tells how Whitefield, " in a ministry of thirty-four years, crossed the Atlantic thirteen times and preached eighteen thousand sermons." Whitefield's dust, however, is not Whitefield, so Mrs. Müller, turning from the hallowed bones, quotes the noble words which the

ing to preach next morning at Newburyport. Fifteen miles on, at Exeter, he was persuaded to halt and preach, coining, in answer to a sympathetic remark, a phrase that has become famous : " Lord Jesus, I am weary *in* Thy work, but not *of* it." Accordingly he preached, from a barrel-top, for two hours, to an immense multitude. Reaching Newburyport, he went to the manse, and took some food. The people, hearing of his arrival, crowded even into the house itself, anxious to hear some word from those eloquent lips. " I am tired," he pleaded, " I must go to bed." Taking his candle, he made his way to the staircase, but the sight of the crowd touched him ; he stopped, began to preach, and went on till the candle burnt out and expired in its socket—an emblem (reminding us of Henry Martyn's " Let me burn out for God ") of the ending of his own life. He went up to bed ; in the night he was seized with an attack of asthma ; before morning dawned he was at rest in God.

warrior of God addressed to Howell Harris :—" Show the people, in the ' map' of the Word, the kingdoms of the upper world, and the transcendent glories of them ; and assure them that all shall be theirs, if they believe on Jesus Christ with their whole hearts. Press them to believe on Him immediately. Intersperse prayers with your exhortations, and thereby call down the fire from heaven, even the fire of the Holy Ghost. Speak every time, my dear brother, as though it were your last ; weep out, if possible, every argument ; and as it were, compel them to cry : ' Behold how he loveth us.'"

The tour extends far afield, from Florida to California, and from New Orleans to Chicago—where Müller preaches in "Mr. Moody's Tabernacle" to a great audience. In all these labours no account is taken of denominational difference. Müller's own words are : "As I love all who love our Lord Jesus Christ, and as I habitually seek more and more to promote union amongst all the children of God, I preached among so-called Episcopalians, Presbyterians, Congregationalists, Episcopal Methodists, Lutherans, and Baptists." At length, sailing from New York and giving, during the journey, three addresses, he arrives in Liverpool, whence he goes on to Bristol, being greeted with many shouts by the orphans. The record of the tour is : addresses given, 308 ; distance travelled, 19,247 miles. Statements have been given currency in the Press to the effect that, during this tour, "very large sums have been obtained for the orphans." The Press is in error.

THE PREACHING TOURS

Müller declares : " All the donations handed to me for the Institution would not meet one-half of its average expenses for one single day." Having trusted the Living God thus far, it is not likely that in his old age he is starting upon a begging tour.

Eight weeks and three days in the Orphan Houses and at Bethesda, and then he is afield again, this time to the Continent once more, through France, Switzerland, Spain, and Italy, returning to England, once more, in time for the Mildmay Conference. The tour is notable for bringing Müller afresh into touch with the superstitions of Romanism, and for the warm encouragement he gives to Protestant stalwarts. Indeed, he is himself a protagonist in the struggle for light and liberty, since the Scriptural Knowledge Institution maintains ten Day-schools at Barcelona—where the parents of the children, Mrs. Müller particularly notes, are without exception Romanist or infidel—and five in Madrid.

The influence of Müller upon Spain must not be lightly passed by. When the reign of Isabella II. came to an ignominious end, in 1868, and the queen went into exile, her unhappy dominions were in a terrible state. Her behaviour had come to be one of the scandals of Europe, but her departure did not bring peace. Civil turmoil ; furious struggles between the Republicans and the various Monarchist groups ; mutiny and assassination, wrote their red record upon the annals of Spain. The fall of Isabella, however, at least opened the way for the distribution of the

Scriptures, a condition which continued until the restoration of the monarchy, under Alphonso XII., in 1875. Later years, again, brought renewed and increased opportunities, to some extent under Queen Christina, and to a greater under Alphonso XIII.

Immediately the "open door" in Spain was perceived, Müller was prompt with aid; indeed, with all energy he began to circulate copies of the Word—particularly of the Gospels and the New Testament. "Large editions," testifies Henry Payne—who became acquainted with Müller in 1869 and was thereafter in frequent communication with him—"were printed and circulated by him. The schools were opened in the year 1870, and for twenty-two years were supported by Messrs. Müller and Wright, at a cost of £13,000. During the twenty-two years about twenty thousand children were received into the schools."[1]

[1] The accounts of work in other lands, given by Müller in his annual Reports, and the letters sent home by missionaries, were in the early days the chief links between Christians at home and those labouring in other lands. An instructive booklet, entitled *Thou Shalt Remember*, traces the rise of missionary literature among Brethren: "For some years, from 1854, a little paper called *The Missionary Reporter* was issued, in which, besides news from India, some of Mr. Hudson Taylor's earliest letters appeared, and somewhat later a *sheet* called *The Gospel in Italy* was circulated. In 1872 *The Missionary Echo* was begun by Mr. H. Groves and Dr. Maclean, the title being taken from 1 Thess. 1 : 8, where the apostle speaks of the Word of the Lord being *echoed forth* from this newly-formed assembly of believers. This also gave letters about China from Mr. Hudson Taylor, though his work soon required a paper to itself. In 1885 *The Missionary Echo* was enlarged and called *Echoes of Service*, and in 1890 it was again enlarged and—chiefly on account of the new work in Central Africa—began to be published twice a month." This excellent magazine grows in usefulness.

254

THE PREACHING TOURS

At the time of this tour, then, the days are dark in Spain, but the good seed is being sown; another generation shall witness the glorious harvest and the decay of the long and tenacious absolutism of the Pope in the land of Loyola and Torquemada.

In Switzerland, and particularly at Berne, a week or so is so crowded with meetings that it is marvellous how his strength lasts out. The farewell sermon, "to an immense audience," is on the "Second Coming of the Lord." During this tour, the warm sympathies of Müller with brethren persecuted for righteousness' sake are shown by his visit to the tomb of Manuel Matamoros[1] at Lausanne; by the interest with which he notes, at Florence, the prison in which Francesco and Rosa Madiai[2] had been confined; and by his visit to the Waldenses in their secluded valleys.

[1] The heroic witness of Manuel Matamoros, the reformer, shines with lustre amid the gloom of Jesuitry and its natural product—infidelity, in the story of modern Spain. "The rule of my faith is the Word of God," he declared; but this was not to be tolerated by the priests' party. He was thrust into an underground dungeon, at Granada. The Evangelical Alliance and many of the Brethren championed his cause and helped him, but the sufferings he endured at the hands of persecutors ultimately caused his death. The Evangelical Alliance organised a deputation of chosen representatives of nine European nations, to Queen Isabella. "What!" said the Queen, "do the Protestants believe I shall let this man out? I would sooner have my right hand cut off!" However, after a week of prayer by the Christian Churches, on Matamoros' behalf, the Queen, with that same right hand, signed the order of release, on commuting his sentence, of nine years at the galleys, to one of banishment.

[2] Francesco and Rosa Madiai were poor shopkeepers at Florence, who, convinced of the errors of Roman Catholic teaching, left the Papal Church, and were immediately subjected to intense persecution. They read the Scriptures in their own house, and witnessed for the truth. They were

THE LIFE OF GEORGE MÜLLER

So busy and so public is the life which Müller now lives—a constant succession of journeys, meetings, and interviews, that Mrs. Müller thinks it well to record the question : "How does Mr. Müller find time to attend to his *own* spiritual welfare?" She also supplies the answer :—

"Through the goodness of the Lord, he is a man *given* to the reading of the Scriptures and to prayer. Whether travelling or at rest, a day *never* passes without his devoting as much time as possible to the diligent, prayerful study of the Word of God. He is a man of *one* Book; and that Book is the Bible. Besides our reading the Scriptures regularly together early in the morning, in the course of the day, whenever there is time, my husband employs it in studying the Bible, in meditation, and in prayer. He waits habitually upon *God*, and thus it is that day by day his spiritual strength and vigour are renewed."

Ten weeks in Bristol are occupied with preaching condemned by the Grand Duke of Tuscany to five years, with hard labour, in the galleys. An outburst of indignation followed in England. Lord Shaftesbury was naturally looked to as the leader of public opinion in such a case, and he wrote the Prince Consort, who replied (September 24, 1852) : "The cruel case had already attracted the Queen's notice, and I attempted a personal appeal to the Grand Duke, to which I have not yet received an answer. I tried particularly to impress him (or rather his Confessor, who is the ruling power) that the case will do irreparable mischief to the Roman Catholic cause in England, knowing that for the sake of Christian charity not a finger will be moved. This is the Church that calls us *intolerant*, because we do not choose to be *governed* by it !" All Europe was in commotion over the two poor shopkeepers, and a British deputation, headed by the Earl of Roden, went to Florence ; finally, the Grand Duke, unwillingly enough, liberated the Madiai, commuting the sentence to "perpetual exile" from Tuscany.

and administrative duties; then, on August 28, 1879, another journey is made to the United States and Canada. In every city the story is again of vast crowds gathering to hear, of meetings for pastors, for students, for German-speaking people, for Christian workers generally, and for the public at large. He preaches repeatedly on the Second Coming of our Lord, makes Gospel appeals to the unconverted, and amongst numerous other engagements speaks, by interpretation, in "finger language," to some hundreds of deaf and dumb inmates of the Illinois State Asylum.

An idea of the energy and zeal of this aged saint may be gained from the fact that at Cincinnati, during a ten days' visit, he preaches once at a Congregational Church, twice at a Presbyterian Church, and once at the Friends' Meeting-House; conducts three services for Germans, addresses a meeting of two hundred ministers, darts out to a town five miles out to preach once more in German, and returns to speak to the young people at a Children's Home. No matter whither he goes, his programme is crowded with engagements; and on the voyage home he gives a Bible-reading each day for the passengers, preaches on the Sundays, and addresses the seamen in the forecastle. June 17, 1880, sees him back at Ashley Down; he has visited forty-two different places and preached nearly three hundred times. Yet, in less than three months he is off once more to America, having large numbers of invitations still unaccepted. December finds him in New York, and although the winter is the most severe for many years, and the ice is so thick that the ferry steamer can scarcely force a way through, he remains in the city from December 8, 1880, till March 19, 1881, conducting nearly a hundred meetings in all, many of them involving long drives in the cold. In this seventh tour, he preaches two hundred and forty-four times. Ashley Down is reached once more on May 31, 1881.

Very natural is it that Müller should feel strongly drawn to the Bible Lands; not, however, from lively curiosity or even from reverent interest does he set out; but he has it laid upon his heart to encourage the Protestant missionaries, labouring as they are under tremendous difficulties, and to visit, more particularly, the German colonies.

The entire record of this tour, as of the others, demonstrates the absorption of George Müller in the Kingdom and cause of God. On landing at Alexandria he is immediately busy in the Lord's service; the ten days of the stay see him preaching repeatedly at the Russian Hospital, holding meetings in English at the Scottish Free Church, addressing the children at Mission schools and preaching at the German Church. Immediately on arriving at Jaffa, he preaches to both English and German audiences; then to Arab children, then at the dispensary—to a mixed crowd of Jews, Mohammedans, and members of the Greek Church.

It is interesting to note that, looking carefully

around if haply he may discern signs of the fulfilment of prophecy, in the return of Israel, he sees none, but yet uses the language of faith. "Palestine," he says, "so many times called 'the land flowing with milk and honey,' and 'the glory of all lands,' has now a most barren and rocky appearance, so that one is forced to see that God's curse rests even upon the *land*, and not merely upon the people who once inhabited the country, the descendants of Abraham, Isaac, and Jacob. Nevertheless the day is coming when Jehovah will remember even 'the land,' and when the desert shall rejoice and blossom as the rose." Truly prophetic, for the beginning of the transformation was at hand. Could the aged warrior of faith have looked ahead a little more than thirty years, he might have used the language of "fulfilment commenced"; but "blessed are they who have not seen, and yet have believed."[1]

Amid the scenes of gloom and squalor, and yet believing the sites associated with the greatest events of history, his heart is sad but not cast down. Re-

[1] A missionary told Müller that the Pasha (Governor of Jerusalem) had received orders from the Sultan not to sell any considerable quantities of land to the Jews. Compare this, and Müller's description of the prevailing conditions, with the words of a clergyman who recently visited Palestine : "The Jaffa of to-day is different from the Jaffa of two decades ago. Since then, the Jews have commenced to return in large numbers to their own land, and have made themselves an integral part of the Palestine community by buying thousands of acres and throwing themselves assiduously into the work of cultivation. Round about Jaffa, the land is once more 'a land flowing with milk and honey.' As Jerusalem is reached, further developments, unknown and unthought of a few years ago, are seen to be pressing in the Holy City of to-day, causing it to take its part in history once more."

peatedly he preaches in English and in German; and, as becomes a servant of God, he speaks to the lepers, in the hospital outside the city, of Him to whom the leper cried out of old, and not in vain: " Lord, if Thou wilt, Thou canst make me clean."

A visit is also paid to Haifa, on the sea-shore, close to the foot of Mount Carmel, where there is a large colony of Germans. " There," says Mrs. Müller's record, "the Lord was pleased to grant a particular blessing, for his ministry was the means of bringing about a complete Revival." It is intended to go on to Nazareth, but " that ancient river, the Kishon," is in flood and threatens to sweep away travellers even as it did the smitten forces of Sisera, so, turning north-ward a call is made at Beyrout, and thence the route is by Cyprus, Chios, and Smyrna; thence to Ephesus and back. Next comes Constantinople, where many meetings are held in English, German, and French; hundreds of school children are addressed, and two congregations of Armenians; he is twelve days in the city and speaks in all eighteen times. He is similarly active at Athens, speaking to poor children in a ragged-school, and in the jail to some hundreds of prisoners. Sailing from Corinth, he reaches Brindisi, goes on to Rome and Florence, holding meetings at either place, and finally makes for home, reaching Bristol on May 30, 1882.

Affairs at Ashley Down are, in the light of human reasoning, rather discouraging. Funds are low; the

Lord is trying the faith of His servants, "that we might learn," declares Müller, ever sounding the note of calm and reliant faith, "the lesson which our Heavenly Father meant to teach us." Sundry well-meaning friends of the Orphan Houses, not living in the atmosphere of Faith Triumphant, plainly protest that the reason for the falling off in income is the absence of Müller on the preaching tours. "Out of sight, out of mind—unless the picturesque figure of George Müller is kept before the public, money must needs come in less quickly." Such is, practically, the protesting view.

Müller mildly surveys the field and weighs the facts. The Scriptural Knowledge Institution is under the direction of James Wright; there are efficient helpers; each branch is in as good order as if Müller himself had been personally attending to it. These facts, whatever men may say, are encouragements to him to persevere in the preaching tours. Moreover, can it be seriously contended that his presence at Bristol is vital to the receiving of sufficient means? Assuredly not, for in one of the years that the tours are in progress the income was higher than ever before.

"Real trust in God is above circumstances and appearances," he concludes; wherefore, in a little over two months, he commences yet another tour through Germany, Austria, and Russia. Many of the large cities are visited, among them being Munich, Vienna, Dresden, Berlin, and St. Petersburg. A keen desire to hear him is everywhere manifested by the people, and the servants of God regard Müller himself with affection and his meetings as a rallying and unifying force. At Konigsberg he preaches, in addition to other engagements, to an immense audience, of at least three thousand people ; the same day a smaller meeting is held in a small hall, but hundreds are unable to obtain admission ; two other meetings, on the two succeeding days, are conducted in the large building, which is filled on each occasion. At Lodz, a large manufacturing centre in Russian Poland, the whole town is stirred. The meetings are in a chapel, holding twelve hundred people, which is densely crowded at each service. Müller and his message are the topic of universal conversation. Sceptics and infidels attend eagerly and are moved to tears. The general feeling is evidenced in a note sent by one of the Christian townspeople : "I and almost the whole population of this town entreat, in the name of the Lord Jesus, that you will have the kindness to remain with us till after next Sunday. In the name of many thousands I thank you for your ministry." Accordingly the visit is prolonged, to the great satisfaction of the people. "There is good reason to believe that the Spirit of God moved mightily among them," is Müller's comment.

Despite the power of Romanism in Austria and the strict surveillance of the police in Russia, many thousands hear Müller with profit. In St. Petersburg he is occupied at more than a hundred services or meetings : he is permitted to speak in English, and to preach in the German churches, and—by translation—to the Swedes ; however, on holding drawing-room meetings at the house of Colonel Paschkoff—a glorious champion of the Evangelical faith — he is warned by the police that the permission is being strained—translation into Russian cannot be allowed. Yet, a mighty work is wrought. A touching experience of the tour is a further renewal of memories of his boyhood. Journeying from Leipzig to Berlin he calls at Halberstadt, where he had attended school in preparation for Halle University ; at Kroppenstadt, his birthplace ; and at Heimersleben, whither the Müller family had removed when George was but four years old. Two meetings are held at Kroppenstadt, in a large hall ; Müller describes his life and labours, and preaches the Gospel to overflowing congregations. At Heimersleben, he looks once more upon the pleasant house where he had lived as a child. On the way back to England, a call is made in London, to attend the Mildmay Conference. Finally, Ashley Down is reached on June 1, 1883.

The tenth tour is devoted to India, in the hope of encouraging missionaries. The eleventh, twelfth, and thirteenth—in 1883, 1884, and 1885, respectively —consist of brief journeys, of a month or two only, in Great Britain. Then, November 4, 1885, a start is made from Bristol on a world tour, *via* New York, to California, thence to Australia, and by Java, to Hong-

Kong, through various Chinese cities, and on to Japan, the return journey including visits to Singapore and Penang. Next, after two months at Ashley Down, the fifteenth tour is commenced, August 10, 1887, the itinerary including South Australia and New Zealand, Ceylon and India. Mrs. Müller, ever careful of her husband's health, realises the danger of the extreme heat, while at Calcutta, and arranges a consultation with a physician, who declares : " If you remain here, it is at the risk of your lives."

Although Müller is an excellent traveller—" one of a thousand," his wife earnestly witnesses, " to endure fatigue "—yet on the journey which is at once commenced to Darjeeling he becomes prostrate, but his wife by careful nursing " manages to keep life in him." On arrival, however, the cool air restores him, and in a few days this veteran of the Lord is delivering lectures and Bible-readings, preaching—at Jellapur—in a theatre, and speaking to Germans ; and spending his " odd moments " in writing the fiftieth annual Report of the Scriptural Knowledge Institution.

Delhi, Agra, Cawnpore, and Allahabad are visited, with meetings for Europeans, Eurasians, natives ; students are addressed in colleges, and children in orphanages ; there are public gatherings in churches, and private assemblies for missionaries, at which Müller tells the glowing story of God's faithfulness, and encourages his brethren to fight the good fight of faith. At Jabalpur he preaches fourteen times, greatly helped by the Lord ; on one occasion he is in the vestry, conversing quietly to a minister, just before proceeding into the pulpit, when a message arrives from a missionary at Agra ; it conveys the news, sent by cablegram from James Wright, at Ashley Down, that Lydia is dead. The blow is a heavy one ; but he bows to it, being, indeed, so near to heaven that the moment of reunion seems not far distant.

Lydia had laboured for the orphans for well-nigh thirty years. Always delicate, she was, however, wonderfully active, and her industry was remarkable. An attack of bronchitis and inflammation of the lungs suddenly prostrated her, and she passed away, January 10, 1890, aged fifty-seven. Her very last words demonstrated her unselfish character : anxious lest, in attending to her, her husband should forget the duties of the coming day, she exerted herself to remind him, by words and signs, of an engagement to conduct a wedding on the following morning. Having made her meaning clear, she fell back exhausted upon the pillow, and in a few minutes her gentle spirit had departed.

Naturally, the call of home is strong at such a moment. James Wright, sore at heart although resting in the Divine will, needs counsel and fatherly sympathy. Clearly, their place is with him, so the Müllers set their faces once more towards England. They reach London on March 11 ; Müller preaches once again at Mildmay Conference before proceeding to Bristol.

Four months are spent at Ashley Down. Müller,

who has almost attained the age of eighty-five, pathetically, but by no means sadly, admits that he "greatly requires rest." His method of obtaining it, however, is characteristic. Proceeding to Germany, he learns of the spiritual deadness in the churches, and the inroads of Rationalism; whereupon, having received numerous invitations to visit German and Swiss cities, he realises that God has called him to the Continent at this time for a set purpose.

After preaching at Heidelberg, he goes on to Stuttgart, where such crowds gather that he can scarcely make his way to the front; and great spiritual blessing is given. His physical and mental activity, and his true spirituality of thought, seem to furnish themes for wondering comment on the part of the Protestant Press, one writer confessing to great surprise at "the venerable octogenarian carrying his own carpet bag!" At Schaffhaüsen, Zurich, Basle, Berne, and many other places, thousands of people flock to hear: of Carlsruhe he says: "I preached twenty-three times, in two large halls, in the twenty-seven days we were there."

The tour becomes even more a crusade of Faith Triumphant than any of its predecessors. The vitality of Müller is amazing. He goes on once more into Germany. At Essen, apart from giving addresses at a Conference, he addresses, in four meetings, an aggregate of seven thousand people. A similar story might be told of all the places visited, but Müller is not content with the mere drawing together of multitudes; what rejoices his soul is to know of the unconverted finding the Lord, of blessing coming to the young and uninstructed, of the confirmation of believers in the Faith and of the restoration of backsliders. All the meetings are conducted in German, except one for English-speaking people.

Following preaching at Elberfeld, Barmen, and Cassel, comes a brief interval; then the journeying is renewed. The time originally allotted for this tour has expired, but in consequence of the prevalence of indifferentism and scepticism, it is resolved to start out on another tour—making the seventeenth—without first returning to England. Large numbers of Bibles and Testaments have been distributed, and tens of thousands of tracts in German, French, Italian, Spanish, or English, this further service forming an important auxiliary to the preaching.

Tract distribution, indeed, is a matter of high importance with Müller, else he had not made it one of the chief features, all these years, of the Scriptural Knowledge Institution. The quality of consecrated zeal which, by the grace of God, marks the man, appears in the handing of a tract. The spirit with which he takes up this work appears in the counsels given upon the subject at Clifton Conference: "Wait upon God. Water the tracts with your tears, water them with your prayers. As you give the tract, let your soul go out after it. Cry to God: 'Go with this tract; direct it to the right person.' And when you have given it, or given a Testament, cry to God that He would be graciously pleased to give His blessing; but at the same time labour as if everything depended upon your labour. Put no trust in your labour, but let all your dependence be upon God the Holy Ghost; at the same time pray as if everything depended upon your prayer. Thus work and pray, and pray and work. Again and again work, again and again pray; expect blessings, and blessings assuredly will be granted."

It is a joy to Müller to witness once more at Halberstadt: visiting Heimersleben also, he rents a hall—not obtainable on the occasion of his last visit. Another holy aspiration is satisfied when he comes to Magdeburg, the scene of some of his youthful follies, where he now bears witness for Christ, addressing five meetings, and testifying: "I was exceedingly glad to labour for the Lord in a city where I had formerly dishonoured Him." Numerous other opportunities for witnessing ensue. There are two visits to Berlin, where he preaches many times, to large congregations, and to cities in Brandenburg, Pomerania, and Silesia; then he travels into Austria and Italy. The last city to be visited is Naples, where four months are spent; numerous meetings are held, and the work grows larger and larger, but at length it appears desirable to return home. After an absence of a year and nine months, he reaches Ashley Down. James Wright and the helpers at the New Orphan Houses are passing through the severe trial of faith—which is therefore, primarily, Müller's trial—which eventually ends in deliverance coming through the sale of the surplus land.

The preaching tours are now ended. During the seventeen years, Müller has travelled about two hundred thousand miles, has addressed audiences aggregating more than three millions of people, and has carried to countless thousands a new inspiration of faith, a new delight in the Bible, a new realisation of the meaning of prayer, and a new and reverent anticipation of the Lord's Return. In addition to his speaking in English, French, and German, the addresses have been interpreted into as many as eighteen other languages. The principle of his life, to ask nobody for financial help, applied also to the expenses, which were necessarily considerable, of the preaching tours.

We do well to remember that at the time of his return to England Müller is only a few months short of his eighty-seventh year. The flame of holy zeal and power which came to him long decades before, where, kneeling in the snow, he dedicated himself to the service of God, burns undimmed. The body may indeed be failing somewhat, but he remains unwearied in his testimony to the rich grace which supports him, and in witnessing to the ungodly of the love and mercy of Calvary.

The great message of his life is necessarily that which is embodied in the New Orphan Houses and their maintenance. Men will continue to think of George Müller as the prophet of faith of Ashley Down ; and the fact, while not only natural, but entirely warrantable and right, tends somewhat to obscure the importance of his other labours. Not easily, however, should we forget the service to Christianity rendered by these seventeen years of assiduous and devoted effort in the name of the Lord. In them, also, he was the prophet of faith ; and an object-lesson of God's faithfulness to countless thousands. Yet this has been but one part of the result, for there remains the glorious fact that, alike in lands where the priest has held practically all power, and in communities where the Evangelical faith has been honeycombed by rationalistic thought ; alike among the children of the day as among the children of darkness, he has placed before all who would hear, the apostolic message, the one Evangel, the essence of Bible truth ; he has depicted to the ungodly something of the unsearchable riches of Christ, has bared the cross of the meretricious decorations of men, and riveted afresh the attention of nations upon the fundamental truth that " God so loved the world that He gave His only begotten Son, that whosoever believeth in Him should not perish, but have everlasting life."

CHAPTER XIII

More " Müller Stories "

WHEN a man of God specially distinguished in some aspect of life or work passes to his rest, certain of his characteristic sayings and doings inevitably come to pass current among those who delight to recall his memory, as specially typical of the man. Such is the story of Whitefield and Chesterfield: Whitefield vividly pictures the peril of sinners by imagining a blind beggar, deserted by his dog and wandering at midnight upon the edge of a great cliff; whereupon Chesterfield, aroused from his fashionable frigidity, is so carried away in imagination that he cries aloud in the chapel : "He is gone ! He is gone !" Such is the story of John Wesley preaching in Epworth Churchyard, with his father's tomb as a pulpit. Such is the story of George Fox, asking, in a rapture, of a contemptuous minister : "Dost thou call this steeplehouse a 'Church'? Or dost thou call this mixed multitude a 'Church'?" Such is the story, of the godly Sunday-school teacher, Edward Kimball, going one day into the Chicago store, to speak to young

Dwight L. Moody, and leading him there and then to Christ.

So is it with Müller. As time elapses, people will inevitably be less concerned with the detailed round of his life than with the essentials of his testimony, and these are pointedly and picturesquely illustrated in the stories of his life. The earnest believer finds lively encouragement in them; they warm his heart, for they represent exactly what he wishes to urge upon a cynical and unbelieving world: that God is the Answerer of Prayer. A Christian, indeed, needs not to be assured that God hears; nor has he any doubt regarding God's ability, but he dearly loves to note the actual living proof, both for the new inspiration and gladness which it affords his own soul—bringing, with a fresh glow, a realisation of God's greatness and goodness—and for its power as an object-lesson of faith to an unbelieving world. Such blessed fruits of believing are, as M'Cheyne says, "apples having a taste of heaven in them."

Moreover, not all the Lord's people claim descent from Mr. Greatheart or the heroic Valiant-for-the-Truth. There are still among the band of pilgrims brethren and sisters who, albeit they struggle forward on the upward way, are yet but feeble folk: indeed it is no difficult matter to recognise, with the sympathy that arises from a sense of our own shortcomings when facing the lions in the road, how strong a family resemblance they bear to the ancient lines of Ready-to-halt and Despondency. To such, the stories of Faith Triumphant are like water springing suddenly from the desert's cloven rock. Again; there is the merely nominal religionist who lives in constant fear of God's promises breaking down. However much he strives to live by faith he is anxious and careworn, suspecting that somehow or another it is all too good to be true, and that Eternal Wisdom and Love and Power must needs prove but doubtful supports after all! To such trembling souls Müller was at once a marvel and a delight. As to the attitude of Unbelief, atheists would debate on specified Christian Evidences, but did not on those of the Müller order. The advocates of Atheism and Agnosticism, sufficiently vocal upon occasion, are significantly silent regarding Ashley Down.

Upon all sad and gloomy souls, Müller's stories of Faith Triumphant may well have a healing effect, for the light they bring is from the Sun of Righteousness. Some of the stories indeed are simply of incidents, but they sparkle like diamonds, witnessing to the faithfulness of God; the majority, as we have already seen, bear a strong resemblance one to another; they tell of Müller praying, and the Spirit of God, in answer using human means to provide the needed help exactly at the psychological moment. The circumstances differ: the central fact is the same. One of the simplest might be entitled: "Right to a Shilling." It is a cold December day. There are house-keeping responsibilities and other incidentals to be met. Müller casts up items and calculates that the Lord will need to send him £11 within twenty-four hours. The same night, however, £1 is received from a friend, leaving a balance of £10 required next day.

While Müller, at Bristol, is pleading with his Friend regarding this £10, there is a busy man, yonder at Liverpool, who in the midst of the racket of commercial affairs bethinks himself of a certain £10 note which he has stowed away somewhere in his desk, intending some day to send it to Müller for the orphans. Let us note parenthetically that it is a liberal education in the life of faith to witness the bridging over, by prayer, of the gap between Müller's need and a donor's money. It is as though God placed in the Orphan Houses, in time of need, a compelling magnet, to the holy drawings of which, gifts must obediently fly.

"Lord," urges Müller, "Thou knowest our need. We must have £10. Thou wilt not disappoint."

"Where is that £10?" ejaculates the busy man. There are many calls upon his time; he is a person of affairs; but—God first; here is the true business; let commerce wait at the door a little. And so the busy man pens a brief epistle: "I have had the enclosed £10 note in my drawer for some time, intending to send it to you for the orphans; but my time is so occupied that I have overlooked it. I now enclose it"!

O busy man, hadst thou but known, wouldst thou not have underlined that little word "now"? For George Müller, next morning, having prayed again and again for the £10, rises from his knees, calm in the Lord, and expecting—looking for—*immediate* help. "Immediate"! cries Faith Triumphant. "Immediate"? Yea; count but sixty seconds and—see, there is a messenger at the door, bearing the busy man's letter. Opened by Müller, it yields up the £10; the precise sum required. "How exactly to the very shilling!" comments George Müller.

The next story may be entitled: "George Müller Declines to Say." A friend inquires: "Mr. Müller, have you any *present* need regarding the Institution? I know you do not *ask*, except indeed of Him whose work you are doing, but to *answer when asked* seems another thing and a right thing." Another reason for obtaining the information is, that if the Orphan Houses are not in need, the money can be sent to some other worthy object. Müller *is* in need, for he is about to start an Infant-school, and he also requires Bibles for the Circulation work. Nevertheless, he realises, what his inquiring friend fails to see, that here is a question of fundamental principle. The basal idea of the Orphan Houses being to demonstrate the power and faithfulness of God, who is Himself to maintain the work, the explanation of the needs, to men, would be an abandonment of vital principle.

Wherefore, excellent as this good friend's intentions

are, Müller replies, in effect : "While I thank you for your love, nevertheless I am not at liberty to speak about the state of our funds, since the primary object of the work in my hands is to lead those who are weak in the faith to see that there is reality in dealing with God alone."

Thus is it that "George Müller declines to say," even at the risk of losing a donation. But, if he will not declare the facts to men, he declares them to God. On such terms are Müller and his Divine Lord, that it is easy to think of him as talking with God as Abraham did with his Friend in the fields of Mamre. The intending donor has been "put off"—but the need remains; what is God going to do? "Lord," pleads George Müller, "Thou knowest that for *Thy* sake I did not tell this brother; it was for Thy glory; now show afresh that there is reality in speaking to *Thee only*, about our need : speak to this brother Thyself, that he may help us."

The letter from Müller to the kind inquirer remains unanswered. At the end of nine days, there remains not one penny in hand for the Orphan Houses; nor is the Infant-school established; nor are the required Bibles ordered. But the answer is at hand. So far from Müller's letter giving offence, it brings a hearty response, with a gift of £100. The Infant-school is commenced; the Bibles are bought; and there is money enough remaining to maintain the orphans for a week, and this in answer to a letter declining a request for information which the average man would assuredly describe as "eminently reasonable."

Not only in financial affairs is prayer answered, as a story of "The Leaky Boiler" testifies. The boiler of the heating apparatus of New Orphan House No. 1 is reported "out of order," one cold day towards the end of November, 1857. It seemed an excellent boiler, in good condition, so far as can be judged, but something must be done, and that promptly, for the weather is bitter. Examination, however, shows that the leak is a great one, and the question arises, which will be best, to install a new boiler—a work which will take many weeks—or to strip away the brickwork, uncover the present boiler, and proceed to repair it? Even the latter arrangement will take some days. Meantime, what shall be done to warm these rooms for the three hundred children? "Gas stoves might do," thinks Müller, but, he reflects, there is not enough gas to spare from the lighting apparatus; moreover, chimneys would be needed, and the arrangement, however suitable for a shop or a public hall, is not ideal for the Orphan Houses.

"Let us fall into the hands of God," says Müller, thinking of David and the threatened plague of old; "let us see what can be done to repair the boiler, at any rate to manage through the winter." The arrangements are made; the workmen will be due in a few days. Just then a bleak north wind sets in. Two things at least are needed: one, that the workmen shall do the repairs swiftly; and the other, that the cold wind, which would nip the young children keenly were there no heat in the rooms, shall be changed to a warm one. Let us watch this north wind, and listen to Müller's prayers regarding it.

At this time, people have been admiring the tender beauty of *In Memoriam*, as it has come increasingly into public notice; and the famous phrase acclaiming "the faith that lies in honest doubt" is supplying a school of rationalistic pulpiteers with a convenient quotation, clothing agnosticism in a picturesque robe. Did great Tennyson but know, however, he might, stirring among his laurels, refer Honest Doubt to George Müller's leaky boiler for a homely but intensely practical solution of misgiving—at any rate regarding Answers to Prayer.

Let us by all means imagine Honest Doubt at Ashley Down, peering and poking about among the bricks and trying the leak to make sure there is no Cagliostro deception or jugglery; moreover, turning those anxious and suspicious eyes upwards now and again to watch the vane. Honest Doubt—always a trembler—shakes in this bitter wind! It is Friday afternoon; the fire is to be allowed to go out on the ensuing Wednesday. George Müller's prayer is, for the wind to veer completely round, from north to south.

Saturday comes; the wind is still north; but the fire is kept up, the leak being controlled as best may be; Sunday comes, and still blows the north wind;

Monday—and Honest Doubt shivers again at the thought that we are now in December—the same; Tuesday the same—yea, this Tuesday night there comes a wind "like the tenfold blast of the arctic zone"! Run, O Honest Doubt, fetch blankets, fur coats, aught that will warm thee in this night vigil, for we are to watch until morning. But in the morning—Wednesday—the day when prayer is to be answered, Honest Doubt may put away his furs. A south wind is blowing, and no fire is needed; the orphans are warm; the boiler is being repaired.

Let us remember, too, that other prayer of George Müller's, that the repairing gang, like Nehemiah's of old, may have "a mind to work." Some there are to whom the ways of British workmen—particularly men of repairing duty — supply thoughts for humorous dialogues and ballads, or even for the sardonic play of facile draughtsmanship; but here is the British workman wrought upon by the power of the Living God. Let us see how things go. George Müller dives down to the cellar, and makes inquiry as to progress. Says the Principal of the firm, in reply : "The men will work late to-night, and come early to-morrow." This might seem satisfactory even to a writer of squibs. Clearly, the men "*have* a mind to work"; but, mark the further word of the foreman : "Sir, *we would rather work all night!*" This they do; by the morning the leak is stopped; soon, the brickwork is up again; and all the time the sweet south breeze comes tenderly, so that, under the sheltering wing of Jehovah, Ashley Down is as balmy, in December, as if it were

> the island-valley of Avilion
> Where falls not hail, or rain, or any snow,
> Nor ever wind blows loudly.

By the time the north wind sweeps Ashley Down again, the boiler is sound, the fires are lit, and the orphans are warmed.[1]

The gifts that come by faith in God, who answers prayer, are sweet indeed; perhaps there is a more delightful satisfaction, however, in noting, not only faith's fruit, but faith's restraint. In 1865, Müller is needing, at one of the stages of extending the New Orphan Houses, not only a large sum of money for these enlargements, but a good deal for current expenses. His thoughts turn to a certain Christian man of business, who has several times sent donations. Müller has never seen him, but yet prays that God will incline him to give. Within a day or two comes

---

[1] The story of the changing wind suggests, naturally enough, that of the contrasting change from south-west to north-east in the prayer of James Turner, the apostle of the coast towns of Elgin, Banff, and Aberdeen. When the Revival at Findochty had just begun, the fishermen were due to put to sea, on a certain day, but their going would have meant the suspension of the work. The friend with whom Turner was staying bewailed the fact when the day broke fine. "Never fear," replied Turner, "not a boat will go out to-day." At eight o'clock, and again at half-past nine, the weather, his host lamented, was still favourable to going, but Turner silenced him with : "Never fear, you will *not* go." At eleven, the "honest doubter" found that a slight breeze had arisen from the north-east—that is to say, the wind was directly unfavourable. Three hours later, a furious tempest raged. Not a boat could leave, so the fishermen crowded to the meetings, and the Revival went on.

£100 with the plain statement: "I believe it is through the Lord's acting upon me that I enclose you a cheque"; and he adds: "I hope your affairs are going well." Now, this Christian brother does not definitely ask: "How are things going with you? He does not seek information, but expresses a kindly hope. Doubtless, if the need of a large sum were mentioned to him, he would give a further and larger amount; so, in enclosing a receipt to him, may not some indication of the need be made? Nay; that is not George Müller's way; the acknowledgment is duly sent, but not with any suggestion of an implied " beg."

Here, then, is the restraint of faith: " In truly knowing the Lord, in really relying upon Him, and upon Him alone, there is no need of giving hints, directly or indirectly. My practice is, never to allude to any of these things in my correspondence with donors. When the Report is published, every one can see, who has a desire to see, how matters stand; and thus I leave things in the hands of God, to speak for us to the hearts of His stewards. And this He does. Verily we do not wait upon God in vain."

In all Müller's faith, there is the note of satisfaction not only with the amounts, large or small, which come in, but with the time at which they arrive. In the winter of 1842–43 a certain person, who is apparently quite poor, declares that, having £500, it is her intention to devote it to the work. Müller hesitates to receive it, but, convinced of her earnestness, agrees, after some correspondence has passed, to accept the sum. Unexpectedly, a delay arises. Müller has been depending upon it, needing a considerable amount for the replenishment of stores for the orphans. But he lays hold of the apostolic word: "We know that all things work together for good to them that love God"; and with his soul in peace, he "has grace to delight himself in the will of God." Next day there comes a donation of £100, and then £50, and other amounts, so that, within a week, about £200 is received— sufficient to meet all the expenses of replenishment. In due course—three months later—the £500 is duly received also.

There is one day, April 3, 1866, the story of which might be labelled: "George Müller Asking for More." The work is large; the expenses heavy; the "day of small things" being past, considerable donations must needs be received. The first postal delivery brings £26. George Müller, with a grateful heart, "asks Him for more." At eleven o'clock, comes £10 more, whereat, he records: "I thanked God for this donation and asked for more." At two o'clock, there is another £14. Praise and prayer follow again, and at three o'clock another £20 arrives. As the need, so the prayer; and so the man of God, needing the money for God's work, is waiting at His feet, and pleading. Shortly, a further £6 is given. "Yet," declares Müller of this day of singular experience, "I asked for more, and another £5 was left at my house." At seven o'clock in the evening, £16 more is brought in, when, praising God for His goodness, he reminds Mrs. Müller: "Even now He can send us more than we have had all day." Assuredly, He can. An hour afterwards, there arrives a little box, containing banknotes for £100, endorsed "Matthew 6 : 3." Thus, beginning with £26, Müller is so wonderfully led of the Spirit, to "ask for more," that the day ends with a total receipt of close upon £200.

The stories of Müller and his influence have not all to do with money. His record arouses a great revival of faith in God, not only the Provider for His people's needs, but as their Friend. Christianity becomes a throbbing, vital force in homes and communities where it has hitherto been merely a lifeless form, a dead belief. God is very near ; He is nigh at hand ; what may not be asked of Him in the Name of His adorable Son ? Will He not send, not only supplies, but a Revival of spiritual religion ? Müller's own labours among the orphans, by which many are converted, and his missionary tours, are themselves such a Revival ; but there is also the story of James M'Quilkin.

A young Irishman, unconverted, M'Quilkin was one of the numerous class who are splendid champions of sound doctrine but are strangers to saving grace. One day, at a tea-table, he meets Mrs. Colville, of Gateshead, an earnest Christian who is engaged in preaching the unsearchable riches of Christ in and around the little town of Ballymena, County Antrim. He commences a doctrinal battle; but Mrs. Colville, declining to be drawn aside from the main object of her life, gives him a thrust: "If one were to tell me what he knows of the state of his heart with God, I think I could tell him whether he knows the Lord Jesus savingly." M'Quilkin is silenced, and sits tremblingly, with the arrow of conviction fixed in his heart. Now speaks a lady in the company who describes the state of her own soul. Had she been describing M'Quilkin's it could not have been more exact to truth; wherefore he waits breathlessly to hear what Mrs. Colville will say. "My dear," is her quiet remark to the lady, "you have never known the Lord Jesus." Here is another terrible arrow. It quivers in M'Quilkin's heart. For two weeks he has no peace, day or night. Then he wins his way to Calvary, and is saved.

This is in November, 1856. Two months after, M'Quilkin reads the first two volumes of Müller's "Narrative," and reasons: "If George Müller is heard and answered, I, too, may obtain blessing by prayer." Wherefore he prays, and rallies three other young men to pray, telling them of the inspiration he has won from the experiences of Müller, and urging that they shall work for God, and more especially exercise believing prayer, meeting regularly for that purpose. At this time comes the news of the extraordinary spiritual movement in the United States—the Revival of 1857. Salvation by faith is there the absorbing subject. Ministers find their churches crowded with anxious listeners, and their homes besieged by inquirers. Midday meetings in New York city are attended by not less than twelve thousand business men. All classes are touched by the heavenly breeze. Christ and His salvation is the absorbing topic of conversation. The secular papers find their chief subject of news and comment in the Revival.

From the Atlantic to the Pacific, indeed, a spirit of repentance and prayer and hope in Christ sways the land. "There was such confidence in prevailing prayer," said Charles G. Finney, describing, in after days, the movement at Boston, " that people seemed to prefer meetings for prayer rather than for preaching. They said : ' We have had instruction until we are hardened ; it is time for us to pray.' Evidently in answer to prayer, the windows of heaven were opened and the Spirit of God descended like a flood."

Meanwhile, here is James M'Quilkin studying the news from America, and meeting with a little company in the schoolhouse of an Ulster village ; and he asks himself : " Why may we not have such a blessed work here, seeing that God did such great things for George Müller, simply in answer to prayer ? " So the dauntless four pray on.

Presently there come conversions, and the little group enlarges. In Ballymena and other places a marvellous work breaks out. It might almost be said that a nation is born in a day. The whole country is stirred. The drink traffic is paralysed. On every hand are heard the cries of seeking souls and psalms of praise from the people of God. Churches are crammed with hearers who, with tremendous earnestness, have come, not to listen to some dry-as-dust moral essay or exercise in philosophy, but to the saving message of the Cross. Religious services, once begun, will go on for hours, while weeping inquirers are pointed to the Lamb of God. Open-air meetings are held, attended by vast throngs of people, in places of popular resort, at which hundreds are converted. The churches are suddenly reinforced by many thousands of new and zealous members; a new impetus is given to Christian work at home and abroad, and the land that was dry as a desert blossoms as the rose. This mighty movement of the Spirit spreads to parts of England and Scotland : in days to come men shall call it " the Revival of 1859."

George Müller, as we have seen, longed in his heart of hearts to preach the Gospel to the masses, and see a mighty ingathering, like Whitefield of old : God has called him to witness in other ways—nevertheless the Spirit thus uses the " Narrative " as one chief means of inspiring the greatest religious movement Ireland has ever known.

It is not surprising, considering the triumphs of faith at Bristol, that a rumour finds credence regarding Müller possessing some secret hoard treasure, or perhaps underground cave, flashing with jewels and ingots, of the " books of adventure " order. These monstrous legends are met with an amused smile. His storehouse is not earthly but heavenly. Many, too, are the expressions of profound sympathy which reach him regarding the "enormous burden" which he has to bear. But the idea of Müller living a mournful life, incessantly apprehensive of being forgotten by God, is preposterous to him. Not a sparrow falls from heaven unmarked by the All-seeing eye : wherefore he declares, with a sunny smile : "I cannot tell you how happy this service makes me. Instead of being the anxious, careworn man many persons think me to be, I have no anxieties and no cares at all. Faith in God leads me to roll my burden upon Him ; for I have hundreds of necessities, besides those connected with money. In every way I find God to be my Helper, even as I trust in Him, and pray to Him in childlike simplicity, about everything."

"The Story of the Auction Sale" is that of a gift, which Müller himself calls "one of the most remarkable I ever received," from a certain unbelieving business man. One of the annual records falls into the hands of the man in question, who, reading some of the "Müller stories," regards them as preposterous, and with a touch of scorn rejects the idea that the orphans are really maintained in answer to prayer. Yet he cannot get away from the thought; for, after all, behind the question of the orphans' bread and butter there lies the mightier one of God's reality— and of His readiness to hear the cry of His people.

This business man is a nominal Christian, which is to say, not very far removed from unbelief and materialism; but here are matters which may well appeal to a business man; for the Orphan Houses are no fairy vision, the orphans are no pixies and fairies, but sturdy British children, with amazing appetites, as appears with sufficient clearness at meal-times. The problem appears insoluble; for the orphans are fed, clothed, and educated, yet the business man can find no one of whom George Müller has ever asked a penny.

"Now," he reasons with himself, "I will put the matter to trial, and see for myself if God does actually help George Müller. Here is a property which I wish to buy. I have had it valued, and if, at an impending auction, I can buy it for a certain low figure, I will give George Müller £100."

The sale is to take place at a distant town; the business man instructs an agent to bid for him up to the figure named. As the day approaches, however, the business man becomes so intensely interested that, immediately after the auction, he makes the journey to the place, in order to learn at once what the result has been. On arriving he finds that the property has been obtained for him, at the exact amount he has agreed to give.

The surprising result works a complete spiritual revolution in the business man. He sees "how right and proper it is to trust God," and marvelling that he could ever have been unbelieving, sets out for Bristol to pay the £100. George Müller is away—gone to Ilfracombe for a few days' quiet. "Give me his address," says the business man, and, obtaining it, he sets out in pursuit, finds Müller, tells him the whole story, and pays the £100. But this is not all. "I am not surprised at God working for me in this way," says Müller, "for day by day I seek His help, and He sends help from all sorts of unlikely persons—even from entire strangers."

The business man listens intently, but says no word. Müller goes on: "For instance, from the very place whence you come I have had a letter from a lawyer asking me for a proper form for a legacy to be left to the orphans, as a certain client—unnamed—wished to bequeath them a legacy of £1000. Now, see how God works : I know nobody at that place, nor do I know the name of the person who wishes to leave this £1000." The business man knows, however. He himself is the man. After the auction sale, with its remarkable result, he was so ashamed of his scepticism, that, although in good health and by no means an old man, he resolved to have his will drawn at once, with a legacy of £1000 for George Müller's orphans : which fact he straightway confesses.

Other stories, or chains of incident, might well be entitled "Lord's Day Manna." Obviously, it is necessary that sufficient money must be received during the week to provide for the Lord's Day also, even as, of the manna which fell in the wilderness, "it came to pass that on the sixth day they gathered twice as much bread," and Moses said : "That which remaineth over lay up for you, to be kept until the morning. And they laid it up till the morning, as Moses bade. . . . And the house of Israel called the name thereof, Manna."

Exquisite indeed, to faith, are these stories of George Müller's Saturday nights. On a certain Saturday, a few shillings only are received—although each little gift is regarded by Müller as "a further sweet proof of our Father's loving remembrance of our need." There is not enough, however, to purchase bread for the Lord's Day. About eight o'clock, Robert C. Chapman is expected from Barnstaple, to stay at Müller's house. "Come home with me," says Müller to one of the workers, "and we will see what the Lord may send—by post or otherwise."

A quarter-past eight; no money; half-past—here comes Robert Chapman, who, after being in the house only a few minutes, gives Müller ten shillings—which, with the cash in hand, is enough to buy all that is needed for the Lord's Day. "Observe," says Müller, "for the trial of our faith the Lord had allowed us to be kept waiting so long: when, however, Brother Chapman arrived, he could not delay giving it at once!"

On another Saturday, there is not enough money in hand, in the early morning, to meet the day's necessities, so that the Lord's Day manna has yet to fall. In the course of the morning comes £2. 10s., but this will not suffice. The day wears on. About eight o'clock in the evening, a gentleman calls, apologising for his lateness, and gives £2. He is asked for his name, but his reply is: "If the giving of it would be of any benefit, I would do so, but as it will not, please put it down as 'Sent,' for I am sure the Lord has sent me." George Müller entirely agrees: the manna is "sent," according to the promise of the Everlasting One.

Equally pointed, in the "Müller stories," are those regarding prayer for the conversion of individuals—and some of these go back to his student days. Soon after his conversion, when at Halle University, out of 1260 students, there are only about half-a-dozen who care for the things of God. Müller speaks to two of them—in fact, is so concerned that he falls upon his knees before them and prays for them. Then he rises, goes to his bedroom and pours out his soul before God in their behalf.

About ten minutes passes thus; then he returns to the two astonished students; what they have said to one another during his absence we know not; but they have found peace in God. Both of them afterwards became clergymen. "Ask, and it shall be given you; seek, and ye shall find; knock, and it shall be opened unto you" (Matt. 7: 7); here is the absolute promise claimed by Müller; it specifies nothing regarding the *time* of fulfilment. Sometimes, as in the case of the two students, it may be immediate; sometimes it may be "after many days." An illustration of the latter is found in a story which we may call: "The Bargain in Prayer." It harmonises happily with Matt. 18 : 19 : "If two of you shall agree on earth as touching anything that they shall ask, it shall be done for them of My Father."

Müller has a certain friend, whose father, a wealthy and influential landowner, in Wales, is living in conditions of a particularly flagrant character. Müller's friend is the heir to the estates—and has become a Christian—truly converted to God. The news of the transformation reaches the father, who threatens to disinherit his son, and even refuses to see him. At this the family lawyer, anxious for peace and to save a scandal, urges: "You should at any rate see him; public feeling will be stirred if you refuse and the fact leaks out." "Well," says the father, "he may come and see me if he likes to do so."

Accordingly, the son goes to see his father, but breaks his journey to Wales in order to call on George Müller, at Bristol. The result of their conversation and prayers is an agreement to pray for two things: first, that the son may have a kind reception, and then that both parents may be converted. The "kind reception" comes to pass, but there is no sign of repentance for sin. Seven or eight years elapse: the squire is now eighty-eight years old: "I am very ill," he writes to his son, "come and see me." The son finds him under deep conviction of sin; he eventually died, rejoicing in Christ. The mother is highly moral, but has no idea of a new creation in Christ Jesus. Ten years pass, but at length she, too, is brought to the Lord—"it shall be done for them of My Father."

To trace the daily labours of George Müller is to see how wonderfully the Lord provides, not only in affairs of breakfasts and dinners and teas, but in every one of the multifarious needs that arise.

Here is a small boy who is shortly to go out as an apprentice. This Young Hopeful eagerly awaits the day when he is to commence the battle of life. The happy youth is to have a complete outfit, for George Müller does nothing by halves; every boy and girl must have a sufficiency. The day arrives, but— where is the money for the outfit? While Müller waits upon the Lord, the Spirit works upon a Christian brother who, industrious and frugal, has saved up a sum of £150, and has duly placed it in a savings bank—but he is led to ask himself: "Cannot *God*, who has been looking after you in the days of your strength, also look after you in old age or sickness? Will it not be more for the glory of God to devote the money to the work of the Lord, than to keep it hoarded up in a savings bank?"

Thus does God bring together the thrifty man's money and eager Young Hopeful at Ashley Down, waiting for his outfit. The time nears: the day is come: £10 of the money is sent to George Müller; and our blithe young apprentice, smart in his new clothes, and carrying his bag, goes out into the world to earn his daily bread. Thrifty man and little boy, it seems, know nothing of one another; one of these days there may be a trio, of Müller and thrifty one and erstwhile little boy, in the streets of the New Jerusalem, talking these things over, tracing the hand of God in them, and giving glory to Him for all the stories of George Müller.

Finally, as a lovely example of self-denying devotion on the part of a poor donor, let us record the story of The Poor Woman's Half-Crown. The woman in question has a consumptive husband, unable to work, whose illness finally becomes so serious that she must needs give up her own humble occupation of charwoman, in order to minister to him. A parish allowance of 3s. 6d. per week is made to the husband, and to the wife, as his nurse, of 1s. 6d. Christian friends are glad to help them a little, as occasion offers, particularly as they have a delicate child to support; nevertheless, this does not seem an income out of which to devote a donation to philanthropy, but, so deep is this charwoman's sense of gratitude to God for all His goodness to her and her family that the question rises in her mind: "The Lord has proved His love to me; how can I prove mine for Him?" So she decides, this ex-charwoman with the weakly child and the dying husband, that it will be well to give a halfpenny out of every shilling to the work of God. Her husband consents, and the first-fruits—half-a-crown—are sent to George Müller.

MORE "MÜLLER STORIES"

Such are some of the picturesque stories, illustrative of the life of faith, of a man whom God raised up as it were from the grave—for George Müller had been warned, as a young man, to expect an early death from consumption. This sickly young fellow, smitten by the feebleness which ofttimes overtakes those who tarry long at the wine and give their days to revelry, has found it well, both for body and soul, to serve the Living God. His ransomed life has been given to holy service, and the stories of his experiences in the realm of faith are touched by a golden simplicity and beauty. He thought of himself as nothing and of God as All-in-all. As James Wright said of him : "He saw in Christ his Coming Lord, and in that light he lived from day to day. To him it was of no importance how man might judge, if only he might please the Lord." Wherefore he by no means said, with Emerson :

> It is time to be old,
> To take in sail,

but, as the years passed, his zeal waxed yet stronger, and he sought more and more to know and to do the will of God, crying, from his inmost soul, as he looked upon the Finished Work of Christ: "This makes my precious Lord Jesus Christ so dear to my heart; it is on account of this that I see such comeliness in Him ; and He is coming to take me to Himself. In the degree that we are entering into this by appropriating to ourselves these glorious things, the joys of heaven commence already !"

CHAPTER XIV

Müller as Teacher

NO view of Müller's life-work is complete which fails to take account of his influence, as a teacher, upon the great body of Evangelical Christians, and more particularly upon the leaders of that body as they, in turn, moulded Christian opinion and led the way in Christian work. To hear Müller addressing the orphans is to learn how wisely and well he instructs the young and seeks to build up sterling Christian character : to hear him preach at Bethesda is to be impressed by his spirituality and power as a Bible expositor and soul-winner : to accompany him upon the preaching tours is to recognise that vast numbers of people, the wide world over, reverence him and receive his words as those of a prophet; but we must not miss the fact that in his addresses upon Christian truth, delivered more particularly at Conferences in Great Britain and Ireland, he is exercising a ministry whose results tell in an inspirational way upon the whole Christian life and experience of the people of God, and react upon the generations following. If we would understand the man, we must note his warm evangelistic glow, his whole-hearted devotion to the cause of Christ. He is no superfine centre of an eclectic circle of self-satisfied expositors, out of touch with soul-winning. He is toiling for God; listening, too, for the leadings and admonitions and instructions of the Spirit. The streams of world-thought and world-politics sweep by, but he heeds them not: is he unconcerned for the welfare of humanity? No: mark his eager attitude of soul; amid all his innumerable activities, he is waiting for the Spirit to bid him go forward, this way or that, in the service of the Lord: he is waiting for "the sound of a going in the tops of the mulberry trees."

During the first of his preaching tours, he makes a halt in London and is one of the speakers at the Mildmay Conference. Thereafter he often speaks at that Conference or preaches at the regular services in the Conference Hall. Thus, he is a Conference speaker in 1875; his second preaching tour in the later part of the same year also commences at Mildmay—with meetings for Moody's converts; the third tour likewise concludes at Mildmay, in 1877; and after the exhausting activities of the fifth tour, upon the Continent, he times his return to England so as to be present once more at the Conference, addressing four meetings, in June, 1879. Again, in May, 1883, when passing through London, he speaks on no fewer than seven occasions in the Conference Hall, although a little earlier in the year than the date of Conference.

Mildmay may therefore be regarded as the scene of Müller's chief public appearances in London. To understand the force of his testimony there it is necessary to realise the spirit and influence of the Conference itself. The day of Keswick Convention is not yet; and there are practically no Conferences on so large a scale as those of Mildmay, although important gatherings are held, year by year, at Perth and Dublin. Mildmay, then, is the rallying-place, at this time, for the people of God, in all Evangelical denominations, who desire to gather for holy encouragement and counsel, for reaffirming the verities of the Faith, for renewed personal dedication to the service of the Lord, and for emphasising, in such an atmosphere of spiritual blessing and power, the instruction to evangelise all nations, and the assurances: "I will come again. . . . Behold, I come quickly."

Mildmay Conference is an ideal assembly, with its enormous attendances, its earnest spirit, and its atmosphere of love and unity, for George Müller. He is not slow to take advantage of the opportunity. True, he is sixty-nine years old before the way opens, but George Müller is quite "young" at sixty-nine.

In the visit of August, 1875, he preaches for a fortnight—commencing August 15—a few days after Moody and Sankey, amid the hymn-singing and handkerchief-waving of thousands of converts and friends, have left the Mersey on their journey homeward. Gawin Kirkham, a gifted and godly evangelist

—the first secretary of the Open-Air Mission—gives an interesting sketch of these meetings of Müller's, saying :—

"Mr. Müller's appearance is striking; he is tall and commanding. He is in his seventieth year. He has a strong German accent, though he is easily understood by any English hearer. In his public ministry, he is emphatically a *teacher*, yet he frequently brings in the way of salvation, in a clear, sweet, persuasive manner. Preachers may learn much from his *method* of preaching. He first of all gets a message from the Lord : *i.e.* he waits upon the Lord, by reading the Scriptures, meditation and prayer, till he realises that he has the mind of the Spirit as to what he shall say. He has sometimes been in doubt till almost the last minute, but never once has the Lord failed him. He strongly advocates and practises expository preaching. Instead of a solitary text detached from its context, he selects a passage, it may be of several verses, which he goes over consecutively, clause by clause. His first care is to give the meaning of the passage, and then to illustrate it by other Scriptures, and afterwards apply it.

"This is done sentence by sentence, so that it is definition, illustration, and application all the way through. Yet there is no uncertainty to his hearers as to when he is coming to a close, as he intimates at the outset how many verses he purposes to consider. His illustrations are occasionally taken from history, biography, or nature, but chiefly from the Scriptures or his own personal experience. One of the most striking things about Mr. Müller's preaching is the way in which he induces his hearers to *reconsider* what has already been said. He frequently says : 'Let us ask ourselves, Have *I* understood this ? How does it apply to *me* ? Is this *my* experience ? ' "

His teaching also, and inevitably, made much of the Bible. Addressing young converts—also at Mildmay—he gave a powerful address, of which the following is an outline :—

Read the Word of God with meditation and prayer (1 Pet. 2 : 23).

1. Read the Word *regularly through*. Begin with Genesis in the morning, and Matthew in the evening, making a mark where you left off. When you have finished the Old and the New Testaments, begin again. As an earthly Will is always read through with great care, so this "Will" ought to be read entirely through with reverence and godly fear. Consider the advantages of this plan :—

(*a*) We are kept from making a system of Divinity of our own, and confining ourselves to a few favourite doctrines and truths : we become lovers of the *whole* Word.

(*b*) Variety is pleasing.

(*c*) When we have finished reading through, we shall be glad to begin it again. In forty-six years I have read my Bible through a hundred times ; yet it is always fresh and new when I begin it again.

2. Read in a *prayerful spirit.*

3. Read with *meditation.* Ponder over what you are reading.

4. Read *with reference to your own heart.* So many preachers read for their hearers ; parents read for their children ; teachers read for their scholars. Ask yourselves : "How does this suit *me?* How does this warn *me?* How does this rebuke *me?* How does this comfort *me?*" If you do this, God also uses the Word, by you, for others.

5. Always seek to mix *faith* with your reading.

6. *Practise* what you read. We must carry out what God tells us. He expects us to be obedient children : "If ye know these things, happy are ye if ye do them." Come in childlike simplicity to the Word of God ; give heed to it with all earnestness, and let it settle all questions.

Naturally, the counsels touch next upon Prayer. He puts the matter thus : Prayer must be (1) according to the will of God, (2) offered in the name of the Lord Jesus, and (3) mixed with faith. Further, (4) it must be persevered in until the answer comes. "When these conditions have been complied with," he declares, "I have never known a single instance of failure. I have had not only hundreds and thousands, but literally tens of thousands of answers to prayer! When I began to pray about the orphans, forty years ago, I asked for a House, and for £1000. I never doubted the £1000 would come ; I had to wait eighteen months before the last of it was received, but it came. Since then I have received £650,000 in answer to prayer."

An even deeper impression is made when he speaks upon Phil. 4: 6, 7: "Be careful for nothing; but in everything by prayer and supplication with thanksgiving let your requests be made known unto God. And the peace of God, which passeth all understanding, shall keep your hearts and minds through Christ Jesus." The deduction is: The child of God ought not to have a single care about anything. If we begin to carry our own burdens the Lord will add to them, but in love, so that when crushed by the increasing weight and overwhelmed by our trouble we shall at length be obliged to cast all our care upon Him.

The people listen, profoundly attentive. This man who is speaking to them might well be regarded as the heaviest-burdened man living, in all work for God. He has the care of two thousand orphan children; in the Day-schools ten thousand children are being educated; he circulates over three millions of tracts every year, and thousands of Bibles and Testaments. He is the means of maintaining missionaries, partly or entirely, in many parts of the world. Only a few weeks before, the orphan ranks have been devastated by an outbreak of typhoid fever, in which many of the children have been stricken down, and several have died. Many, therefore, are his responsibilities; but God supports him.

Another illustration of his teaching is the address at the Conference of 1876, of which gatherings the basal thought is Paul's word to the Philippians : "That I may know Him, and the power of His resurrection, and the fellowship of His sufferings, being made conformable unto His death" (Phil. 3 : 10).

It is urged by Müller that in this passage the Holy Spirit, speaking by the Apostle, is making no especial reference to that measure of knowledge which is absolutely needful with regard to the salvation of the soul, but to a higher, further, and more particularly intimate acquaintance with the Lord Jesus Christ, even as a friend is intimately acquainted with his bosom friend. What is it, then, that the Apostle is particularly desiring ? Is it not that, while yet in the body, he may be more intimately acquainted with the precious and adorable Lord Jesus Christ, in all His loveliness, so that he may in goodly measure see the King in His beauty as the saints see Him in the world to come ?

Then, what would be the *results* of this intimate knowledge of the Lord ? (1) *Increased conformity to His image.* On this account this knowledge is of immense moment. God's ultimate object regarding us is not simply our salvation, but the glory of His Son ; and will not this be served by our conformity to His image ? (2) *Increased spiritual power and comfort.* Isaiah describes the Lord Jesus (Isa. 50: 4) as One who "speaks a word in season to him that is weary."

Coming to Him when we are weary, we know the blessedness of having Him as a bosom Friend in trial, in difficulty, in labour, in sore temptation, in conflict against the powers of darkness, and against the natural tendencies within. Again and again and again the child of God who desires to walk in the ways of the Lord will find himself spiritually weak and worn, but if he will come to the Lord Jesus he will hear the " word in due season" for him.

(3) *The realisation of the state described in Ps. 9 : 10—" They that know Thy name will put their trust in Thee."* How blessed to be able to confide in the Lord at all times and in all circumstances! The world looks on and wants to know whether our religion is any more than a mere difference of creed between itself and us. It wants to know how much we have of the reality of the things of God. If it finds that here is a man or woman who is able at all times and under all circumstances to come to Christ as a bosom Friend, and continually receive help and succour and watchful care, it will know that there is a blessed reality in the things of God. On this account it is of vast moment not to be satisfied with knowing the Lord Jesus Christ for the salvation of the soul, wonderful as that is, but to be intimately acquainted with Him as the Friend in whom we are always able to confide. (4) *That, being, as believers, in fellowship—which is to say, " in partnership"— with God we may know who our Partner is, His*

wealth, His disposition, His ability. How wondrous is God's condescension to bear towards us such a relationship, and how blessed to know that in our weakness, our helplessness, our necessity, our trial, we may betake ourselves to our infinitely rich, kind, gracious, wise Partner, for support, for comfort, for strength, for everything that we can possibly need as strangers and pilgrims here.

Such being the results of this intimate knowledge of the Lord Jesus Christ, how shall we *attain* to that knowledge? By the putting aside of everything that hinders. The pleasures of this world, the fashion, the riches, the honour of the world—all that the natural man craves after or desires, must be laid down at the feet of Jesus, in order that we may be able to say, with the Apostle: "I count all things but loss for the excellency of the knowledge of Christ Jesus my Lord . . . that I may know Him" (Phil. 3 : 8, 10). So, for the remainder of life we shall have but *one single* object—not five or four or three or two, but ONE SINGLE OBJECT, *to live for God.*

At the Conference of 1877, George Müller is increasingly a centre of interest and regard, as he speaks upon the theme of "The Transformation"—"Be not conformed to this world: but be ye transformed by the renewing of your mind" (Rom. 12 : 2). His points are: "(1) *It is the will of the Lord that we should be transformed.* In our natural state we go the way of the world—which is to say, bringing the facts home to our own hearts, that we 'go our own way.' We may be amiable in the eyes of our fellow-men; we may be honest and moral; every one may speak well of us, even while we are unconverted, but yet—we go our own way. In such a state it is impossible for us to please God, because we do not set Him before our thoughts. Bodily strength, mental powers, all talents and gifts are used to please and gratify ourselves. That is how all 'natural' men, through living to themselves, and not living unto God, do dishonour unto Him.

"And, until we are renewed by the Holy Ghost, things will go on in this way. Thus do we go on until convinced that we are sinners needing a Saviour, and, putting our trust in the Lord Jesus Christ, we accept salvation through His Atoning Sacrifice alone. In this way we are by the Spirit's power renewed. We obtain spiritual life. Only in this way the true foundation can be laid.

"The world wants to see whether our lives witness for Christ. In order, then, that we may more and more aim at conformity to the image of God's dear Son, and that we may make progress in this conformity, it is a matter of deep moment that, day by day, we seek to keep before us, what we have been redeemed from, and into. We are no longer the slaves of Satan, the world, and our own wicked hearts. All our sins are forgiven; we are justified before God through faith in the Lord Jesus Christ, begotten again, renewed, children of God for time and eternity, heirs of God and joint-heirs with Jesus Christ. Ere long we shall sit with Him on the throne, and with Him judge the world. Our eyes shall see that Blessed One, our own hand shall touch Him, and in seeing Him we shall be like Him—not only obtaining a glorified body but being perfectly free from sin. And the more this is kept before us, the more shall we be constrained to seek to glorify God in this present world.

"(2) *It is the will of God that man should not be happy, if walking in separation from Him.* This should be a settled conviction in our minds, that God is determined that man shall be miserable in going his own way, peace and joy in the Holy Ghost only being obtained by walking in the fear of the Lord. Therefore, we should have this settled purpose of heart, that we will live for God and Him only, that we will dedicate the whole heart to Him—and that is what He looks for. In thus giving ourselves to Him, we must not forget that, having no strength of our own, we must use certain means whereby we shall be helped and kept in this frame of mind, not merely for an hour or two, or a year or two, but every day.

"Thus, we must be given to prayer, day by day going to our Heavenly Father for help, for strength, for support, for comfort, for wisdom, for everything we need. Coupled with this, we must let Him speak to us : we must be men and women who love the Word of God. It is a matter of the deepest moment that we should be given to the reading, regularly and consecutively, of that Word; and with this should be coupled meditation, every day, and always with reference to our own heart. *How* is the Bible to be read? As the *Word of God*, so that our fallen reason bows before it. It is God who speaks; that should be sufficient, whether we can clearly understand, with our fallen reason, or not—for 'What thou knowest not now, thou shalt know hereafter,' is applicable in this respect also. We should patiently, prayerfully, believingly await God's time, when we shall clearly know why this is so and why it is expressed in this way and not in another. We should always have it before us that the Holy Scriptures contain the Word of God, and therefore it becomes us fallen beings to bow before it. But we should mix with the Word, faith, reading and meditating with *the desire and object of carrying it out in our lives*—for, if *this* is neglected, prayer will profit little. Reading the Word is little use if we do not mean to act according to its teachings. It is given to us that we should act according to it, and in so doing there comes blessing to the soul—our peace and joy in the Holy Ghost are increased more and more."

Finally, going on in this way of trust and obedience, "we shall have (3) *the fulfilment of the Lord's promise*: 'Whosoever hath, to him shall be given, and he shall have more abundance.' To walk in this way is to be less and less conformed to the world, and more and more transformed, more and more like Jesus.

And He is worthy, that Blessed One who laid down His life for us, that we should seek to live for Him. It is a blessed thing, even for this life, to walk in the ways of the Lord. What He looks for is that our whole heart should be given to Him."

Such is a simple outline of Müller's teaching on the relation of the soul to Christ. The substance thereof is to be found in many of his addresses, given in many parts of the world. It is sometimes charged against Brethren, although quite erroneously, that while an intense love for Scripture and a wonderfully developed skill in exposition mark their Assemblies, yet there is a tendency to rest satisfied with a statement of correct doctrine, and to allow the ideal of a full and glorious dedication of heart and life to God to become a little dim. To get back to Müller is to realise afresh that the Brethren knew no parley with the world. Nothing in the teaching of Müller, whether to great assemblies in the chief cities of Europe or America, or to the saints at Bethesda, has any of that faint odour, as of the charnel-house, which clings to the endeavour to maintain the profession of a godly walk while the heart and life are on the plane of greed and indulgence. Nor is any touch of Antinomianism here. "Other foundation can no man lay than is laid"; then, the foundation being laid, here are the commands of God to be marked, here are His promises to be accepted and translated into godliness of life and earnestness of service.

THE LIFE OF GEORGE MÜLLER

In the Conference of 1879, Müller gives, in his own sunny way, some very practical hints to Christians, in which he traces much of the joylessness of professors to their refusal to act simply as stewards instead of "proprietors": "They act as if it were all their own, forgetting that they have nothing whatever which is their own, that they are bought by the precious blood of Christ, and that all they possess—their bodily strength, their talents, their business, their profession, their eyes, their hands, their feet—belongs to the Lord Jesus Christ: because He has bought them with His precious blood. They are not their own; they belong to the Lord, with all they have and are. Now, beloved saints, I am persuaded many are depriving themselves of great spiritual blessing, because they act as if they were owners instead of stewards."

Not only that the work of God at large may prosper increasingly, but that they themselves may richly partake of His blessing, Müller proceeds to urge: " I affectionately beseech and entreat my beloved Christian friends to take this blessing, and consider that they have been depriving themselves of vast spiritual blessings, because they have not followed the principle of giving systematically, giving as God prospers them and according to a plan: not as they are moved by a missionary or charity sermon, but systematically and habitually, on principle, just as God enables them. If He entrusts to them a sovereign, to give a proportion, accordingly; if He entrusts them with £10,000, or whatever it may be, still to give accordingly. I believe if we realised the blessing, we should give thus on principle; and if so, we should give a hundred times more than we do now."

But is this a mere matter of "paying out"? Not at all: "We give, just as we are constrained by the love of Christ." And he gives his own experience: "for your comfort and encouragement, to stir up your hearts that you may consider yourselves henceforth as stewards and not as owners. See the blessedness, the privilege, the wondrous honour, that a poor man, as I am, should thus be entrusted by Him. By the grace of God I desire to be nothing but poor. I wish to be nothing but a poor man, having nothing, no house of my own, no money in the Funds, not an acre of land—a poor man altogether; day by day waiting upon God for all I need, for the very clothes I wear. I wait on God for everything, and yet He has allowed me the great honour and blessed privilege of *giving* more than £40,000 within the last fifty years. I began in the year 1830 to live thus as steward for the Lord.[1] In the little way I could, I gave, but God increased my ability more and more. Why do I say it? To encourage the hearts of my beloved brethren to seek

[1] This passage beautifully harmonises with Müller's words, years before, of the light which came to him at Teignmouth: "The Lord . . . led me, in a measure, to see what is my true glory in this world, even to be despised, and to be poor and mean with Christ. I saw then, in a measure, though I have seen it more fully since, that it ill becomes the servant to seek to be rich, and great, and honoured, in that world where his Lord was poor, and mean, and despised."

to give systematically. If you have not done so hitherto, do begin now. I do not say : 'Imitate me, George Müller,' but I do say, seek to give, if it be ever so little, systematically ; if it be only the twentieth part of your income, give systematically."

From this great subject he turns to that of the Christian ministry. Standing upon that high platform at Mildmay he looks upon a throng of Christian workers, many of them young and eager souls, all around him, and to them he turns: " I have been engaged for fifty years in pastoral labours, and therefore I would say a word of encouragement to younger brethren. The first thing I have to say is : see that the truth is enjoyed in your own soul, and that it is a reality to you, so that, with the Apostle Paul, you can say : 'We speak because we believe.' Another point of great importance, is to wait upon God for the right message. We may suppose a certain subject will do, but perhaps another would be more profitable, and our business is to wait upon God for the right message, for He alone knows who will come to hear, and He alone knows the state of heart in which they come, and what word is suited to their need. Another deeply important point is the opening up of Scripture and exposition of the Word. When I first began to preach, in my own country, I used to write out my sermons and then deliver them from memory. I learned the truth more clearly when I came to England; and then from principle I began an expository ministry. One verse, two or three verses, or more—a short Psalm, or half a Psalm, or sometimes a chapter or a whole Epistle, I went through, and obtained great blessing to my own soul; but the greatest blessing came to those to whom I ministered. When I first began my ministry in England, fifty years ago, I came to a congregation where scarcely any had Bibles in their hands; but, four weeks after, when the text was announced, hundreds of Bibles were opened; and that was not all—it created a love of the Word in the hearts of the hearers."

Finally: "The grand point is this: Are we preaching Christ? When the crucified and glorified Christ is preached, there is a blessing: it is always the experience of ministers of the Word, wherever Christ is preached. This should be done with the greatest simplicity; as Luther used to say: 'I preach every Sunday before doctors of divinity and professors, and learned men, but I preach every time so that the maid-servant behind the door, who brings her master's children, may, together with the little children, understand me; and if they can understand, those great and learned men will also be able to understand.' I know this is very simple, but there is a vast deal in it, for if you will make inquiry you will always find there are numbers of persons unable to take in that which is not in the most simple way expressed, therefore this cannot be a matter of little account. Christ as the Saviour is to be preached, and, whether it is liked or not liked, we are here to be faithful to our Master."

THE LIFE OF GEORGE MÜLLER

The addresses which Müller gives, also, at Bethesda or at other centres in connection with the work of God at that place, are all marked consistently by these great thoughts of faith and consecration and service. Some of his especial texts are : John 3 : 16 ; Matt. 6 : 33 ; John 14 : 13, 14 ; 2 Cor. 12 : 9 ; Heb. 12 : 8, 13 : 5, 6 ; 1 Pet. 5 : 7 ; Rom. 8 : 28 ; Jas. 1 : 2–4 ; and 1 Cor. 15 : 58 ; but we need to remember that Müller is always strong against detaching a phrase ; he desires rather to take a passage and consider the whole, rather than a small section. " A text without a context is a pretext." It is a poor ideal which regards a text simply as a peg upon which to hang flower-wreaths of man's rhetoric ; rather let the aim be to bring forth "things new and old" from the inexhaustible treasure - house of the Word of God. That is Müller's foundation thought in all his preaching, public or private.

Since Müller's influence was so unifying, it may well be asked : " What had he to say upon the subject of Christian Unity ? " Speaking upon the " Closer Union and Fuller Co-operation of Believers in Christ," he sensibly and pointedly said : " What will help us, who believe in Christ, to be more united together ? One might say : ' Oh, we must give up our differences.' Allow me affectionately and humbly to say : ' I do not think so.' According to my judgment, a closer union would not be brought about by our giving up our own views of what we consider to be taught us by God and the Scriptures. Not thus, but the great point is to let the foundation truths of our holy Faith have their proper place. We have not to say: 'Now I will put away for the time being all that I hold distinctively from my brethren.' No; nor do I expect this from other brethren. With great diligence and prayerfulness, and, if necessary, great sacrifice, ought we to 'buy the truth'; but, having obtained it, for no price whatever is it to be sold.

"This is *one* side of the truth; the *other* side is this : The foundations of our holy Faith are so great, so momentous, and so precious, so altogether superabounding in comparison with anything else, that, if we lived more under their influence, and more valued and enjoyed them, we should be constrained to love one another, to be knit together in love. We have the one, selfsame Saviour; by faith in the Lord Jesus we are all introduced into the same family; through believing the Gospel we become the children of God, and members of the same heavenly family. Now, if this were present to our hearts, that we all have one Father in heaven; one Saviour; are all bought by the same precious blood, and baptized by the Holy Ghost into one Body; are all walking the same road to heaven, and ere long shall all reach the same Home— if all this were present to our hearts, I say, this or that difference of opinion would not separate or alienate us. There is a blessedness and sweetness connected with really holding the membership of the Body, and loving our fellow-believers, though we differ from them, that brings unspeakable joy to the soul."

Amid such glorious thoughts of true unity in Christian love, he never loses sight of the blessedness of single-handed conflict for God : " Let no man say : ' I am single-handed ; what can *I* do ? If there were a hundred others with me, I might accomplish something !' Never say this. Think what Hezekiah accomplished single-handed, and Josiah, and Martin Luther : see what such men did. Oh, if we cry mightily to God, and 'expect great things from Him,' what may not be accomplished through us. Look at our beloved Wesley, and Whitefield, too ; they were comparatively single-handed, and yet what great things were accomplished through their instrumentality. But there must be a right beginning, and the right beginning is at home—with *ourselves*. Let us, then, 'expect great things,' and *ask* them of God, who delights in bestowing abundant blessings."

If, however, we are to think of all that Müller teaches we must take into consideration the man himself and the whole of his work. When he appears upon the platform, every eye is turned : "That is *Mr. Müller.*" When he speaks, it is impossible to think of him only as a Christian brother who expounds Scripture with reverence and insight and holy ardour. He is the apostle of faith, the man of Ashley Down. Moreover, his Annual Reports, apart even from the triumphs of faith of which they consistently tell, contain numerous digressions, in which Divine principles are applied, to the glory of God. All of it, assuredly, is sound teaching, so that we cannot easily take George Müller's various spheres of labour, and treat them in "watertight compartments" under this or that heading. What he *is* appears in every activity of his life : the unifying golden twin-thread of faith and consecration runs through all.

It is possible for a godly and gifted man to pass a long and useful life, preaching and exhorting among the saints, and yet to be little known outside his own circle ; but George Müller's name becomes a household word, and a subject for much marvelling. Wherefore we judge that George Müller's teaching derives intensive force from the facts of what George Müller is and what George Müller does. Clearly it exercises a powerful formative influence upon Christian life and thought throughout the world, particularly as Müller is truly "a catholic Christian." At Plymouth, in the early days of the Brethren Movement, a certain official, preparing statistical returns, is in doubt as to "what Denomination these people belong," and can obtain no definite information ; finally he enters them as : "Catholic, Non-Roman." A particularly shrewd statistician was this, or he wrote better than he realised. This is assuredly George Müller's "Denomination" : he is essentially Catholic, and—by all means holding to the Book and to the Revelation of the One Mediator between God and men—Non-Roman.

CHAPTER XV

"That Blessed Hope"

THE Brethren Movement, bringing primarily a revival of spiritual religion, and laying emphasis, as we have seen, on the teaching of apostolic days, naturally led to a re-studying of the truths embodied in the Acts of the Apostles and the Epistles. What had been vital in the eyes of the Thessalonians or Corinthians, was therefore vital also in Dublin or Plymouth; what had stirred the believers of the First Century stirred also those of the Nineteenth. Time can set no freezing grip on truth; indeed, the tremendous declarations regarding the spiritual struggles of the saints with the forces of evil, which are prefigured in the words of our Lord Himself, in the teaching of the Apostles, and in the Apocalyptic Vision, must remain urgent until all be fulfilled.

In a renaissance of spiritual thought, the minds of men, desirous of apprehending, so far as may be, the whole body of Christian truth, naturally desire to study, not only the commands and counsels of the Book regarding Christian life and service, and its sweet assurances of Divine guidance and support and help, but also the terrific panorama of "things to come" which it so solemnly unfolds: the Great Tribulation; the man of sin, his attributes and reign and his final destruction; the Coming of the Lord in manifested glory; Babylon, drunken with the blood of witnesses; the new heavens and the new earth.

When the Church of Christ waxes cold and worldly, spiritual vision grows dim, and the seemingly far-off events which Scripture indicates as "things to come" are regarded as of small importance. "My Lord delayeth His coming": indeed: "How shall we know, amid all this sombre and mysterious record, what is actually the truth regarding that Coming?" The study grows arduous; the laugh of the world irritates and its fascinations at length allure the soul into carelessness regarding even so stupendous an event as the Coming of the Lord. But the Brethren, with tender hearts and solemn thoughts, studied and hoped and looked for His appearing. Redemption was drawing nigh. The Lord, many held, might appear at any time; others judged that certain prophecies must first be fulfilled; divers schools of interpretation arose; nevertheless, all that the Brethren did and taught was illuminated by the light shining down the centuries from Olivet: "This same Jesus, which is taken up from you into heaven, shall so come in like manner."

This Nineteenth Century revival of "that Blessed Hope" as a living reality, giving a fresh outlook, brightening as with the foregleams of the new Epiphany the whole field of Christian activity, was further intensified during the spiritual awakening of 1859–60, when, both in Ulster and in Great Britain, the Gospel testimony and Bible teaching of that wonderful day was largely maintained by Brethren.

That men should be divided upon a subject so solemn, so awe-inspiring, as the Second Advent, was a profound sorrow to George Müller; still more, perhaps, was he grieved when the marvels of the Unveiling were made the subject for childish guess-work in the spirit of the manufacturing and solving of Christmas conundrums. Hence, we trace, in all his references to the Blessed Hope, a spirit of peculiar reverence, as of one who puts off his shoes in the presence of the bush of Divine truth —which burns but is not consumed. He held, with Tregelles, that: " Prophecy has been bestowed on us in order that we may know how, in the midst of confusion and the varied forms of Satan's workings, we may stand and act as those who belong to Christ. We know as a simple fact how the Church has greatly overlooked this important portion of revealed truth. We know also how the enemy has sought to cast a kind of discredit upon every effort which is made either for any to understand and use prophecy themselves, or to give instruction to others therein. But this, instead of leading us to overlook this precious deposit of God's truth, ought to make us the more earnest in not neglecting that which is so important." Whenever

Müller touches upon the subject of the Lord's Return
—and he frequently does so—it is with a special guard
upon his words; yet with a thrill of joy.

Müller's interest in the subject was kindled during
that visit to Devonshire, in 1829, when he first became
intimate with Henry Craik. How great a blessing
came to Müller through the ten days spent with Craik
under the same roof, we have already noted. That this
blessing carried a new realization of spiritual truth and
led him to cry: "Behold, He cometh with clouds,
and every eye shall see Him!" is clear from his
own testimony :—

"I had believed what others had told me, without
trying it by the Word. I thought that things were
getting better and better, and that soon the whole
world would be converted. But now I found in the
Word, that we have not the slightest Scriptural warrant
to look for the conversion of the world before the
Return of our Lord. I found in the Scriptures, that
what will usher in the glory of the Church, and uninterrupted joy to the saints, is the Return of the Lord
Jesus, and that, till then, things will be more or less
in confusion. I found in the Word that the Return of
Jesus, and not death, was the hope of apostolic
Christians; and that it became me, therefore, to 'look
for His Appearing.' And this truth entered so into my
heart, that though I went into Devonshire exceedingly
weak, scarce expecting that I should return again to
London, yet I was immediately, on seeing this truth,

brought off from looking for death, and was made to look for the Return of the Lord."

The Blessed Hope was to Müller no mere sentiment, however ethereal; it had the practical effect, for him, of which the Apostle spoke : " Every man that hath this hope in him purifieth himself, even as He is pure." Its fruit was action, not ease ; zeal, not self-congratulatory laziness. " Having seen this truth," he says, " the Lord graciously enabled me to apply it, in some measure at least, to my own heart, and to put the solemn question to myself : What may I do for the Lord, before He returns ?—as He soon may come."

The same consistent balance, the same practical application of truth, regarding the Lord's Coming, to his own heart and life are illustrated throughout his career. Not, indeed, that clearness of view was instantaneously attained during those days in Devonshire ; but the Hope became a living reality to him, and so it remained, illuminating his soul continually. At Clifton Conference, in 1869, he speaks upon Elijah's reply, in the cave, to God's question : " What doest thou here, Elijah ? "—" The children of Israel have forsaken Thy covenant, thrown down Thine altars, and slain Thy prophets " (1 Kings 19 : 9, 10). Depicting the approaching end of the age, Müller's underlying thought is that the people of God, realising their position, and having their pathway lit by the revelation that Christ's Appearing nears, should be zealous for Him, despite solitariness and persecution, in a godless world :—

"THAT BLESSED HOPE"

"There never was a time when the statement of the Apostle John, regarding the world, was not true : 'The whole world lieth in wickedness' (1 John 5 : 19). Hence the deep importance that all the children of God in this rebellious world should seek to bring honour to Him, should live for Him, should be as lights in the darkness, should manifest their zeal for His glory. In seeking to do so, they may meet with many difficulties, but God will help them and strengthen them, if they pray to Him for help, and expect help from Him. They may find themselves, sometimes, almost alone, or quite alone, in their path, in seeking to glorify God, as was the case with men of God of old ; but the more solitary, the greater the importance to live for God, to seek zealously His glory—and the greater the reward of grace at last for doing so."

What, then, is Müller's outlook ? It is clear to him that civilisation can never save : else, indeed, were no Redeemer needed ; humanitarian transformations, however beautiful outwardly, cannot touch the soul, but leave it sadly surveying its own sinfulness. What men sometimes call "increased light" is but a delusion if it be the glory of man's accomplishments in the flesh, rather than the illumination of the Holy Spirit. Moreover, all human opinions and views apart, what is the plain declaration of the Word ?

"As we are drawing nearer and nearer the close of the present Dispensation, spiritual darkness, departure from the Holy Scriptures, and consequent ungodliness, we have reason to believe, will increase more and more, though coupled with a form of godliness (2 Tim. 3 : 1–5); therefore the path of a true disciple of the Lord Jesus will become more and more difficult; but for this very reason it is of so much the more importance to live for God, to testify for God, to be unlike the world, to be transformed from it. If we desire that thus it may be with us, it is needful that we give ourselves to the prayerful reading of the Holy Scriptures with reference to ourselves. The Bible should be to us the Book of books; all other books should be esteemed little in comparison with the Bible. But if this is not the case, we shall remain babes in grace and knowledge."

Thus he contrasts the ungodly characteristics of these closing days with the opportunities of the believing soul. Are the days dark? Then let the Christian shine the brighter :—

" Beloved fellow-disciples, how many of us are in heart purposed to live for God, to be zealous for Him, and to be truly transformed from the world? We have but one brief life here on earth. The opportunities to witness for God by our life will soon be over ; let us therefore make good use of them. Let none among us allow his life, or even a small part of it, to be wasted, for it is given to us to be used for God, to His glory, in this godless world."

At the same Conference, in another address, he looks

for the mighty deliverance that is to come, and delights in the blessings given even now to the pilgrim of Christ :—

"Faith says : 'Rest upon that word : "Lo, I am with you alway, even unto the end of the age."' And thus the heart is made happy by the belief in a present, living, loving, Almighty Saviour. The Lord Jesus has not yet taken His power to Himself manifestly ; He does not yet manifestly reign, but faith looks for the fulfilment of all that which is said of the Return of the Lord Jesus ; and, therefore, though we are not yet actually with Him on the throne, reigning with Him, we believe that He will come again, and we comfort ourselves, whilst yet in conflict, in poverty, meanness, and suffering, by the precious statements made in the Holy Scriptures regarding the time of His Appearing, and we walk thus in peace and joy, though we do not yet *see* His glory with the natural eye."

Now comes the shout of faith regarding the day when the Blessed Hope shall be realised, and when this body of humiliation shall be changed for a glorious body :—

"The manifestation of the sons of God has not yet taken place ; we are not yet in our glorious body, such a body as the Lord Jesus has had since His resurrection : we have not yet entered upon the possession of this inheritance : we are yet poor, mean, without possession at all, it may be, so far as *sight* is concerned ; we have, therefore, to exercise faith in this

Promise, to lay hold on it, to seek to enter into it, in order that we may be full of peace and joy in the Holy Ghost. The Holy Scriptures tell us of Satan being bound, yea, bruised under our feet (Rom. 16: 20); but this has not yet taken place; we are yet in the warfare, we constantly experience his power still; we have, therefore, for our comfort to lay hold on the blessing promised in this respect; and thus our hearts will be cheered."

The Coming of the Lord in power is always a sweet thought to Müller. At the Clifton Conference of 1870, he breaks out, in one of his addresses, to depict the day when his Lord shall triumph, speaking of: "the bright and blessed prospect, with regard to the Coming of our Lord Jesus Christ, when Himself shall put away war, Himself shall take the power and reign, and all the kingdoms of the world shall become the kingdoms of the Christ of God; when the blessed Jesus will come, not in the character in which He came before, but as the King in His beauty. How the heart, with joyful anticipation, should look forward to the day when He will come and reign, and take the power to Himself, and subdue everything that is contrary to Himself. This is the bright and blessed prospect before us, and most blessed with regard to our own hearts now. He will subdue in us individually everything contrary to His own blessed mind. The Lord Jesus will have His own blessed mind, to the full, seen in us. Precious, bright, glorious, is the prospect! After waiting yet a little while, we shall see Jesus as He is, and be made like Him."

It is a common charge against those who are students of Scriptural teaching regarding the Second Advent, that they are over-curious, and that their over-emphasis of one aspect of Biblical truth renders them introspective and unpractical. The basis for such a charge is small indeed; it will rather be found that those who are most in earnest regarding the Blessed Hope, are likewise most in earnest regarding soul-winning. Clearly it was so with George Müller. The Coming of the Lord was a subject almost too solemn for words; yet he says, at the same time :—

"The consideration that 'the whole world lieth in the wicked one' does not allow us to go on dreaming, to go on slumbering; and if we are not affected by it, it is a plain proof that as yet we have not apprehended what is contained in that solemn statement. In the measure in which the soul does apprehend it, the soul cries to God: 'Lord, help me to deliver my poor fellow-sinners out of their present condition,' and the Lord condescends to use us as the blessed instruments to win souls to Him. Now, in this state of mind we are to continue. Not now and then, 'by fits and starts,' but day by day, as an habitual thing, this should be foremost in our hearts. The most important point is, that we are earnest in prayer. But we are not to be satisfied simply with praying. The example of our Lord is ever before us. He told

His disciples—we have it in Matthew—to pray for labourers to be sent forth; and immediately He sent them forth. Then He Himself went forth, through every city and town, preaching the Gospel" (Matt. 9 : 38 ; 10 : 1, 5 ; 11 : 1).

Müller is ever careful lest the eager desire for the Lord's Return should lead any to sink into that other subtle materialism which is more concerned with arithmetical calculations of date than with the great fact itself. On this point, the address which he gave at Clifton, in 1872, upon the words : "Watchman, what of the night?" (Isa. 21 : 11), may be taken as typical of views which he expressed again and again.[1] The full wording of the passage runs : "The burden of Dumah. He calleth to me out of Seir, Watchman, what of the night? Watchman, what of the night? The watchman said, The morning cometh, and also the night : if ye will inquire, inquire ye : return, come" (*vv.* 11, 12).

The question put to the prophet—the spiritual watchman—is practically, as Müller says : "'When shall these terrible judgments come to an end?' In New Testament language: 'When will this Dispensation end? When shall our sorrows cease, and we be "for ever with the Lord"?' Now, observe particularly the answer of the watchman. He does not say it is the second or third watch of the night. How deeply important it is to notice this. Again and again it

[1] See *Jehovah Magnified : Addresses by George Müller.*

has been the inquiry among Christians: 'How far are we from the close of the present Dispensation? How near is the Return of the Lord?' And repeatedly calculations have been made with the view of fixing the precise date, or nearly so, of the fulfilment of the prophetic predictions; and this political event or that religious movement has been taken as an indication of the speedy approach of the end; and statements have been made: 'So many years, or months, or days will elapse, and then the Dispensation will close.' Now, how, beloved, are we to decide when we hear such statements? I judge we should be guided by the answer of the watchman: 'The morning cometh, and also the night.' Nothing was declared concerning the *time*."

On this matter, he gives a wise word from his own experience at the time when, with an eager and thankful heart, he first realised the teaching of Scripture regarding the Blessed Hope:—

"At that time there was war between the Ottoman Empire and Russia; and many good, excellent Christians said: '*Now* is come the time that the Euphrates shall be dried up': '*Now* the Ottoman Empire will be destroyed, and Israel will be restored,' and so on; and I, as a young disciple, very naturally took up the views and repeated the words of my elder brethren. Well, what followed? Before six weeks were over, peace was proclaimed, the Ottoman Empire remained, and remains to this day, and Israel is still not restored to their land. Now, I firmly believe that Israel *will* be restored to their land; but I refer to this mistake of my earlier years to illustrate the point to which I am referring. Not that we should never look at political events in connection with the prophetic Word, but that we should use the greatest caution before we conclude that such-and-such events must surely usher in the end. I judge that when the time really comes, Christians shall be so guided by such events, the signs will be so plain, so decided, that *all* who love the Lord Jesus will be able to see that *now* truly He is at the door. But *before* this time comes, until these things come to pass, let us be cautious how we make such statements as: 'In so many days, or so many months, or before this generation passes, such-and-such events will happen'; but rather let us say with the watchman: 'The morning cometh, and also the night'—that is to say, the great, the all-important point is, the *certainty* of our Lord's Return: 'this same Jesus . . . *shall* so come in like manner' as He went into heaven."

And to any who say: "Why make so much of the Coming of the Lord? Is not death the same thing, for it is our going to Him?" Müller's reply is: "I once thought so myself; but I was led to see that there is a vast difference between the two. The hope of the Church is not death, but the Return of the Lord. If I am taken out of the world by death, I shall *myself* be happy so far as regards the soul;

but, blessed as I shall be, my happiness, even as regards myself alone, will not be full; for I shall not yet have my glorified body, my redeemed body. But when the Lord comes, it is the whole *family* brought into happiness and blessedness — the whole family gathered home. 'The morning cometh'—that is, the morning of that day which will be 'without clouds' (2 Sam. 23 : 4)—of that day which will never end, in which the whole heavenly family will share together eternal happiness."

During the preaching tours, the subject is ever before him—which is to say, the Blessed Hope is a living truth to him. Of a certain Sunday evening at Clifton Springs Sanatorium, the famous Christian and missionary centre of the Eastern States, Mrs. Müller says :—

"His subject was the Second Advent, on which he spoke for an hour and a quarter with great liberty, earnestness, and joy, breaking out into fervent prayer that Christ would graciously revive the Church, and arouse His slumbering Bride to look, and watch, and wait, for her absent Lord's return."

A few weeks later, he is invited to a Christian Conference at Toronto. He speaks several times upon the subject of the Second Coming of Christ, and, at a later meeting, replies in public to a number of written questions bearing upon the same sacred topic. Of these questions, Mrs. Müller preserved one, with her husband's answer :—

Question : "Are we to expect our Lord's Return at

any moment, or that certain events must be fulfilled before He comes again ? "

Answer : " I know that on this subject there is great diversity of judgment, and I do not wish to force on other persons the light I have myself. The subject, however, is not new to me ; for, having been a careful, diligent student of the Bible for nearly fifty years, my mind has long been settled on this point, and I have not the shadow of a doubt about it. The Scripture declares plainly that the Lord Jesus will *not* come until the Apostasy shall have taken place, and the man of sin, the 'son of perdition' (or personal Antichrist) shall have been revealed, as seen in 2 Thess. 2 : 1–5. Many other portions also of the Word of God distinctly teach that certain events are to be fulfilled before the Return of our Lord Jesus Christ. This does not, however, alter the fact, that the *Coming of Christ,* and not death, is the great Hope of the Church, and, if in a right state of heart, *we* (as the Thessalonian believers did) shall 'serve the living and true God ; and wait for His Son from heaven '" (1 Thess. 1 : 10).

The subject of the Blessed Hope is necessarily one of vivid contrasts, the light and glory of our Lord's Coming being in opposition to the darkness of this present world. Writing with this fact in view, Mrs. Müller says, in her account of the tour in India, 1883–84 : " Though multitudes may yet be converted before the Lord Jesus comes, the Word of God plainly declares that no improvement of a *universal*

character is to expected *before* that event, but that
spiritual darkness will increase, and that iniquity will
abound more and more, as the present Dispensation
draws nearer and nearer its close.   There will be no
Millennium until *Jesus comes*; but at His Appearing,
a glorious period will be ushered in, when 'the knowledge of the Lord shall cover the earth as the waters
cover the sea.'   Oh, what a sunrise will that Advent
be !"

These, doubtless, are practically George Müller's
own words ; the quotation of Hab. 2 : 14—evidently
made from memory, in the course of an arduous
journey—is in harmony with its use by Müller himself in the announcement preliminary to the commencement of the Scriptural Knowledge Institution,
long years before.   And it is also in harmony with
Müller's teaching, that the admonition is added :
" But *until* that blessed event shall come, and
because this poor earth is in its present deplorable
condition of spiritual darkness and of death, true
believers should be most earnest and unceasing in their
efforts to win souls for Christ, and should seek to
become the instruments, in His hand, of gathering out
His own elect, before the end of this Dispensation
comes."

CHAPTER XVI

At Home with God

THE death of the second Mrs. Müller, January 13, 1894, leaves the patriarch lonely again. He makes his home at New Orphan House No. 3; and, despite his great age, still fills, with zeal and acumen, his accustomed place as director. His voice is still heard on Sunday mornings at Bethesda, or Alma Road or Stokes Croft. Quiet days are these for the aged warrior of faith—not, indeed, without alternations of trial, yet not one word fails of the Divine promises. If the morning's post brings only a few pence, his heart, as in the olden days, suffers no shock; after the waiting shall come the receiving.

The winter of life, while slowly exhausting his physical resources, has no frosts for his soul; the Lord God is his Sun as well as his Shield. Jehovah is the Covenant-keeping God; and His promises are Yea and Amen in Christ—in witnessing to which Divine assurance perhaps there was never orator like George Müller in these islands. He is a speaker of weight, of precision, whose wise sayings are fraught with spiritual illumination and instruction : yet his chief words of witness to the world are expressed upon Ashley Down, in terms of Orphan Houses, and in the daily provision, through faith, for the great throng of orphans.

His peculiar gift, in the assemblies of the godly, lies in the inspiration of saints, by the prayerful exposition of Holy Scripture. The majesty of Truth; the glory of the Lord's Return; the privilege of responding to the call of God with a whole-hearted cry of: "Here am I, send me"; the joy of obedience to the Spirit's leading and of sheltering in the tent of God's care; such are some of the subjects upon which Müller loves to dwell. The years have not brought him the rushing oratory of Whitefield, to sway a godless crowd and change the ribald shoutings of unregenerate mockers into groans of repentance and songs of praise; yet, from Chrysostom, preaching the everlasting Gospel to thrilled thousands in St. Sophia's, to the ex-tapster of Gloucester weeping over ochred mountebanks upon Moorfields, was there ever expressed a more scathing rebuke to unbelief, or more potent testimony to the grace of God, than is given in these "sermons in stone" upon Ashley Down—which still declare, to all who have ears to hear: "The Lord, He is God"?

Now come to be one of the best known of mankind, Müller, however, desires neither homage from the saints nor recognition from the world. What are the smiles of the great to the heir of glory? The apostle of faith will pull no wires to secure an official endorsement or a newspaper puff or to influence Dives to dole him some miserable shekels. As well might John the Baptist have requested a testimonial from Herod, or Paul have hawked about an "appreciation" from Festus, as George Müller have built upon the opinion of a fellow-worm of Mayfair or Kensington. The endorsement of Heaven is sufficient: indeed, is not the whole work of the Scriptural Knowledge Institution the creation of God?

In the silver dignity of old age, reverenced by the people of God in every land, he walks in the power of the Spirit. Familiarity with finance has brought no materialistic influence into his life; book-keeping for God has not made him presumptuous. His soul is preserved in peace; his mind is alert and perceptive as ever; but there are symptoms of physical failure. Certain attacks of heart-trouble, and the irregularity of the pulse, he takes as intimations that the earthly tabernacle wherein dwells George Müller's bright spirit must shortly dissolve, but as the frail frame grows weaker the ardent determination to do God's will glows the brighter, ever looking in faith for the day of Christ's final triumph. In his prayers and testimony, high aspiration to achieve great things for God is mingled with the sweet note of lowly simplicity. Some visitor, using a stereotyped form of kindly, but fulsome, compliment, declares: "When God calls you Home, beloved brother, it will be like a ship going into harbour in full sail." But George Müller will receive no such vain thought. "Nay," he retorts, "it will be just poor George Müller, who needs to pray: 'Hold Thou me up, that my footsteps slip not.'"

His final word in public is given on Sunday, March 9, 1898, when he preaches at Alma Road Chapel, the subject being the Vision of Isaiah (Isa. 6), linked with the reference thereto by John (John 12: 37–41). Picturing the scene in the Temple when Uzziah, in autocratic vehemence, and swollen with a sense of his achievements in military organisation and engineering, thrust himself into duties sacredly reserved for the Temple priests, and was swiftly smitten of God with the leper's whiteness, George Müller characteristically says: "A very profitable lesson to us all, to seek for a lowly mind, and to pray that we may be kept from pride and high-mindedness—the faults of Uzziah." Then, he soars to the Theme of themes, the Man of Sorrows Himself: "As the 'live coal from off the altar,' touching the lips of the prophet, and taking away all vileness and sin and transgression, made him clean before God, so the precious blood of our adorable Lord Jesus Christ, though our sins are numberless, removes all spiritual defilement from us, and makes us clean and spotless in the sight of God."

There, at the Cross, behold George Müller, in his last days, adoring his Saviour. Although he knows not that his call Home is speedily to sound, he is resting, in the end of his pilgrim career, as at the outset, upon the

Atoning Sacrifice. In the last words of all, his soul seems to catch the rosy glow of the glory into which he is soon to enter. By faith he catches a new fragrance from the Lily of the Valley, sees a new vividness of beauty in the Bright and Morning Star.

Like a tired traveller who, having scaled the last height and crossed the last river, is about to make a final descent into the shadows below, but lingers a moment to glance back where the rays of the setting sun gild the long line of the grey, stony road, George Müller stands here, thrilled afresh with a rapt sense of gratitude for the mighty work of Calvary, and for all that "It is Finished" has meant for his own heart and in his own life. Then his looks turn forward, where no mist of earth can obscure the Light of Life : and he cries : "Oh, the bright, glorious prospect which we poor, miserable sinners have through faith in Christ Jesus ! At last taken Home to be for ever with the Lord, and to see that lovely One who laid down His life for us, ourselves being permitted to kiss His feet, ourselves being permitted to kiss His hands. Oh, the precious prospect that awaits us ! Yet a little while, yet a little while, and all will be fulfilled. How full of gratitude our hearts should be that now, guilty, wicked transgressors that we are by nature, and numberless though our transgressions have been, by the power of the blood of Christ we have been made as clean, as spotless, as if we had never in our whole life been guilty of one sinful action ; as if we had never uttered in our whole life one single unholy word, and as if there had never been found in us a thought contrary to the mind of God. This is the position into which we are brought through faith in the Lord Jesus Christ, so that during the remainder of our life, and throughout eternity, never one single sin shall be brought against us. Oh, the precious blood of Christ!"

On the following evening, he attends the prayer-meeting at Bethesda—so rich with memories of departed saints and of strenuous days of Christian witness and warfare. The next day, Tuesday, sees him busy at the Orphan Houses; but on the Wednesday morning he is so weak that he is scarcely able to dress himself. Recovering strength, however, he cheerfully declares: "I feel quite myself again"; but he gives way to the urgent request of his friends to have a night attendant with him in the bedroom. Hitherto he has not cared for this, but decides to have one the next day.

The attendant is not required. On the Wednesday night, Müller manages to lead the usual weekly prayer-meeting at New Orphan House No. 3; then he says "Good-night" to James Wright, and retires to rest. Early next morning, Thursday, March 10, 1898, a cup of tea is taken into his bedroom as usual, but the attendant finds the man of God lying dead on the floor. He has evidently risen, in accordance with his custom in later years, to take a glass of milk and a biscuit, probably about five or six o'clock in the morning, but has fainted, and clutched at the table for support; then, dragging at the cloth, he has fallen by the bedside in a final collapse. The serene face is pale in death. The long journey is ended. George Müller is at Home with God.

Four days later, a service is held around the coffin, in one of the Orphan Houses, a thousand of the elder boys and girls being present. Then the remains of the beloved patriarch are taken through Bristol streets to a solemn meeting at Bethesda. The procession includes, for part of the distance, the orphans, in their homely and picturesque outdoor attire. There are crowds in the streets; a flag flies at half-mast over the cathedral; church bells are tolling; tram-cars pulling up in a long line; onlookers are wiping away their tears as the boys and girls whom the dead saint befriended come pathetically into sight. Here is the bizarre mingling of death's solemnities, awakening memories of well-nigh a century, with the bustle and scurry of humanity in the city street.

A huge crowd is assembled at Bethesda. It parts reverently to make way for the dead. In the course of the service James Wright gives a characteristic glimpse of Müller's ways of life: "I hardly ever went into his room but the Bible was open before him; and when no break in his ordinary life occurred, seven, eight, or ten chapters a day were his ordinary reading. Reading systematically, he applied the teachings of

Scripture to his own state of life. He fed on the Bread of Life; that is why he was strong. He said: 'I am a lover of the Word of God'; and to this he added a living grasp of the Person who was the centre of that Word. This was the secret of the power of his testimony for God." And again, with a felicitous sense of the need at such a moment to touch afresh the keynote of Müller's life, there is added the appropriate word: "I feel it important, as the mouthpiece of my beloved father-in-law, to emphasise that Philanthropy was not the leading feature of his life. I must give his own words: 'When I began this orphan work, I aimed from the beginning at the salvation of the children . . . Yet my great desire was, that it might be seen that *now* God is still the Living God, and that *now*, as well as thousands of years ago, He listens to the prayers of His children, and helps those who trust in Him.'"

The procession is re-formed and moves onward to Arno's Vale Cemetery, where the sacred dust is to await the resurrection of the just. The throng of people is enormous. Another simple service is held at the grave; George Frederic Bergin tells of Müller's life of faith and prayer and adds one of Robert C. Chapman's[1] sayings of only a few days before: "If I were asked to write Brother Müller's life, I should

---

[1] Robert Cleaver Chapman, for so many years the friend of George Müller, passed to his rest in 1902. He had lived on, in gracious ministry, into his hundredth year. Converted at the age of twenty, he had thus been enabled to devote nearly eighty years to the service of God. His ministry at Barnstaple is one of the most beautiful memories in the

say, he brought everything to God, small and great, temporal and eternal, and brought God into everything."

A plain tombstone, the simplicity of which is in harmony with the man of whom it is a memorial, marks the burial-place. The inscription reads :—

" In loving memory of GEORGE MÜLLER, founder of the Ashley Down Orphanage. Born September 27, 1805. Fell asleep, March 10, 1898.

" He trusted in God, with whom 'nothing shall be impossible,' and in His beloved Son, Jesus Christ our Lord, who said, 'I go unto My Father, and whatsoever ye shall ask in My name, that will I do, that the Father may be glorified in the Son,'

" And in His inspired Word, which declares that 'All things are possible to him that believeth,'

" And God fulfilled these declarations in the experience of His servant by enabling him to provide and care for about ten thousand orphans.

" This memorial was erected by the spontaneous and loving gifts of many of these orphans."

The question will inevitably be asked, from generation to generation : " How did this man, who preached devotion and self-sacrifice, act with regard to his own

annals of spiritual work in Britain. How well he and Müller would agree regarding the teachings of Holy Scripture, may be guessed from the fact that he carried, as his constant companion, a Bible, in a leather case ; if asked whether he had read some new book, he would quietly lay his hand on his favourite volume, remarking : " I have not finished this yet."

income?" The question is easily answered, for in the mingled simplicity and business-like accuracy which marked all his financial dealings, Müller kept an exact record of his personal income and expenditure. The teaching of that record may be summed up in the one word : "Stewardship." For God he received; for God he spent. It was a matter of conscience with him to take no salary; being a child of God, would not his Heavenly Father, without whose knowledge not a sparrow falls to the ground, care for him? Even regarding the money sent by friends for his own support, he refused to say : "This is mine own ; I may treasure it." On the contrary, if more came in than he actually required at the moment, it was a matter of conscience with him to give, to the work of God, or to the needy ones of the Household of Faith, that which he himself could do without. Thus, he gave largely, not merely as a kindly Squire Bountiful, liberal in harvest suppers to "sun-burnt sicklemen, of August weary," or in Christmas goodies to village children ; but systematically, to young and old, in the name of the Lord Jesus Christ.

In his old age, he stood for the principle of steward-ship, as earnestly as when, half a century before, he cried : "The child of God has been bought with the precious blood of Christ, and is altogether His property, with all that he possesses : his bodily strength, his mental strength, his ability of every kind, his trade, business, art, profession, property." And he still stood, regarding the systematising of giving, where he did when he declared, likewise : " If it be asked : 'How much shall I give of my income—the tenth part, or the fifth, or the third, or a half?' my reply is : 'God lays down no rule concerning this point. What we do we should do cheerfully and not of necessity. But if even Jacob, with the first dawning of spiritual light (Gen. 28 : 22), promised to God the tenth of all He should give to him, how much ought we believers in the Lord Jesus to do for Him ?—we, whose calling is a heavenly one, and who know distinctly that we are children of God and joint-heirs with the Lord Jesus.'"

When his yearly income was £151. 18s., he gave away £50; when it rose to £195, the gifts rose to £70; when it amounted to £267. 15s. 8¼d.—we mark the true Müllerian scrupulosity of correctness even to the farthing—he gave £110. In the course of time, as people sent to him from near and far, the income increased; so, too, did the giving, and with Christian consistency, even the legacies which came from relatives of his second wife were treated just as any other income; as also was a sum of £400 from Bethesda, presented to him in commemoration of his eightieth birthday and of fifty-three years of pastoral labour.

With the frankness of an ingenuous soul, he took all the world, so to speak, into his confidence, desiring to display the beauty of a life of Faith Triumphant. Anybody might know how much George Müller received; for he set it all out in print. When his income was £781. 0s. 7d. he "had the joy and privilege of being able to give away £500 during that year." In 1857, he received £836. 2s. 1¼d. and distributed £566. There was no touch of stinginess about Müller, nor of luxury; wherein we see the spirit of true stewardship; of nothing whatever that came to him did he regard himself the owner. It was not that, if money came, he sought to get rid of it straightway, "as if it were a crime to possess a five-pound note"; for, since it was the Lord who sent the money, and since He held Müller as steward, then He would also indicate, in answer to prayer, the ways in which it should be expended. We are apt to think and speak of these financial matters in a cold spirit of accountant-office discussion, as though God were somehow apart from it all. To George Müller, however, God was not a long way off; He was near at hand. Christ being his intimate Friend, how could such a man—who realised the Presence of the Saviour as much as he realised that of his own family—incline to luxury and sit down to a dinner of style? It could not be done; much more, it was foreign to his spirit. To go to the foundation of things, Müller could truly say, in the great Pauline phrase: "Old things are passed away; behold, all things are become new." Earthly wealth and gorgeous feasting were in complete antagonism to the spirit of such a man.

Objection is sometimes taken to this method of life, on the ground that no one knows how much a man receives, who lives according to this method. Such a criticism can in no case lie against George Müller. Moreover, the gifts he received were the outcome not only of confidence in his integrity, but of the determination of the saints to uphold and strengthen one who was giving so glorious a witness to the reality, the power, and the faithfulness of the Living God.

"Saving up for a rainy day" or "for the evening of life," then, was in direct opposition to Müller's principles. He saved nothing, but still said: "The Lord is my shepherd, I shall not want." Nor did he want. The "evening of life" inevitably came, and to Müller it was a long, long twilight; but when he realises that the sun is westering, what says he? After referring to those little account-books of his, he computes that from the year 1831 to the year 1885, he has been enabled to give away about £57,000, of which £45,000 was devoted to the orphan work and other branches of the Scriptural Knowledge Institution. "Do you suppose I regret to have given away this sum?" he quaintly asks all and sundry; and he " answers his own question " with characteristic simplicity and trust: "Verily not. I thank God for the honour bestowed upon me, in allowing me to do so, and I am not the least tired of this way; while, at the same time, I need to pray still : 'Hold Thou me up, and I shall be safe.'" He has peace in his heart; his Fountain of supply is still—the Living God.

Thus, while he continually received, he continually gave : a man who makes large donations may yet have enormous resources left, but it was not so with George Müller; literally, he deemed it his privilege to be a channel of blessing, but by no means a cistern. " Buy land for New Orphan Houses ? " By all means. " Buy a house for George Müller ? " By no means. Whether it were a Queen Anne villa with a rose garden and a sweet lawn, or a grim little house in a Bristol street, he will have no house of his own possessing. A man must, indeed, live somewhere, under present conditions, but he need have no possessions or hoarded or put-by treasure. Such a man is Müller, whose Friend has told him : " I go to prepare a place for you, that where I am, there ye may be also."

It is delightful to note how, amid all Müller's activities and his concern for others, he promptly seizes upon and rejects any suggestion of gain for himself, or any departure from his principle of living by faith. A well-meaning and kindly friend, expressing " admiration of the services you have rendered to poor orphans and to mankind in general," suggests the formation of a Fund " for the maintenance of yourself and family," and sends £100 as a commencement. Müller seeks neither admiration nor, in this way, money. Some may regard his objection as somewhat of a hair-splitting character, and may ask: " Why receive a series of gifts but yet object to a permanent Fund ? Well, George Müller looks upon the proposal as a temptation to trust in a Fund rather than in God. It would mean, practically, the possession of property, the receipt of a sort of " stated salary "; and these things are anathema to him. When needing anything his plan is to "ask God for it, and the Lord puts it into the heart of some one or other to help me." All his wants are supplied; nothing is lacking. To live so, is to live blessedly, in very real dependence upon God, in very real receipt of daily maintenance; wherefore from this life of faith he will by no means depart.

Doubtless, at the faintest hint of such a Fund, thousands would haste to contribute, but Müller, clearly, will countenance no such plan. Anything given by those who have it in their heart to help him he will thankfully accept, as from the Lord, but a method which seems to "make provision for his future" would be "displeasing to my Heavenly Father, who has so bountifully given me my daily bread." The brother —an entire stranger—who has made the offer accordingly desires the £100 to be devoted to the orphans. Seemingly, he is a little puzzled over Müller's plain statements and is thinking the matter out; for, next day, he sends a further £100. Clearly, however, the more he ponders, the less subtle does the position become; he is persuaded that a man who refuses money in this fashion is a man to be trusted; so, four days later, he sends yet a third £100.

The whole story of Müller's personal experiences conveys a beautiful contrast of faith with the surrounding materialism of the world and the carnal Christian. This faith of his is like the rainbow in the great landscape of Rubens, dominating the whole picture. The idea that to walk with God in the path of simplicity and self-denial brings any touch of dour discontent or hard unreality is scouted. Very plain-spoken is he to any worldly Christian who says : " I seek to enjoy life ; I live up to my income." It is quite evident that Müller not infrequently comes face to face with such pitiful representatives of a Faith the very essence of which is, not getting but giving; and upon occasion he smites them hip and thigh.

" ' Live up to your income ? ' " he cries, " well, I have not so learned of my adorable Lord and Master, the Lord Jesus. True enjoyment of life does not consist in seeking how much we can spend on ourselves, but how much we can minister to the comfort and happiness of others, both temporally and spiritually."

Müller's childlike trust in God, expressed in his matter-of-fact way of regarding resources unreceived as yet, as though they were actually received, has a way of reflecting, as if in biting satire, upon the selfishness of the world. While the world is eagerly set upon grasping at more and more wealth, more and more pomp, George Müller waits before the Lord, and money comes to him ; and the only pageantry of earth that he cares for is the sight of the orphans marching to the Assembly of the people of God.

It must be cheerfully admitted, that he does now and then speak of certain "investments" of his. "Precisely," taunts elegantly agnostic society, "we suspected something. Besides, you suggest he did not live up to his income : what, then, became of the balance ? Job will not serve God for nought ! "

Let us look into this. Will some committee of financial experts examine these investments, and ascertain if, for example, they have anything to do with stocks and shares ?

Yet—stay; no need is there for a committee to analyse the affairs of Faith Triumphant; we may solve the mystery for ourselves. Let us go back to the Bristol of mid-Victorian days. Here are Mrs. Müller and Lydia, in one of the Orphan Houses, discussing the needs of this or that little girl or boy just received from a poor home. Meantime, Lydia is pouring out a cup of tea for her mother, and another for herself. Suddenly, George Müller himself looks in at the door. He is on the way to give a Bible-reading to a troop of boys, and tell them once again the blessed story of Redeeming Love ; but he cannot pass the door without a kindly word for his cherished ones. But, note that he speaks to his wife and daughter, in passing, about "investments."

Now we are on the scent. Let us listen keenly. "My dears," he says, "I propose to make two 'investments'—to put £100 to missionary work and £100 to the orphans, and so lay up more treasure in heaven !" They look up with a smile, for they hear such "investment news" with fair frequency : then they turn again to their stocking-mending and frock-making, while George Müller, with a quiet smile, goes his way to pay the money into the funds. The explanation is, people have sent him more money for his personal use than he requires, wherefore he "invests" it, in sending out heralds of the cross to the heathen, and in saving and maintaining the orphan children of Britain. So, the treasure is laid up, not in commercial syndicates and dead-certain twenty-per-cents., but in heaven ! What sayest thou, O Throgmorton Street, to this?

About a year before his passing away, he gave a sort of "review" of his life (at the Gospel Hall, St. Nicholas Road, Bristol) to the glory of God, in which he touched upon the several departments of the work, saying: "God has led me to the founding of many schools. In England, Scotland, India, Straits of Malacca, British Guiana, Essequibo, Belize; in Spain, in France, in Italy, and other parts of the world, there are these schools, 117 in number, and in them there have been educated a hundred and twenty-two thousand young people; out from among whom, more than twenty thousand have been converted (the masters have so reported); but in heaven I expect to meet more than forty or fifty thousand. In regard to the Holy Scriptures: 279,000 Bibles, in various languages, and 1,440,000 New Testaments, have been circulated, to His glory: God abundantly blessed this part of the work, particularly in Spain, in Italy, and in Ireland. As to missionary operations, through the goodness of God, sums amounting to £258,000 have been sent out to Missions, alone. In the circulation of tracts, which was particularly laid on my heart, God has granted me to circulate 109,000,000 of books, pamphlets, and tracts. More than twenty thousand persons have been brought to the Lord Jesus through the instrumentality of the four hundred or five hundred missionaries for whom the Lord sent means. Out of the 9750 orphans that I have been enabled to receive, between four and five thousand have been brought to the knowledge of the Lord; and we have at the present time about 1600, in the Orphan Houses, who are believers."

George Müller began his career without resources, and after his death his sole possessions proved to be just a few items of furniture and a few books, with about £60 in ready money—which, according to his regular practice, would doubtless have been spent within a few days on the poor or one of the various branches of the Scriptural Knowledge Institution, for James Wright is witness that, of all the sums given to Müller for personal maintenance, he retained, during all the years, only such amounts as his simple needs called for, giving away the entire balance.

The exact sum he had devoted to the work of God, keeping private record of the items, was £81,490. 18s. 8d. —which, to use the phraseology of the world, he had every right to regard as " absolutely his own property." It belonged to God, George Müller having nothing apart from Him; owning nothing; being simply a steward of the Lord. Of this large sum, £17,000 represented the total given to the poor, and the balance went to the Scriptural Knowledge Institution —most of it to the Orphan Houses. His practice of systematic giving, then, was maintained to the end.

To have been entrusted with so much is in itself humanly speaking, a glorious record; to have given it all to the work of God is the natural act of the Christian pilgrim. But these particulars represent only small sums compared with those which, by the grace of God, he was enabled to raise. He died, as we have seen, in March, 1898. Reckoning, for convenience' sake, from the date of the work's commencement to May 26, 1898, the total sum received for the orphans was £988,829. 0s. 10½d.; the total for the other departments of the Scriptural Knowledge Institution— missionaries' support, Bibles, schools, and tracts, was £392,341. 18s. 7d.; so that the total income received, solely in answer to the prayer of faith, no person being solicited to contribute, was £1,381,170. 19s. 5½d. Other receipts—the sales of Bibles and tracts, and the payments received from the children in the Day-schools —amounted to £72,342. 13s. 9½d.; hence the total income of the Scriptural Knowledge Institution, to the year in which Müller died, was £1,453,573. 13s. 3d. Over ten thousand orphans had been received and shepherded; and all the property connected with the Orphan Houses on Ashley Down had been vested in trustees, and the deeds enrolled in Chancery.

THE LIFE OF GEORGE MÜLLER

"Treasure in heaven!" George Müller, simple-minded Anglo-Prussian or Prusso-Englishman, servant of God, friend of the poor, having laid down his pilgrim staff, goes, by the grace of God, where his treasure is.

To all who love this present world, such a view of life as that held by George Müller is of course the distortion of a prejudiced or a deluded mind; in either case is monstrous nonsense. Yet it is worth while to pursue for a moment the contrast which the position suggests. "I have made my pile," says Love-the-World, shouldering his billiard-cue. And he prattles on: "I have a few millions at the bank, and some fair investments in——" "No," interrupts a rude and fantastic visitor, who, though no hall-porter has admitted him, has climbed the staircase, "you have nothing; you are a pauper." "I shall pull down that crazy Jacobean manor," pursues Love-the-World, oblivious of interruption, "and put up a modern, stylish affair, with plenty of room for entertaining and ample stabling for the hunters." "You will do nothing of the sort," retorts the visitor, "you have nothing; come away." "Who are you?" inquires Love-the-World, amazedly, "I am not accustomed——" "My name is Death," says the visitor; "come away."

"It is time for me to depart," says George Müller, in effect, "my Father is calling me; there is a place at my Saviour's right hand; I shall see Him as He is." "Treasure in heaven!" . . . "Where your treasure is, there will your heart be also."

CHAPTER XVII

The Man and his Work

MÜLLER had lived on into a generation widely different from his own, and, in a historical sense, was like a strange visitor from a dim, romantic past. He could recall the overthrow of the First Napoleon; and he had outlived the Third by a quarter of a century. He remembered Waterloo; and his days lasted past the Jameson Raid. When he landed in England there was no telegraph; no steam communication with America; to send a letter from London to Brighton cost eightpence; the stage-coach and the carrier's wagon were the regular means of travel; yet he lived into the era of the mammoth liner and the corridor express. In the history of his native land his record reads still more strikingly, for his long span of life covered the terrific stroke of Jena and the paralysing counter-stroke, long years after, of Sedan; the flight of the King of Prussia before Napoleon I., and the crowning of William I., as German Emperor, in the Palace of Versailles.

Of historic allusion, however, the "Narrative" is bare. Müller's swift perception, calm reason, and sound judgment fitted him to give, in his own exact and informing way, a terse and reliable account of men and events in an era of extraordinary human interest—but he remains silent. Whether men approve or are irritated, there is but one theme for George Müller, and that is Jesus Christ, crucified, risen, returning. In the midst of an unbelieving world, he gives himself to a living demonstration of the reality and power of God and of His willingness to answer prayer. Of such a man, called of God, and so zealous in His cause as to be entirely absorbed therein, who shall say that he is either dense or dull if, in proclaiming such a Gospel, if, in declaring the inexhaustible treasure and loveliness and glory that are in Christ, he stays not to chronicle even the surrender of Napoleon on the *Bellerophon*? The Pauline "needs must" is upon him—"Necessity is laid upon me; yea, woe is unto me, if I preach not the Gospel."

George Müller dull or dense? Nay; see him visiting among the poor during the cholera outbreak, see him weep over the sorrows of a ragged, destitute, deserted little girl, and take her up in his arms to be saved, as one might lift a white blossom fallen upon a muck-heap. Nay; not dense, not dull. Let those who will take the platform—and George Müller has no word of criticism for those who are thus led, like Shaftesbury, to enlist the forces of the Constitution for the lessening of human woe and the remedying of human injustice,—but, as for him, he has a great work to complete, and, like Nehemiah, he will not be drawn down into any plain of Ono, from that particular sphere, of building, and watching, and exhorting, and pleading, to which God has called him.

In this, he stands by the principles of the circle of the early Brethren; and his aloofness from public affairs was perhaps sufficient explanation of the small notice taken of him by distinguished politicians and leaders of society and the stars of literature. Thackeray could give a dry giggle at the Evangelical curate "dribbling tracts"; Disraeli could vivaciously depict the Romanist dignitary, worldly and subtle; but none of the great Victorian writers seems to have anything to say or hint about George Müller. He was, indeed, remote from Pall Mall and Fleet Street. What average club-man, even of the Athenæum, knew much—or anything at all—in the earlier days, of the philanthropist of Ashley Down, the Bible expositor of Bethesda, the meek and quiet preacher among Brethren? We wonder if Palmerston ever heard his name. Yet the memory of George Müller is one of the most fragrant in the annals of England.

To say, however, that Müller was little concerned in the warfares of Westminster is by no means to say that he was indifferent to the sorrows of humanity or the welfare of the nations. His life contradicts such an assumption. It is still a cheap sneer of the ungodly that Christians as a body are "other-world" enthusiasts who reply to the shriek of suffering with a droning psalm, mock the shiverings of a homeless outcast with tales of the sweet fields of Eden, and fob off a tract —probably against dancing—upon a pain-tormented cripple. To such fantastic ideas the spirit of Christianity and its records of beautiful and loving service might well be a sufficient answer; but if a demonstration of the power of the Christian faith to prove itself by its works be called for, let one answer, at least, be— George Müller.

To understand such a proof it is obviously necessary to understand what Christianity is—which is to say, pure religion and undefiled, and free from the admixtures which a gay and godless world would mingle therewith. Müller will by all means let humanity have a Psalm of Hope; but it is: "Blessed is the man that walketh not in the counsel of the ungodly."

He has a message for the man who has sunk to the depths, whether through iniquity or misfortune; he will indeed encourage such with the thought of a Land where wretchedness has no place, and nothing enters that defileth, or maketh a lie; but he will also point the man to the one Power which, by bringing a change of heart, of necessity brings not only content- ment and peace, but the assurance that the child of God shall lack no good thing. He will indeed give a poor cripple a tract—also, probably a dinner and a new crutch; and the tract shall tell of the great Consoler, who knew how it felt to have grim nails hammered through His hands and feet.

THE MAN AND HIS WORK

Year after year, with no further note than a scribbled entry in his diary of so much money expended this or that morning or afternoon, George Müller delightedly ministers to thousands of the needy; poor families are made glad; suffering seamstresses saved from starvation; little toes blue with cold, stockinged and shod; struggling fathers and mothers helped to start their youngsters in life. Then come fiery souls who strive to tear him away to public platforms for the advocacy of this or that unfailing means of making men happy and contented, or to this or that admirable cause; but Müller has only one life to live; he is the comrade of all who labour for the Lord; but he must needs walk in the path whereof the Spirit says to him : "This is the way, walk ye in it." Wherefore he maintains the testimony of faith to which he is called by God.

Unbelief, being spiritually blind, cannot perceive the spiritual meaning of the Orphan Houses. In one sense its request to " show us God " is not unreasonable, if it is meant to be translated to a challenge to Christianity, to justify itself in the living present by deeds which demonstrate its vitality and evidence the truths of its assertions. Such justification did George Müller put forth; such evidence he furnished. Nay, he rode out into the lists as challenger—George Müller against all comers if need be, declaring that he, ex-good-for-nothing, prodigal-come-home, erstwhile companion of tipsy revellers in continental inns, child of God, teacher of holy truths that make men wise unto salvation, would, there and then, in a world tournament, so to speak, with all humanity, half-wondering, half-amused, looking on,

> "assert eternal providence
> And justify the ways of God to men."

Would demonstrate, indeed, that God, here and now, answers prayer, and is kind.

With such a subject, such an aim, absorbing the man and all his powers, we need scarcely wonder that the "Narrative" takes no heed of the Reform Bill, the Indian Mutiny, the American Civil War, or the creation of modern Germany ; he is dealing with eternal verities, and soars above men's wranglings, having the strong persuasion that the way to human happiness lies by the Cross, and not in the perfecting of human civilisation ; for man's devices, at best, would yet leave the carnal mind unspiritualised, and—tragedy of tragedies, remembering Calvary—still at enmity with God, for : " The natural man receiveth not the things of the Spirit of God : for they are foolishness unto him : neither can he know them, because they are spiritually discerned. But he that is spiritual judgeth all things."

Müller's attitude to his fellow-men was determined by his fellow-men's attitude towards God. Broadly, he saw God's message of Redemption ignored, and, realising the reality, the nearness, the willingness, of the Lord to hear and answer prayer, he forsook all that he had, in the way of earthly possessions, and starting without a friend or a penny, set out upon the mighty work of arousing the world to a sense of God's goodness. This, surely, was work enough for one man's lifetime, albeit one so long as George Müller's proved to be; and the motto for such a modern apostle of faith could not be less than the Pauline: "One thing I do." A lesser resolve, a weaker motto would have meant failure. But: "One thing I do"—thereby George Müller leaves a glorious record of Faith Triumphant.

Not easy to gain is this victory: many a groan, many a tear, when words fail; many a silent presenting of petitions before the Lord; many a lowly reminder; many a pleading of promises; all these have been, year after year. The Orphan Houses did not drop from the clouds at the wave of the umbrella of the elderly gentleman in spectacles who preached o' Sundays at Bethesda Chapel. God, it is true, requires not to be persuaded into willingness; but He has laid down a law of Prevailing Prayer; He will be inquired of—by the soul that seeks first of all His glory, that bases prayer upon the assurances of Holy Scripture, and that "holds on" for the answer—being, however, in the meantime, as certain of receiving it as though it were already received.

In Müller's prayers we trace the working of these principles, inspired by the Spirit. No charlatan is he, aspiring to cut a figure before an admiring world; his aim is all for God's honour. All that he does makes for the one grand end of demonstrating to a cold and unbelieving race, that God is as ready to answer prayer in Bristol streets or upon Ashley Down as He was upon the heights of Carmel; that He is as able to send serge coats and apple dumplings for the orphans of Britain as He was to revive the fainting Elijah in the scorched wilderness below Beersheba.

Quietly he worked; quietly he passed. Yet the day is assuredly far removed when men will cease to ponder the legacy of example and precept which George Müller has left them. His counsels, his example, are not merely stirring in their spiritual wisdom and human interest; they are character-moulding forces, and the children of God who desire to learn the lessons of his life will do well to note them.

The emphasis of his life was ever upon the Bible. Upon this Book George Müller built, as upon the rock; this he trusted in, as the Divine Word to his own soul. "I thought the Bible a 'dry' Book," said Moody, "until I was converted; then it *lived*." So it was with George Müller; and, reading it, he found it to be his unfailing guide, and of a truth the lively oracles of God. "Whatever we neglect," he says, "let us not neglect the Word of God—which men are in great danger of doing in these days of activity and of immense literary output. To neglect God's Word is to grow cold and lifeless and careless in the ways of the Lord. What should I do without this blessed Book in my possession, to which I can come day by day?

"But we are not simply to read. We must *pray over* what we read. We need the teaching of the Spirit of God when we go to this blessed Book. Without the Spirit's teaching we may not expect to be guided aright, for our mental powers are not able to fathom the mysteries hidden there; but, with the blessing of God, through the teaching of the Holy Ghost, what may we not find in this blessed Book?"

What is in the mind of God, we ought to practise and carry it out in our lives. "How vast is the importance of this! If we do not live according to the light the Lord gives us, we cannot be happy. If we fall at any time, as all more or less do, what have we to do? Just to make honest confession before the Lord, and lay hold afresh on the power there is in the blood of the Lord Jesus Christ to make us clean, knowing that the Lord Jesus Christ, as our High Priest, makes intercession for us continually. Then there must come the surrender of the heart afresh to the Lord, asking Him to help us for the time to come, that we may be more guarded in our deportment. If any will go on in this way, their peace, joy, and happiness in the Lord will increase more and more."

His experiences in the path of faith made him acquainted also with the trial of faith: hence, it was laid upon him to emphasise, again and again, the truth contained in the Apostle's words: "Let us not be weary in well-doing; for in due season we shall reap, if we faint not" (Gal. 6 : 9). "Sooner or later will come the trial of faith and patience in connection with our service. Therefore we need to see to it, that we do not lose sight of the promise here made to all who are engaged in any way in labour and service for the Lord. In *due season*, remember. Not at that time that *we* think would be the best time, but at *the Lord's* time—and that is *always the best time*. Our business is to give ourselves to prayer, in order that we may keep from fainting, and that we may go on in our service for the Lord."

Müller's counsels are never obscured by clouds of theological phraseology. He is all for the simplicities. The danger is rather that any reader who anticipates electrical shocks of emotionalism will cry : "Is that all ? I learned it at Sunday-school." Yet the things learned at Sunday-school are vital—if only they be translated from theory into actuality. And to these fundamentals Müller insistently returns. He is determined that none who hear him shall go forth to build upon sand. For example, after these counsels on holding fast, he suddenly stops short to declare : "It is absolutely needful, if we are labourers for the Lord, that we should know Him for ourselves, and that we should *know*—it is a point of vast importance—our interest and standing in Christ ; in other words, that we should know our sins forgiven." And : "The next point is that the peace and joy and happiness in the Lord, which we obtained at the first, shall be maintained ;

that we are not deprived of them after a few months, or perhaps after a year or two; but that they should increase more and more."

Long years he has served the Lord: what is the sage record of his experience? Has he a doleful tale to tell, of pilgrims overcome, of wild beasts' howlings, of demons' gibes? Was he silenced by the dolours of the Slough of Despond, by the bitings of the fires of trial, by the withering storms of bereavement? Nay, white and wrinkled as he is, his failing voice still declares: " In all these things, we are more than conquerors."

Immanuel has been his Guide: they have held sweet converse by the way, in the green pastures of the Land of Beulah; and the same Blessed One has been his shield in withstanding the onset of the prince of this world, in the day of battle. Wherefore, his plain word is: " By the grace of God I can say, after knowing the Lord fifty-three years and seven months, that I am far happier than when I was converted, or than I was fifty years ago, forty years ago, or thirty years ago. I say this for the encouragement of my younger brethren and sisters, that they may give no heed to statements that 'their happiness will decrease after awhile.' On the contrary, it will *increase* more and more; it may be thus; it ought to be thus."

What, then, is the summing up of the whole matter, for the Christian worker? Just this: " We must, from the beginning to the end of our pilgrimage, or till the Lord returns, seek to live a life of faith.

We must not suppose that after a year or two we shall have some store of strength of our own. We depend on God day by day. The longer we walk in the ways of the Lord, and the more the Lord has done for us, the more abundantly ought we to give ourselves to prayer; because the devil's hatred will be all the greater against us, and if he can cast us down after we have walked for twenty or thirty years in the ways of the Lord, he will have a greater victory than if he cast down a young convert—grievous and terrible as that would be. Therefore let us give ourselves to prayer, day by day, that we may be strengthened and kept by Him, that we may be fruit-bearers to the praise and glory of His Name—sixty, seventy, eighty, ninety, ninety-five-fold, yea, not to be satisfied with anything short of a hundredfold. Let us be encouraged to expect great things from God through the instrumentality of prayer."

In the west country, Müller moved and preached in the midst of many reminders of the dry days of Unbelief and Deism, and the marvellous change wrought by the gracious showers of spiritual Revival. Not many miles distant was the parish of which Hannah More once declared to Wilberforce: "We went to every house in the place, and found each a scene of the greatest ignorance and vice. We saw but one Bible in all the parish; and that was used to prop up a flower-pot." It was in Gloucester that Whitefield served in the bar of an inn; and it was there, too, that he preached that wonderful first sermon of his, at St. Mary-le-Crypt. Kingswood, with its memories of both Whitefield and Wesley, was close at hand; it was through being excluded from Bristol pulpits that Whitefield, aged only twenty-four, went out into the fields, that bleak February morning in 1739, and began those astonishing services in the open air which were not only a distinguishing feature of his career, but were, in association with the labours of Wesley, the beginning of that mighty movement of Revival which transformed England.[1] The thought of such days and such wrestlings with the powers of darkness might well be as a trumpet-call to a servant of God.

Müller's own peculiar gift was in Bible exposition; nevertheless, so great, so varied, and so ripe was his experience, that he was specially qualified to advise all preachers regarding the ministry of the Word and doctrine. He was evangelist as well as expositor. None could hear him, whatever the subject, without hearing the Gospel. At the same time, none could hear him without feeling the force of his appeal for consecration to God's service. And again and again he came back to the Scriptures of Truth, and the proper method of reading them. Thus, he urged: " Some take the Bible and begin to read just where it opens. If it opens on Psalm 103, they read Psalm

[1] " I thought," declared Whitefield, " that I might be doing service to my Creator, who had a mountain for His pulpit and the heavens for His sounding-board ; and who, when His Gospel was refused by the Jews, sent His servants into the highways and hedges."

103; if at John 14 or Romans 8, then they read John 14 or Romans 8. By degrees, the Bible opens naturally on such portions of Scripture. Let me affectionately say that it ill becomes the child of God thus to treat the Father's Book. There is a special purpose in the arrangement of the Scriptures. They begin with the creation of the world, and close with the end of the world. As you read a book of biography or history, commencing at the beginning and reading through to the end, so should you read the revelation of God's will; and when you get to the end, begin again and again. But this is not all. When you come to this blessed Book, the great point is, to come with a deep consciousness of your own ignorance, seeking on your knees the help of God, that by His Spirit He may graciously instruct you."

Müller's own experience in thus studying the Bible is illuminating: "I had been a student of Divinity in the University of Halle, and had written many a long manuscript at the lectures of the professors of Divinity; but I had not come to this blessed Book in the right spirit. At length I came to it as I had never done before. I said: 'The Holy Ghost is the Teacher now in the Church of Christ; the Holy Scriptures are now the rule given by God, and from these I must learn His mind; I will now prove it.' I put my Bible on the chair. I fell down before the chair, and spent three hours, prayerfully reading the Word of God; and I unhesitatingly say that in those three hours I learned more than at any previous three, six, or twelve months of my life. This was not all. I not only increased in knowledge, but there came with that knowledge a peace and joy in the Holy Ghost of which I had known little before. Since that time, for more than forty years,[1] I have been in the habit of regularly reading the Scriptures."

And the result of his experiences is the " confident recommendation to my beloved fellow-disciples to read carefully, comparing Scripture with Scripture. If you do not understand some portions, be not discouraged, but come again and again to God, and He will guide you, and further instruct you in the knowledge of His will. But this is not all; for with an increasing knowledge of God, obtained in a prayerful, humble way, you will receive, not something which simply fills the head, but which exercises the heart, and cheers and comforts and strengthens."

His public ministry testified clearly to the blessing that came through his expository method. Taking a selected portion, he would treat it, whether synthetically or analytically, so that the attention and interest of all were riveted upon the Bible. Having been guided, through earnest prayer, to what he believed to be the subject chosen of God for him, he went on, as he said, " to meditate, with my pen in my hand, writing down the outlines as the Word is opened

---

[1] Müller related these experiences at a Bristol prayer-meeting, in 1870.

to me. This I do for the sake of clearness, as being a help to see how far I understand the passage. I very seldom use any other help besides the little I understand of the original of the Scriptures and some good translations in other languages. My chief help is prayer. No one ought to expect to see much good resulting from his labours, if he is not much given to prayer and meditation."

The expository method, he readily admitted, was apt to be lightly esteemed by the unenlightened and careless; nevertheless, it tended to the true benefit of all hearers. Moreover, he warmly insisted, again and again, upon simplicity and clearness, so that all should understand—"so far as the natural mind *can* comprehend the things of God." He declined to make his sermons mere moral essays, decorated with literary scraps. Not that he despised learning or scorned the forces of holy oratory sweeping a crowd Godward. Whitefield was orator indeed, but Whitefield was simplicity itself, in the declaration of his message. Spurgeon's silver-tongued gift was an attraction to vast numbers, but never was preacher clearer in proclaiming the majesty and power and love of God, than Spurgeon.

By no means did Müller scorn learning and oratorical power, but he saw the uselessness of a discourse in which the flowers of rhetoric obscured the Cross: time was too precious to be spent in entertaining and pleasing the mind; the preacher's business was to be an instrument in the hands of God—"a sharp instrument, having teeth"—for the conversion of sinners and the edification and inspiration of the pilgrims and soldiers of faith.

All that he says and writes upon the subject of Prayer rings with special urgency. He will have every Christian put God to the trial, and that at once. "With all the efforts that are made to spread the truth, let us specially keep before us this, that the Lord will be sought for blessing, and that if there is little prayer there will be little result; whilst the more abundant prayer there is, the more abundant blessing may we reckon on." Nevertheless, he will have them also understand clearly the Divine rules by which prayer is governed. Dependence must be on the Lord Jesus Christ, solely, as the one ground of acceptance, before God. The subjects of prayer must be to God's glory. There must be patient continuance in prayer, until the answer comes. All must be ventured upon the Living God. "The more we know of the temptations without, the more shall we be conscious, day by day and hour by hour, how weak we are in ourselves; and therefore how we need the strong One whom we have in Jehovah-Jesus. Oh, the preciousness that we have not to do with a *dead* Christ! Though He was crucified and put into the grave on account of our numberless transgressions, yet He rose from the dead, He ascended on high, and there at the right hand of God He is, for us who put our trust in Him, as the Living One, as the Mighty One, who takes delight and joy continually in helping us amidst all our weaknesses and frailties. When Paul stood alone, and every one of the brethren, by reason of the danger, had forsaken him, there was One who stood with him, there was One who was at his side ; there was the King in power—that Blessed One who never leaves us, never forsakes us."

Müller's counsels, then, regarding prayer, are never in the nature of arithmetical calculations ; he gives advice for the glory of God and the encouragement of believers, but while he thus speaks from the human standpoint, he is also bowed in adoration and reverence and love ; for prayer is not to be described in the terms of the Harley Street consulting-room and the hospital surgery-theatre. Prayer was a living, throbbing, vital fact, and God was near, to answer; he believed God ; he walked by faith, declaring : "Faith has nothing to do with feelings or with impressions, with improbabilities or with outward experiences. If we desire to couple such things with faith, then we are no longer resting on the Word of God, because faith needs nothing of the kind. Faith rests on the naked Word of God. When we take Him at His word, the heart is at peace." The trial of faith shall come, but the trial of faith is the very food of faith, whereby it is strengthened and increased, as also it is by the reading of the Scriptures, whereby we may acquaint ourselves with the character of God. "And what," demands

THE MAN AND HIS WORK

Müller, "shall we find regarding Him? Not only that He is the Almighty God, and the righteous God, but how gracious He is, how gentle, how kind, how beautiful —in a word, WHAT A LOVELY BEING GOD IS!"

It is in such words as these, that we come at the very heart of George Müller's life and testimony. Walking in the light, with a life surrendered to Him, proving His faithfulness, building on His promises, the living God is his All-in-all. We may find a fine fascination in his devoted life, a lively interest in his extraordinary experiences, and a wonderful attraction in the lowly simplicity of his sayings, and yet miss the spiritual glow of his being; but here as he speaks of his Heavenly Friend, here as he seems to enter the holiest and is lost in adoration, we have the key of all. George Müller, loved much, loves in return, being governed now by God, who is Love. And so, with a heart illuminated with the Spirit's beams and a tongue touched with the Spirit's fire and tenderness, he pleads as though he would address every living soul individually: "Are you able to say, from the acquaintance you have made with God, that He is a lovely Being? If not, let me affectionately entreat you to ask God to bring you to this, that you may admire His gentleness and His kindness, that you may be able to say how good He is, and what a delight it is to the heart of God, to do good to His children."

Much might well be added of Muller's connection with the missionary enterprises of Brethren. Crowded as his life was, he encouraged, inspired, and helped to maintain, in all parts of the world, godly men who sought above all to preach the Word of Life and win souls for Christ. Hundreds of zealous workers were thus aided, and it would be difficult to realise, at this day, how much his help and encouragement meant to men and women of God, toiling amid the horrors of heathenism.

Now and again we catch a glimpse of him, studying the work of God, which reveals as in a flash the larger aims of his soul. For example, on October 6, 1879, his comment upon receiving £1000 for Foreign Missions and £500 for the Spanish work particularly, is: "In every way I have sought to press in to every open door, with reference to Foreign Missions; and God has supplied me with means accordingly." It is also impossible to say how much the Missions of the Brethren—for example, in British Guiana and the West Indian islands—owe to Müller. That remarkable pioneer, Leonard Strong, of Demerara, who, about 1827, gave up a Church living worth £800 a year to labour with the Brethren, and was enabled to raise up a mighty band of converts, was encouraged by Müller, who, year after year, sent him financial support, and workers, and Bibles and tracts: "Our tract and Bible stock is [September 7, 1844] very small, as we have much reduced it on account of sending supplies to Demerara." Much the same might be said of Gospel work in Canada and Australia, but few details are given: names are not mentioned; it is sufficient for Müller that money has come, in answer to prayer, and has been duly expended upon the work of God. This is no ordinary man, who, in the midst of engrossing activities, and while bearing vast responsibilities in the philanthropic and educational spheres, takes upon his shoulders the great questions of grappling with Rome and evangelising, as far as he may organise and direct and supply, whole nations.

The Orphan Houses, however, remain, as heretofore, the centre around which human interest in Müller chiefly gathers. "What will become of the work when you are gone?" was a question frequently put to George Müller by the doubtful and unbelieving. The reply was, that the work was not George Müller's, but God's, who was well able to carry on what He had Himself begun. That answer has been justified by the event. George Müller has been called to higher service, but the Orphan Houses remain as strong, in the receipt of the gifts of God's people, as ever; and a godly succession of directors has been raised up to continue the management of the institutions according to the principles of the founder. The testimony of faith is maintained; the orphans are trained in the way of righteousness; and Müller's own striking phrase still holds good in this later generation: "Only the Living God is our Patron."

"No man," says the old proverb, "is a hero to his valet"—meaning, when translated, that human nature breaks down, under close inspection, amid the bustle and grind of heavily pressing daily duties. But George Müller's testimony did not break down. There was no seamy side of personal aggrandisement, or frivolity, or behind-the-scenes indulgence; no whispered : "But—— !" His life was transparent; he had nothing to conceal. The longer he lived—and his final years were passed amid the domesticities of Ashley Down—the more fragrant was his spirit and the brighter was his zeal. Old age sometimes brings a petulant and impatient touch, particularly to those who for long years have been accustomed to issue directions which are accepted without question and immediately obeyed; but no declension from high ideal marked George Müller's waning days of strength. Indeed, the longer he lived, the deeper was his humility. He issued orders, not as an autocrat, but as an elder brother in the Lord, as a trustee for Him.

Deep was the veneration in which he was held by great numbers of people, but any suggestion of adulatory expression horrified him, and his simple soul cried : "See thou do it not : I am thy fellow-servant, and of thy brethren that have the testimony of Jesus : worship God." So he was the lowly brother of all who loved the Lord; and yet was the strong warrior of faith, even to the last, "bearing all things, believing all things, hoping all things, enduring all things." Wonderful things had he seen of the workings of the Spirit; wonderful was it to look back to the time when that first donation of one shilling, for an Orphan House, was handed him by the German missionary. To the very end, too, he is engrossed in the glorious work of proclaiming the Gospel. Here is George Müller, past his ninetieth year, urging all Christians to give themselves increasingly to prayer, especially for the conversion of sinners; and he encourages all who hear him with the story of his own experience: " When I came to Bristol, and, after I had been labouring for some time, we first met for the Breaking of Bread in the Lord's Supper, there were just seven of us. Since then, there have been received into fellowship by us, as a Church, more than six thousand, and when the branch Churches that have sprung out of Bethesda are taken in—for we not only meet in four different places, but there are five branch Churches—if these are taken in, oh, how many thousands more! Let this, then, be a great encouragement for prayer; at first only seven, and since—how many thousands more! See what God is willing to give and to do in answer to prayer, see what He is willing to give to you. I am only a poor miserable sinner myself, but see what God has given me, simply for Christ's sake; and what He has given to me, He is willing to give to others. Oh, expect great blessings from Him, and He will give them to you, when you seek them by earnest prayer."

The suggestion was made, by some who failed to realise the spirit and testimony of the man, that a statue should be erected to his memory; but the well-intended proposition was very properly rejected. The plain gravestone in Arno's Vale Cemetery, indicating where his dust lies, is sufficient. Those who desire a monument have but to stand on Ashley Down and look around; yea, and there are living monuments also, a succession of godly men and women labouring and witnessing for the Lord, who learned to love and honour His name, in the days when they were sheltered as orphans at "George Müller's." But to speak of monuments, in the presence of such a life, is distasteful; being foreign to its spirit and witness. George Müller's life made for the exaltation, not of George Müller, but of Immanuel the Prince. "Not unto us, O Lord, not unto us"—children of a day so brief— " but unto Thy name give glory."

The honour in which Müller was held by Christians, the esteem manifested for his labours in the Lord, clearly made him apprehensive quite early in his experience of being regarded as some marvellous specimen of humanity, possessing peculiar powers of exercising faith, to which ordinary mortals might not attain. Accordingly we find him declaring, again and again, that the faith he possesses is of the selfsame kind that is to be found by all; moreover, that it has by no means to do with temporal necessities only, but is demonstrated, by the grace of God, in many circumstances of soul-trial: when the way has been hidden in storm-clouds he has laid hold of God's mighty power, unchangeable love, and infinite wisdom, saying : "God is able and willing to deliver me, for it is written: 'He that spared not His own Son, but delivered Him up for us all, how shall He not with Him also freely give us all things?'" And deliverance has ever come.

Thus, in all things God is his helper: if money be needed for potatoes or for overcoats, he asks the Lord for it; if he fails to understand a passage of Scripture, he waits upon God for instruction; if he is to minister the Word at Bethesda, or in some great assembly at home or abroad, and yearns for the unction of the Spirit, he seeks Divine help, having only one Storehouse, only one Refuge, and so he breaks out to his brethren: " Oh, I beseech you, do not think me an extraordinary believer, having privileges above others of God's dear children which they cannot have : nor look on my way of acting as something that would not do for other believers. Make but trial!" And again: "There is none in the whole wide world who can say that I ever asked them for a penny. To God, and to God alone, I went. And this I did because I knew, ever since my conversion, that one of the greatest necessities for the Church of God to learn, and the world at large to learn, is— real, true, lasting dependence on God."

Müller gives these counsels, not as one who is publishing pet theories, but as the pilgrim-warrior of faith, who knows the road full well, and, at the pleadings of would-be travellers to whom the way is known only by such " maps " as are furnished in guidebooks, he relates his experiences, and gives his plain assurance that there are no intricate paths to thread; one has only to march boldly along the King's highway of faith. And when the Fainthearts among the pilgrims fancy they see threatening monsters in waving boughs and Diabolonian spear-heads in glistening dew, and despondently cry to him : " Art thou not terribly frightened ?" the reply of the man of God is : "By God's grace I have been enabled to continue to trust in Him alone, and, though failing and weak in many ways, yet by God's grace I have been enabled to walk uprightly, hating sin and loving holiness, and longing after increased conformity to the Lord Jesus."

Thus he struggled, fought, conquered ; thus he met and vanquished the foes of his own soul ; thus he put away the gloomy whispers of the unbelieving. His earthly tabernacle became fragile with age, and at last fell broken to the hearth ; but to the end there was no lapse in his simple trust ; his spirit was serenely triumphant, hoping in the Lord, triumphant all the way. The world, boasting its own practicalness, challenges faith and demands evidences ; it has little interest in the pearly gates of the New Jerusalem, but will believe, say, in stone and mortar. Well, here, let us in conclusion remind ourselves, are stone and mortar ; here are Orphan Houses, to which no worldling, or, for that matter, any other person has been asked to contribute one splodge of mortar or one chimney pot, one leg of mutton or one apple dumpling. And the dominating thought in the internal management of these Orphan Houses is to guide little feet into the Way of Life.

Thus, God confounds the materialistic spirit, the calculating shrewdness of this present world, by raising up plain, unassuming, zealous George Müller, who has no resources of his own, but who, scorning all patrons but the Living God, is yet enabled to uprear one of the most remarkable monuments of God's faithfulness the world has seen. This story of George Müller adds another chapter to the history of God's warriors of faith, who fought and conquered the alien armies of unbelief. Their strength was their simple confidence in the unfailing promises of God. "Carnal" Christians accept the record of God being faithful in times past; they do not deny that He will be faithful in times future; but they deem Him sure to fail in times present. But George Müller's life glows with the holy fervour and triumphant faith of one who takes God at His word now, and is secure and strong in the simple, vital, dynamic fact, that He remains faithful. Here shines again the living truth apprehended of old by Abraham, going out not knowing whither he went; by Moses, esteeming the reproach of Christ greater riches than the treasures in Egypt; by Paul, declaring amid a thousand perils and sufferings, "our sufficiency is of God." That truth, being eternal and unchangeable, is the same whether working in the plain Anglo-Prussian of the Victorian time, or in the Apostle of the Gentiles ; also, whether early or late, as we reckon the passage of time, the glory is God's.

Not for us is it to pluck the curtain which, till the hand of God draws it aside, hides from our vision the things of the eternal world ; but of this we may be confident, that if we could exchange quiet confidences with George Müller, in the place where faith dissolves in sight, and ask him whence he learned this heroic measure of glowing faith and glorious achievement, the answer would needs be that God condescended to call him and he followed on ; that it was all of Grace. And if, in turn, we ask ourselves how it came about that this man shone with so steady and so clear a light amid the darkness of the world, we must needs say : God raised him up from the grave of sin, and, seeing him to have the spirit of a little child, and to be—through the Divine grace which transforms and illumines—humble, faithful, constant, and sincere, God also made him to be a witness in these latter days, of Divine love and Divine faithfulness. God led him, taught him, equipped him, upheld him, implanted the treasure of faith in his heart ; both the treasure and the earthen vessel which carried it were of God : to whom be glory for ever.

*   *   *   *   *   *

"Ask, and it shall be given you ; seek, and ye shall find ; knock, and it shall be opened unto you : for every one that asketh receiveth ; and he that seeketh findeth ; and to him that knocketh it shall be opened."

" Sell that ye have, and give alms ; provide yourselves bags which wax not old, a treasure in the heavens that faileth not, where no thief approacheth, neither moth corrupteth. For where your treasure is, there will your heart be also."

INDEX

I

INDEX

INDEX

INDEX

INDEX

INDEX

INDEX

THE CHRISTIAN LIBRARY

Classics of the Christian faith in deluxe, hardcover, gold stamped, gift editions. These beautifully crafted volumes are in matching burgundy leatherette bindings so you can purchase a complete set or pick and choose. All books are complete and unabridged and are printed in good readable print. **Only $7.95 each!**

ABIDE IN CHRIST, Andrew Murray
BEN-HUR: A TALE OF THE CHRIST, Lew Wallace
CHRISTIAN'S SECRET OF A HAPPY LIFE,
Hannah Whitall Smith
CONFESSIONS OF ST. AUGUSTINE
DAILY LIGHT, Samuel Bagster
EACH NEW DAY, Corrie ten Boom
FOXE'S CHRISTIAN MARTYRS OF THE WORLD,
John Foxe
GOD AT EVENTIDE, A.J. Russell
GOD CALLING, A.J. Russell
GOD OF ALL COMFORT, Hannah Whitall Smith
GOD'S SMUGGLER, Brother Andrew
HIDING PLACE, THE, Corrie ten Boom
HIND'S FEET ON HIGH PLACES, Hannah Hurnard
IMITATION OF CHRIST, THE, Thomas A. Kempis
IN HIS STEPS, Charles M. Sheldon
MERE CHRISTIANITY, C.S. Lewis
MY UTMOST FOR HIS HIGHEST, Oswald Chambers
PILGRIM'S PROGRESS, John Bunyan
POWER THROUGH PRAYER / PURPOSE IN PRAYER,
E.M. Bounds
QUIET TALKS ON PRAYER, S.D. Gordon
SCREWTAPE LETTERS, C.S. Lewis
WHO'S WHO IN THE BIBLE, Frank S. Mead

Available wherever books are sold.
or order from:

Barbour and Company, Inc.
164 Mill Street   Box 1219
Westwood, New Jersey   07675

If you order by mail add $2.00 to your order for shipping.
Prices subject to change without notice.